S0-ABC-927

Street, MD 21154

30 COMPUTER PROGRAMS FOR THE HOMEOWNER, IN BASIC

Other TAB books by the author:

No. 1275 *33 Challenging Computer Games for TRS-80™/ Apple™/PET®*

No. 1276 *Computer Graphics—with 29 ready-to-run programs*

No. 1380
$18.95

30 COMPUTER PROGRAMS FOR THE HOMEOWNER, IN BASIC

BY DAVID CHANCE

TAB BOOKS Inc.
BLUE RIDGE SUMMIT, PA. 17214

FIRST EDITION

FIRST PRINTING

Copyright © 1982 by TAB BOOKS Inc.

Printed in the United States of America

Reproduction or publication of the content in any manner, without express permission of the publisher, is prohibited. No liability is assumed with respect to the use of the information herein.

Library of Congress Cataloging in Publication Data

Chance, David.
    30 computer programs for the homeowner, in BASIC.

    Includes index.
    1. Computer programs. 2. Basic (Computer program language) I. Title. II. Title: Thirty computer programs for the homeowner, in BASIC.
QA76.6.C428   001.64′25   81-18218
ISBN 0-8306-0050-7   AACR2
ISBN 0-8306-1380-3 (pbk.)

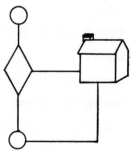

Contents

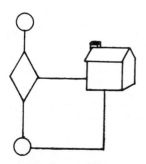

Introduction

Many thousands of homes throughout the world are now equipped with a home computer. Most computer owners are realizing that their computer can be programmed to do more than just play games, although games are very relaxing and entertaining.

Each of the 30 programs contained within this book were carefully thought-out, designed, and de-bugged before publication. Most of these programs are designed for mass storage of computer data. Read through them. You'll find there is a program for almost any part of the home.

This book is not meant to cover every use within the home. With different hardware, software, and interface items, you can program your computer to do everything from turning on a water sprinkler system to locking all your doors and windows.

This book is designed for anyone having the minimum home computer system. The programs were written on a Level II TRS-80, but the BASIC is pretty standard, and you should have little trouble converting them to run on other microcomputers.

Note: Underlined text in the sample runs indicates a user response. <ENTER> indicates that the ENTER key or carriage return was pressed without typing anything else. <SPACE BAR> means the space bar was pressed without typing anything else. Most entries require the ENTER key to be typed, but it is not shown unless it is the only key typed.

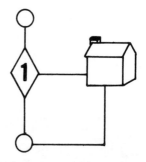

Information before Beginning

Each of the 30 different programs in this book are designed for a different task within your home. Whether you want to build and store Cooking Recipes or Warranty Information on Purchased Items you will find programs to meet your needs.

All programs are written in BASIC, meaning that with only a few alterations a program can be adapted to run on your particular home computer. Some programs contain PRINT statements which PRINT data elements at a certain location on the video screen. If your computer does not have this function, you can easily change these lines to just PRINT statements. Each program contains a summary, sample run, a flowchart, and the program listing.

You should never, under any circumstance type a dollar sign, comma, or a colon into the computer when answering INPUT statements unless otherwise told to do so. When inputting money amounts, times, names, or whatever, leave out the dollar sign, comma, and colon. If these need to be inserted (during printout) the program will add them. If you fail to adhere to this, you might lose part of the information you have entered.

At the end of each program summary you will find how much memory space is required for that program. If you need a particular program, but you do not have that much memory available, change the CLEAR statements to a lower amount, use multiple statement lines, delete REM statements, and shorten the questions found between quotes. If the program still doesn't meet memory requirements, you will have to delete some features from the program.

It isn't possible to show everything each program can do with the sample runs, but you'll find that all the programs do what they are designed to do—and much more!

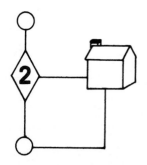

Programs for the Living Room

Phone Directory. Turns your computer into a super-fast, super-intelligent phone book.

Phone Log. Times all your long distance calls for you. Who called, where called, and the date of the phone call will also go into storage for transfer to tape.

Newspaper Clippings. Lets you input any length of clipping you want, from any paper you want.

TV Listings (daily). This program puts an end to those paper airplane pages you've been finding all around the house, from your TV listing booklet!

TV Listings (weekly). Takes the previous program a step further. Lets you input a full week of television programs of your choosing.

Radio Programs. Why a computer storage program for radio programs? Simple. Have you heard all of the interesting shows on the air today? . . . Listen!

Message Center. Gets your message across with ¾ inch high alphanumerics that can't be overlooked!

Arranging Your Furniture. Takes the ache out of your back. Also included is a second part called Computer Drawing. Your computer will draw for you randomly when you tire of fighting with your furniture.

PHONE DIRECTORY

Tired of thumbing through the phone book for a number you use a lot, but can't remember? This program should solve that problem neatly. Names, addresses, area codes, and phone numbers can all be stored and recalled at any time you desire.

All data can be stored on a cassette tape. After loading the program and the cassette containing the phone number data, computer location of the number you need will take almost no time at all. This program requires at least 16K of memory.

SAMPLE RUN
* * * PHONE DIRECTORY * * *
SELECT ONE ITEM:
(A) INPUT DATA FROM RECORDER
(B) SEND DATA TO RECORDER
(C) PRINT INSTRUCTIONS
(D) START A DIRECTORY
(E) REVIEW DIRECTORY
(F) ADD TO DIRECTORY LIST
(G) MAKE CHANGES IN DIRECTORY LIST
(H) END PROGRAM
C

THIS IS A PHONE DIRECTORY PROGRAM.
WHERE YOU CAN HAVE ALL THE PHONE
NUMBERS YOU NEED, AS CLOSE AS YOUR
COMPUTER.
THE DATA FILE WILL BE ENTERED AS FOLLOWS:
NAME OF INDIVIDUAL
AREA CODE & PHONE NUMBER OF INDIVIDUAL

ANY TIME YOU WANT TO EXIT FILE
AND RETURN TO SELECT LIST, JUST
PRESS ENTER FOR A (NAME OF INDIVIDUAL).

PRESS ENTER TO BEGIN
NAME OF INDIVIDUAL? J. DOE
ADDRESS? 123 YOUR LANE
AREA CODE & PHONE NUMBER? 900-555-1111

NAME OF INDIVIDUAL? F.G. BROWN
ADDRESS? 2121 L. DRIVE
AREA CODE & PHONE NUMBER? 900-555-1100

NAME OF INDIVIDUAL? K. MILD
ADDRESS? 8558 HILLTOP
AREA CODE & PHONE NUMBER? 900-555-1200

NAME OF INDIVIDUAL? D. SMITH
ADDRESS? 1212 THEIR LANE
AREA CODE & PHONE NUMBER? 900-555-5555

NAME OF INDIVIDUAL? <ENTER>

SELECT ONE ITEM:

(A) INPUT DATA FROM RECORDER
(B) SEND DATA TO RECORDER
(C) PRINT INSTRUCTIONS
(D) START A DIRECTORY
(E) REVIEW DIRECTORY
(F) ADD TO DIRECTORY LIST
(G) MAKE CHANGES IN DIRECTORY LIST
(H) END PROGRAM
E

(A) SEE THE ENTIRE DIRECTORY
(B) AN INDIVIDUAL NUMBER
SELECT ONE A

NAME	ADDRESS	NUMBER
J. DOE	123 YOUR LANE	900-555-1111
F.G. BROWN	2121 L. DRIVE	900-555-1100
K. MILD	8558 HILLTOP	900-555-1200
D. SMITH	1212 THEIR LANE	900-555-5555

PRESS ENTER TO RETURN TO SELECT LIST <ENTER>

SELECT ONE ITEM:

(A) INPUT DATA FROM RECORDER
(B) SEND DATA TO RECORDER
(C) PRINT INSTRUCTIONS
(D) START A DIRECTORY
(E) REVIEW DIRECTORY
(F) ADD TO DIRECTORY LIST
(G) MAKE CHANGES IN DIRECTORY LIST
(H) END PROGRAM
H

END OF <PHONE DIRECTORY> . . .

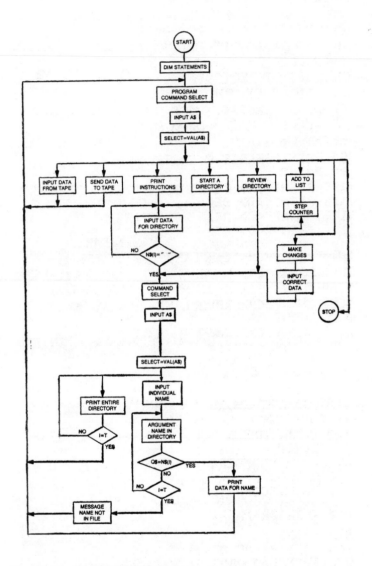

Flowchart for PHONE DIRECTORY

```
10 REM PROGRAM TITLE: PHONE DIRECTORY
20 CLEAR1000
30 DIM N$(50),A$(50),P$(50)
40 REM DIM STATEMENTS - LINE 30
45 REM LET USER INPUT 50 NAMES, ADDRE
   SSES & NUMBERS
50 CLS
60 PRINTTAB(15);"*** PHONE DIRECTORY
   ***"
70 PRINT
80 PRINT"SELECT ONE ITEM:"
90 PRINT
100 PRINT"<A> INPUT DATA FROM RECORDER"
110 PRINT"<B> SEND DATA TO RECORDER"
120 PRINT"<C> PRINT INSTRUCTIONS"
130 PRINT"<D> START A DIRECTORY"
140 PRINT"<E> REVIEW DIRECTORY"
150 PRINT"<F> ADD TO DIRECTORY LIST"
152 PRINT"<G> MAKE CHANGES IN DIRECTOR
    Y LIST"
155 PRINT"<H> END PROGRAM"
160 INPUT A$
165 IF ASC(A$)<=64 THEN 1700
170 ON ASC(A$)-64 GOTO 1000,1200,180,3
    60,600,1400,1800,2200
180 CLS
190 PRINT
200 PRINT"THIS IS A PHONE DIRECTORY PR
    OGRAM."
210 PRINT"WHERE YOU CAN HAVE ALL THE P
    HONE"
220 PRINT"NUMBERS YOU NEED, AS CLOSE A
    S YOUR"
230 PRINT"COMPUTER."
240 PRINT"THE DATA FILE WILL BE ENTERE
    D AS FOLLOWS:"
250 PRINT
260 PRINT"NAME OF INDIVIDUAL"
270 PRINT"ADDRESS OF INDIVIDUAL"
280 PRINT"AREA CODE & PHONE NUMBER OF
    INDIVIDUAL"
```

```
290 PRINT
300 PRINT"ANY TIME YOU WANT TO EXIT FI
    LE"
310 PRINT"AND RETURN TO SELECT LIST, J
    UST"
320 PRINT"PRESS ENTER FOR A <NAME OF I
    NDIVIDUAL>."
330 PRINT
340 PRINT"PRESS ENTER TO BEGIN";
350 INPUT X$
360 CLS
370 PRINT
380 I=1
390 PRINT@64,"NAME OF INDIVIDUAL";
400 INPUT N$(I)
410 IF N$(I)="" THEN 550
420 PRINT@128,"ADDRESS";
430 INPUT A$(I)
440 PRINT@192,"AREA CODE & NUMBER";
450 INPUT P$(I)
460 PRINT@83,"
        ";
470 PRINT@135,"
              ";
480 PRINT@210,"
        ";
490 I=I+1
500 GOTO390
550 I=I-1:T=I
560 CLS
570 GOTO70
600 REM REVIEW DIRECTORY
610 CLS
620 PRINT
630 PRINT"<A> SEE THE ENTIRE DIRECTORY
    "
640 PRINT"<B> AN INDIVIDUAL NUMBER"
650 PRINT
660 PRINT"SELECT ONE";
670 INPUT A$
675 CLS:PRINT
680 ON ASC(A$)-64 GOTO 700,800
```

10

```
700 I=1
710 PRINTTAB(0);"NAME" TAB(20);"ADDRES
    S";
720 PRINTTAB(50);"NUMBER"
725 PRINT
730 PRINTTAB(0);N$(I) TAB(20);A$(I);
740 PRINTTAB(50);P$(I)
745 IF R=1 R=0:GOTO950
750 IF I<>T THEN770
760 PRINT:PRINT:GOTO950
770 I=I+1
780 GOTO730
800 REM INDIVIDUAL NUMBER
810 PRINT
820 PRINT"ENTER INDIVIDUALS NAME";
830 INPUT Q$
840 I=1
850 IF Q$<>N$(I) THEN 870
860 GOTO900
870 IF I<>T THEN 890
880 GOTO920
890 I=I+1:GOTO850
900 R=1
910 GOTO710
920 PRINT
930 PRINT"THE NAME YOU ENTERED CANNOT
    BE"
940 PRINT"LOCATED IN FILE......"
950 PRINT
960 PRINT"PRESS ENTER TO RETURN TO SEL
    ECT LIST";
970 INPUT X$
980 CLS
990 GOTO70
1000 REM DATA FROM RECORDER
1010 CLS
1020 PRINT
1030 PRINT"BE SURE TAPE IS PROPERLY PLA
     CED"
1040 PRINT"IN RECORDER, PRESS THE PLAY"
1050 PRINT"BUTTON, THE PRESS ENTER";
1055 INPUT X$
```

```
1060 PRINT
1070 PRINT"INPUTTING PHONE DATA....."
1080 INPUT#-1,T
1090 FOR I=1TOT
1100 INPUT#-1,N$(I),A$(I),P$(I)
1110 NEXT
1120 PRINT
1130 PRINT"DATA NOW IN MEMORY....."
1140 IF U=1 THEN 1600
1150 GOTO950
1200 REM DATA TO RECORDER
1210 CLS
1220 PRINT
1230 PRINT"PLACE PLAYER IN RECORD MODE,"
1240 PRINT"IF NECESSARY JOT DOWN NUMBER
     ON"
1250 PRINT"TAPE COUNTER, THEN PRESS ENT
     ER";
1260 INPUT X$
1270 PRINT
1280 PRINT"DATA BEING PROCESSED....."
1290 PRINT#-1,T
1300 FOR I=1TOT
1310 PRINT#-1,N$(I),A$(I),P$(I)
1320 NEXT
1330 PRINT
1340 PRINT"PROCESSING COMPLETED....."
1350 GOTO950
1400 REM ADD TO DIRECTORY LIST
1410 CLS
1420 PRINT
1430 PRINT"<A> ADD TO PRESENT LIST"
1440 PRINT"<B> ADD TO PRE-RECORDED LIST"
1450 PRINT
1460 PRINT"SELECT ONE";
1470 INPUT X$
1480 ON ASC(X$)-64 GOTO 1500,1520
1500 CLS
1510 GOTO390
1520 CLS
1530 PRINT
1540 PRINT"TO ADD TO A PRE-RECORDED LIS
     T, YOU"
```

12

```
1550 PRINT"MUST FIRST INPUT THE DATA FR
     OM"
1560 PRINT"TAPE THAT YOU PREVIOUSLY REC
     ORDED."
1570 PRINT"HAVE YOU DONE THIS YET (Y/N)
     ";
1580 INPUT X$
1590 IF X$="N" THEN U=1:GOTO1020
1600 PRINT
1610 PRINT"COMPUTER IS NOW READY TO ACC
     EPT"
1620 PRINT"MORE DATA....."
1630 PRINT
1640 PRINT"PRESS ENTER";
1650 INPUT X$
1660 CLS
1670 GOTO390
1700 REM SELECT AGAIN
1710 PRINT
1720 PRINT"THAT (";A$;") ISN'T LISTED..
     ...."
1730 PRINT"TRY A LETTER FROM A TO H !!!"
1740 FOR X=1TO2500:NEXT
1750 CLS
1760 GOTO50
1800 REM MAKE CHANGES
1810 CLS
1820 PRINT
1830 PRINT"ENTER THE INDIVIDUALS NAME";
1840 INPUT Q$
1850 I=1
1855 IF T=0 THEN 1890
1860 IF Q$<>N$(I) THEN 1880
1870 GOTO1910
1880 IF I<>T THEN I=I+1:GOTO1860
1890 PRINT"NAME NOT IN PRESENT FILE....
     ."
1900 GOTO950
1910 PRINT
1920 PRINT"<A> CHANGE NAME"
1930 PRINT"<B> CHANGE ADDRESS"
1940 PRINT"<C> CHANGE PHONE NUMBER"
```

```
1950 PRINT"<D> ALL THE ABOVE"
1960 PRINT
1970 PRINT"SELECT ONE ONLY";
1980 INPUT X$
1990 ON ASC(X$)-64 GOTO 2000,2020,2040,
     2060
2000 INPUT"ENTER THE CORRECTED NAME";N$
     (I)
2010 IF RR<>1 THEN 2080
2020 INPUT"ENTER THE CORRECTED ADDRESS"
     ;A$(I)
2030 IF RR<>1 THEN 2080
2040 INPUT"ENTER THE CORRECTED PHONE NU
     MBER";P$(I)
2050 IF RR<>1 THEN 2080
2055 RR=0:GOTO2080
2060 RR=1
2070 GOTO2000
2080 PRINT
2090 PRINT"ANY MORE CHANGES (Y/N)";
2100 INPUT X$
2110 IF X$="Y" THEN 1800
2120 GOTO950
2200 REM END OF PROGRAM
2210 PRINT
2220 PRINT"END OF <PHONE DIRECTORY>....."
2230 END
```

TELEPHONE LOG

Almost everyone has been charged for a long distance call that wasn't made by them. If you make a lot of long distance calls, it's hard to remember them all. This program should solve that problem, as you can store all of those calls plus the time for each on a cassette tape. When the monthly bill arrives, all you need to do is load all data tapes that contain your calls and see if they agree with Ma Bell.

To help keep costs down, the program will also time the call while you're making it!

SAMPLE RUN

TELEPHONE   LOG

INSTRUCTIONS? <u>YES</u>

EVER WONDER WHY YOU DIDN'T KEEP
A LOG OF LONG DISTANCE PHONE CALLS
YOU MADE DURING 1 MONTH, THEN RECEIVE
THE PHONE BILL THAT INCLUDED CALLS
YOU DIDN'T MAKE?

THIS PROGRAM (PROPERLY USED) WILL HELP
YOU PUT AN END TO THAT. YOU CAN
LOG EACH LONG DISTANCE CALL YOU MAKE
DURING A 1 MONTH PERIOD, THEN REVIEW
THE ENTIRE LOG WHENEVER YOU CHOOSE.

PRESS ENTER? <ENTER>

WHATSMORE, THE COMPUTER WILL ALSO
TIME EACH CALL FOR YOU, SO YOU'LL
NOT ONLY KNOW ALL OF YOUR CALLS YOU'LL
KNOW THE AMOUNT OF TIME YOU SPENT
ON EACH LONG DISTANCE CALL.

NOW, YOU MUST REMEMBER THAT THE
ONLY TIME YOU'LL USE THIS PRO-
GRAM IS WHEN YOU PLACE A LONG
DISTANCE CALL.
PRESS ENTER? <ENTER>

THE INFORMATION YOU'LL SUPPLY IS:
1) DATE
2) WHO YOU ARE CALLING (NAME/PLACE)
3) AREA CODE & NUMBER
4) CORRECT TIME (INCLUDING A.M. OR P.M.)

WHEN YOU HAVE ENTERED ALL THE ABOVE
YOU DIAL YOUR NUMBER, WAIT UNTIL
WHOEVER YOU ARE CALLING PICKS UP THEIR
RECEIVER, THEN YOU START THE TIMER
BY PRESSING THE <SPACE BAR>, AS SOON AS

YOU HAVE FINISHED (WHEN YOU HANG-UP),
PRESS THE <SPACE BAR> AGAIN. YOU'LL THEN
HAVE A COMPLETE LOG OF HOW LONG YOU
TALKED.
PRESS ENTER? <ENTER>

1) MAKE A CALL
2) PROCESS LOG TO RECORDER

SELECT ONE? <u>1</u>
ENTER DATE (M,D,Y)? <u>10</u>, <u>10</u>, <u>80</u>
ENTER WHOM YOU ARE CALLING (NAME, PLACE)?
<u>J. DOE, SOUTHERN CALIFORNIA</u>
ENTER AREA CODE & PHONE NUMBER? <u>900-555-5555</u>
ENTER THE CORRECT TIME AT WHICH
YOU'LL PLACE THE CALL (WITHOUT THE COLON)? <u>10 P.M.</u>

THE COMPUTER IS NOW READY TO TIME
YOUR CALL FOR YOU . . . . .
DIAL THE NUMBER, AS SOON AS J. DOE
ANSWERS THE PHONE, PRESS THE <SPACE BAR>.
DO THE SAME TO CANCEL TIMING.

/////STOP/////

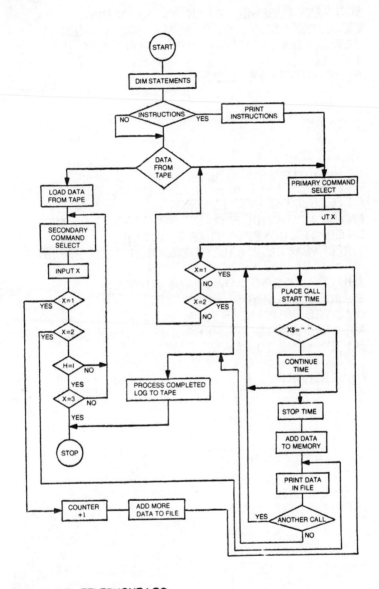

Flowchart for TELEPHONE LOG

Program Listing

```
10 REM PROGRAM TITLE: TELEPHONE LOG
20 CLEAR1000
30 I=1
40 DIM M(30),D(30),Y(30),N$(30)
45 DIM P$(30),PH$(30),T$(30),Q(30),S(
   30)
50 CLS
60 PRINTTAB(15);"T E L E P H O N E
   L O G"
70 PRINT
80 PRINT"INSTRUCTIONS";
90 INPUT A$
100 IF A$="YES" THEN140
110 PRINT"RETRIEVE LOG FROM TAPE";
120 INPUT A1$
130 IF A1$="YES" THEN 1900
135 IF A$="NO" THEN 650
140 PRINT
150 PRINT"EVER WONDER WHY YOU DIDN'T K
    EEP"
160 PRINT"A LOG OF LONG DISTANCEPHONE
    CALLS"
170 PRINT"YOU MADE DURING 1 MONTH, THE
    N RECEIVE"
180 PRINT"THE PHONE BILL THAT INCLUDED
    CALLS"
190 PRINT"YOU DIDN'T MAKE ?"
200 PRINT
210 PRINT"THIS PROGRAM (PROPERLY USED)
    WILL HELP"
220 PRINT"YOU PUT AN END TO THAT. YOU
    CAN"
230 PRINT"LOG EACH LONG DISTANCE CALL Y
    OU MAKE"
240 PRINT"DURING A 1 MONTH PERIOD, THE
    N REVIEW"
250 PRINT"THE ENTIRE LOG WHENEVER YOU
    CHOOSE."
260 PRINT
270 PRINT"PRESS ENTER";
```

```
280 INPUT A$
290 CLS
300 PRINT
310 PRINT"WHATSMORE, THE COMPUTER WILL
    ALSO"
320 PRINT"TIME EACH CALL FOR YOU, SO Y
    OU'LL"
330 PRINT"NOT ONLY KNOW ALL OF YOUR CA
    LLS YOU'LL"
340 PRINT"KNOW THE AMOUNT OF TIME YOU
    SPENT"
350 PRINT"ON EACH LONG DISTANCE CALL."
360 PRINT
400 PRINT"NOW, YOU MUST REMEMBER THAT
    THE"
410 PRINT"ONLY TIME YOU'LL USE THIS PR
    O-"
420 PRINT"GRAM IS WHEN YOU PLACE A LON
    G"
430 PRINT"DISTANCE CALL."
435 PRINT:INPUT"PRESS ENTER";X:CLS:PRI
    NT
440 PRINT
450 PRINT"THE INFORMATION YOU'LL SUPPL
    Y IS:"
460 PRINT"1) DATE"
470 PRINT"2) WHO YOU ARE CALLING (NAME
    / PLACE)"
480 PRINT"3) AREA CODE & NUMBER"
485 PRINT"4) CORRECT TIME (INCLUDING A
    .M. OR P.M.)"
490 PRINT
530 PRINT"WHEN YOU HAVE ENTERED ALL TH
    E ABOVE"
540 PRINT"YOU DIAL YOUR NUMBER, WAIT U
    NTIL"
550 PRINT"WHOEVER YOU ARE CALLING PICK
    S UP THEIR"
560 PRINT"RECEIVER, THEN YOU START THE
    TIMER"
570 PRINT"BY PRESSING THE <SPACE BAR>.
    AS SOON AS"
```

```
580 PRINT"YOU HAVE FINISHED (WHEN YOU
    HANG-UP),"
590 PRINT"PRESS THE <SPACE BAR> AGAIN,
    YOU'LL THEN"
600 PRINT"HAVE A COMPLETE LOG OF HOW L
    ONG YOU"
610 PRINT"TALKED."
620 FOR X=1TO2000:NEXT
630 PRINT"PRESS ENTER";
640 INPUT X$
650 CLS
660 PRINT
670 PRINT"1) MAKE A CALL"
680 PRINT"2) PROCESS LOG TO RECORDER"
690 PRINT
720 PRINT"SELECT ONE";
730 INPUT X
740 ON X GOTO 800,1700
800 REM PLACE A CALL
810 PRINT"ENTER DATE (M,D,Y)";
820 INPUT M(I),D(I),Y(I)
830 PRINT"ENTER WHOM YOU ARE CALLING (
    NAME, PLACE)";
840 INPUT N$(I),P$(I)
850 PRINT"ENTER AREA CODE & NUMBER";
860 INPUT PH$(I)
870 PRINT"ENTER THE CORRECT TIME AT WH
    ICH"
880 PRINT"YOU'LL PLACE THE CALL (WITHO
    UT THE COLON)";
890 INPUT T$(I)
895 CLS:PRINT
900 PRINT"THE COMPUTER IS NOW READY TO
    TIME"
910 PRINT"YOUR CALL FOR YOU....."
920 PRINT"DIAL THE NUMBER, AS SOON AS
    ";N$(I)
930 PRINT"ANSWERS THE PHONE, PRESS THE
    <SPACE BAR>,"
940 PRINT"DO THE SAME TO CANCEL TIMING
    ."
950 X$=INKEY$
```

```
960 IF X$<>" " THEN 950
970 CLS
980 PRINTCHR$(23)
990 Q(I)=0:S(I)=0
1000 PRINT@260,"MINUTES:   ";Q(I)
1010 PRINT@324,"SECONDS:   ";S(I)
1020 X$=INKEY$
1030 FOR J=1TO450:NEXT
1040 IF X$<>" " THEN 1060
1050 GOTO1100
1060 IF S(I)=60 S(I)=0:Q(I)=Q(I)+1
1070 S(I)=S(I)+1
1080 GOTO1000
1100 REM TOTAL TIME
1110 REM COMPLETE DATA PRINTOUT
1120 CLS
1130 PRINT
1140 PRINTTAB(20);"LONG DISTANCE CALLS"
1150 PRINT
1160 PRINTTAB(0);"DATE:" TAB(20);M(I);D
     (I);Y(I)
1170 PRINTTAB(0);"NAME / PLACE:" TAB(21
     );N$(I);"  ";P$(I)
1180 PRINTTAB(0);"TIME:" TAB(21);T$(I)
1190 PRINTTAB(0);"TOTAL TIME:" TAB(20);
     Q(I);" MINUTES" TAB(35);S(I);" SEC
     ONDS"
1220 PRINT
1230 PRINT"PRESS ENTER TO CONTINUE";
1240 INPUT X$
1250 CLS
1260 IF H=1 AND I<>II THEN 1290
1270 IF H=1 THEN 2050
1280 GOTO1510
1290 I=I+1
1300 GOTO1100
1500 REM MORE CALLS ?
1510 CLS
1520 PRINT
1530 PRINT"ANOTHER CALL (Y/N)";
1540 INPUT X$
1550 IF X$="Y" THEN 1570
```

22

```
1560 GOTO1700
1570 I=I+1
1580 II=I
1590 CLS:PRINT
1600 GOTO800
1700 REM PROCESS LOG TO TAPE
1710 CLS
1720 PRINT
1730 PRINT"READY TAPE PLAYER, THEN PRES
     S ENTER";
1740 INPUT X$
1750 II=I
1760 PRINT#-1,II
1770 FOR I=1TOII
1780 PRINT#-1,M(I),D(I),Y(I),N$(I),P$(I
     )
1790 PRINT#-1,PH$(I),T$(I),Q(I),S(I)
1800 NEXT
1820 PRINT
1830 PRINT"DATA NOW ON CASSETTE TAPE...
     .."
1840 PRINT
1850 PRINT"END OF PROGRAM....."
1860 END
1900 REM DATA FROM RECORDER
1910 CLS
1920 PRINT
1930 PRINT"PLACE PLAYER IN PLAY MODE,"
1940 PRINT"THEN PRESS ENTER";
1950 INPUT X$
1960 PRINT
1970 PRINT"PROCESSING DATA TO COMPUTER
     MEMORY....."
1980 INPUT#-1,II
1990 FOR I=1TOII
2000 INPUT#-1,M(I),D(I),Y(I),N$(I),P$(I
     )
2010 INPUT#-1,PH$(I),T$(I),Q(I),S(I)
2020 NEXT
2040 PRINT"DATA NOW IN MEMORY....."
2050 PRINT
2060 PRINT"1) ADD TO FILE"
```

```
2070 PRINT"2) PRINT LOG FILE"
2075 IF H=1 PRINT"3) CANCEL PROGRAM'
2080 PRINT
2100 PRINT"SELECT ONLY ONE";
2110 INPUT X
2120 ON X GOTO 2130,2200,1840
2130 I=I+1
2140 CLS
2150 H=0
2160 GOTO800
2200 REM GOTO PRINTOUT
2210 H=1
2220 I=1
2230 GOTO1100
```

NEWSPAPER CLIPPINGS

Your computer will become a newspaper scrapbook using this program (excluding photos, of course). The clipping can be entered from the headline to its entire length.

You know that while using PRINT # and INPUT # commands to a cassette tape that character length can't exceed 255. This program changes all that. While you are inputting the contents of the clipping, if character length exceeds a certain amount, the computer will let you know. At this point you can either add more to the contents or start another clipping, with no loss of data.

You will also find that when the clipping is printed out, a very impressive format is used. Instead of the entire contents being slapped onto the video, the print format will use the MID$ function, printing one letter at a time.

SAMPLE RUN

NEWSPAPER CLIPPINGS

RECALL DATA FROM TAPE? <u>NO</u>
INSTRUCTIONS? <u>YES</u>

LET YOUR COMPUTER BECOME YOUR
NEWSPAPER SCRAPBOOK WITH THIS
PROGRAM. HEADLINES AND THE TEXT
OF THE CLIPPING CAN BE ENTERED.
THIS WILL PUT AN END TO HAVING
NEWSPAPERS PILED UP IN THE CLOSET.
WHATSMORE, YOU CAN ENTER A FILE
NAME FOR EACH CLIPPING, WHICH
MEANS THAT WHEN YOU RECALL A
CLIPPING FROM STORAGE, THE COMPUTER
WILL 'SEARCH' FOR THE ONE YOU REQUEST.

PRESS ENTER? <ENTER>

WHEN YOU ENTER THE CONTENTS OF THE
CLIPPING: IF THE CHARACTER LENGTH
EXCEEDS 240 CHARACTERS (THE KEYBOARD
WILL SEEM FROZEN) PRESS <ENTER>. THE
COMPUTER WILL TELL YOU HOW TO ADD TO
THAT SAME PARAGRAPH. JUST REMEMBER
IF YOU WANT TO FINISH A WORD, START
THE NEXT <CONTENTS> WITH THE REST OF
THAT WORD. IF YOU WANT TO INSERT A SPACE
PRESS THE <⬆> UP ARROW THEN ENTER THE
CONTENTS RIGHT AFTERWARD (THE COMPUTER
WILL INSERT A SPACE FOR YOU).

PRESS ENTER? <ENTER>
AFTER YOU HAVE FINISHED ENTERING
THE COMPLETED FILE, THE COMPUTER
WILL PRINT-OUT YOUR ENTIRE FILE FOR
YOU. YOU WILL FIND THAT THE PRINT-
OUT WILL BE VERY IMPRESSIVE. ONE OTHER
THING SHOULD BE MENTIONED HERE. WHEN
YOU ARE ENTERING THE CONTENTS OF THE

CLIPPING DON'T WORRY ABOUT THE WORDS
WRAPPING-AROUND THE VIDEO, THE
COMPUTER WILL STRAIGHTEN ALL THIS
UP FOR YOU WHEN IT'S PRINTED OUT.

PRESS ENTER TO START FILE? <ENTER>

TO CANCEL ENTRIES INTO FILE . . . . .
PRESS ENTER FOR <DATE OF NEWSPAPER>

DATE OF NEWSPAPER? 2/2/80
HEADLINE OF CLIPPING? UNREST IN LIBERIA
CONTENTS OF CLIPPING? FEELINGS THAT THE TOLMAN
GOVERNMENT IS UNRESPONSIVE TO TRIBAL NEEDS ARE
INCREASING. AN OVER THROW IN THE NEAR FUTURE IS
FEARED. BLURBVILLE NEWS.
ENTER A FILE NAME (Y/N) ? Y
ENTER A FILENAME FOR "UNREST IN LIBERIA"? LIBERIA
DATE OF NEWSPAPER? 8/24/81
HEADLINE OF CLIPPING? ALASKANS COOL OFF ON NEW
CAPITAL
CONTENTS OF CLIPPING? IN THE ALASKAN WINTER OF
1979 A GROUP OF BUSINESSMEN SET OFF ON SNOW-
MOBILES FOR A SMALL AREA OF LAND 30 MILES NORTH
OF ANCHORAGE. THERE THEY ERECTED A TENT AND PUT
UP A FLAG WITH THE GOVENOR'S SEAL. A SIGN READ
"WELCOME TO WILLOW, CAPITAL OF ALASKA".

YOU HAVE EXCEEDED THE STRING LENGTH 246
IF YOU WISH TO ADD MORE TO
THE SAME PARAGRAPH (ADDED CONTENTS)
ENTER THE SAME DATE FOR THE
NEXT ENTRY. WHEN IT IS PRINTED
OUT THE ENTIRE CONTENTS OF THE CLIP-
PING WILL BE PRINTED TOGETHER.
PRESS ENTER TO CONTINUE? <ENTER>

ENTER A FILENAME (Y/N) ? N
DATE OF NEWSPAPER? 8/24/81
HEADLINE OF CLIPPING? <ENTER>
CONTENTS OF CLIPPING? THE ACTION WAS EVIDENTLY
DONE TO REMIND ALASKANS THAT THEY HAD ELECTED

TO MOVE THE STATE CAPITAL TO THE 100 SQUARE MILE
AREA FIVE YEARS EARLIER. RESIDENTS SAY THAT
JUNEAU IS INACCESSIBLE, BUT COSTS OF BUILDING THE
NEW CAPITAL ARE TOO HIGH. NEWSWEEK.
ENTER A FILENAME (Y/N) ? N
DATE OF NEWSPAPER? <ENTER>
THE ENTIRE FILE OF CLIPPINGS
WILL BE PRINTED BEFORE YOU
SAVE IT TO TAPE, PRESS ENTER?

The printout will be done on the screen using the MID$
function, and will therefore be very neat and justified. After data has
been transfered to tape, you may continue to input clippings. If you
want several clippings for the same date, you may write them to
tape individually (the memory is cleared after each tape dump) or
include the source as part of the date so that dates don't match.

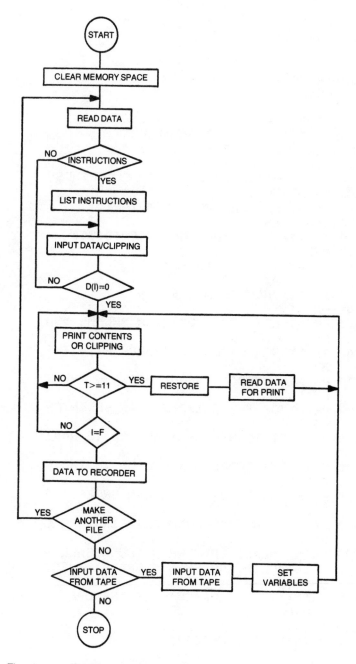

Flowchart for NEWSPAPER CLIPPINGS

Program Listing

```
10 REM PROGRAM TITLE: NEWSPAPER CLIPP
   INGS
20 CLS
30 CLEAR1500
40 FOR I=1TO10:READ U(I):NEXT
50 DATA 257,320,384,448,512,576
60 DATA 640,704,768,832
150 PRINTTAB(15);"NEWSPAPER CLIPPINGS"
160 PRINT
170 PRINT"RECALL DATA FROM TAPE";
180 INPUT A$
190 IF A$="YES" THEN A$="":GOTO1350
200 PRINT
210 PRINT"INSTRUCTIONS";
220 INPUT A$
230 IF A$="NO" THEN 620
240 PRINT
250 PRINT"LET YOUR COMPUTER BECOME YOU
    R"
260 PRINT"NEWSPAPER SCRAPBOOK WITH THI
    S"
270 PRINT"PROGRAM. HEADLINES AND THE T
    EXT"
280 PRINT"OF THE CLIPPING CAN BE ENTER
    ED."
290 PRINT"THIS WILL PUT AN END TO HAVI
    NG"
300 PRINT"NEWSPAPERS PILED UP IN THE C
    LOSET."
310 PRINT"WHATSMORE, YOU CAN ENTER A F
    ILE"
320 PRINT"NAME FOR EACH CLIPPING, WHIC
    H"
330 PRINT"MEANS THAT WHEN YOU RECALL A"
340 PRINT"CLIPPING FROM STORAGE, THE C
    OMPUTER"
350 PRINT"WILL 'SEARCH' FOR THE ONE YO
    U REQUEST."
360 PRINT
370 PRINT"PRESS ENTER";
```

```
380 INPUT X
390 CLS
400 PRINT
410 PRINT"WHEN YOU ENTER THE CONTENTS
    OF THE"
415 PRINT"CLIPPING: IF THE CHARACTER L
    ENGTH"
420 PRINT"EXCEEDS 240 CHARACTERS (THE
    KEYBOARD"
425 PRINT"WILL SEEM FROZEN) PRESS <ENT
    ER>. THE"
430 PRINT"COMPUTER WILL TELL YOU HOW T
    O ADD TO"
435 PRINT"THAT SAME PARAGRAPH. JUST RE
    MEMBER"
440 PRINT"IF YOU WANT TO FINISH A WORD
    , START"
445 PRINT"THE NEXT <CONTENTS> WITH THE
     REST OF"
450 PRINT"THAT WORD. IF YOU WANT TO IN
    SERT A SPACE"
455 PRINT"PRESS THE <↑> UP ARROW THEN
    ENTER THE"
460 PRINT"CONTENTS RIGHT AFTERWARD (TH
    E COMPUTER"
465 PRINT"WILL INSERT A SPACE FOR YOU)
    ."
470 PRINT
475 INPUT"PRESS ENTER";X:CLS:PRINT
480 PRINT"AFTER YOU HAVE FINISHED ENTE
    RING"
485 PRINT"THE COMPLETED FILE, THE COMP
    UTER"
490 PRINT"WILL PRINT-OUT YOUR ENTIRE F
    ILE FOR"
495 PRINT"YOU. YOU WILL FIND THAT THE
    PRINT-"
500 PRINT"OUT WILL BE VERY IMPRESSIVE.
     ONE OTHER"
505 PRINT"THING SHOULD BE MENTIONED HE
    RE. WHEN"
510 PRINT"YOU ARE ENTERING THE CONTENTS
    OF THE"
```

```
515 PRINT"CLIPPING DON'T WORRY ABOUT T
    HE WORDS"
520 PRINT"WRAPPING-AROUND THE VIDEO, T
    HE"
525 PRINT"COMPUTER WILL STRAIGHTEN ALL
     THIS"
530 PRINT"UP FOR YOU WHEN IT'S PRINTED
     OUT."
540 PRINT
550 PRINT"PRESS ENTER TO START FILE";
560 INPUT X
570 CLS
580 PRINT
590 PRINT"TO CANCEL ENTRIES INTO FILE.
    ...."
600 PRINT"PRESS ENTER FOR <DATE OF NEW
    SPAPER>"
610 FOR X=1TO3000:NEXT
620 CLS
630 PRINT
640 I=1
650 PRINT"DATE OF NEWSPAPER";
660 INPUT D$(I):D(I)=LEN(D$(I))
670 IF D(I)=0 THEN I=I-1:GOTO820
680 PRINT"HEADLINE OF CLIPPING";
690 INPUT H$(I)
700 PRINT"CONTENTS OF CLIPPING";
710 INPUT C$(I)
715 IF LEN(C$(I))>=240 THEN 1500
720 PRINT
730 PRINT"ENTER A FILENAME (Y/N)";
740 INPUT A$
750 IF A$="N" THEN 780
760 PRINT"ENTER FILENAME FOR: ";CHR$(3
    4);H$(I);CHR$(34);
770 INPUT F$(I)
780 FOR X=1TO1000:NEXT
790 CLS
800 PRINT
810 I=I+1:GOTO650
820 F=I:FOR I=1TOF:R(I)=I:NEXT
825 I=1:PRINT
```

```
830 PRINT"THE ENTIRE FILE OF CLIPPINGS"
840 PRINT"WILL BE PRINTED BEFORE YOU"
850 PRINT"SAVE IT ON TAPE, PRESS ENTER
    ";
860 INPUT A$
870 CLS:PRINT
880 IF W=1 PRINT"CONTENTS CONTINUED...
    ":FOR X=1TO2500:NEXT:CLS:PRINT
890 REM CONTENTS OF CLIPPING WILL BE P
    RINTED
895 REM USING THE MID$ FUNCTION
900 PRINT"DATE OF NEWSPAPER:" TAB(25);
    D$(I)
910 PRINT"HEADLINE OF CLIPPING:" TAB(2
    5);H$(I)
920 PRINT"CONTENTS OF CLIPPING ";
930 IF F$(I)<>"" THEN PRINT"UNDER THE
    FILENAME: ";F$(I) ELSE PRINT
935 IF W=1 THEN M=0:T=1:GOTO950
940 T=1:V=1:M=0
950 PRINT@U(T),MID$(C$(I),V,1);
960 IF M>=50 AND MID$(C$(I),V,1)=" " T
    HEN T=T+1:GOTO1190
970 IF V<>LEN(C$(I)) THEN 990
980 GOTO1010
990 U(T)=U(T)+1:V=V+1:M=M+1
1000 GOTO950
1010 IF D$(I)=D$(I+1) THEN 1150
1015 IF I<>F THEN 1030
1020 IF J=1 THEN 1700
1025 GOTO1200
1030 I=I+1
1040 PRINT:PRINT
1050 PRINT"PRESS ENTER TO CONTINUE CLIP
     PINGS";
1060 INPUT A$
1070 CLS
1080 PRINT
1090 GOTO900
1150 IF MID$(C$(I+1),1,1)="*" THEN 1170
1160 I=I+1:V=1:U(T)=U(T)+1:GOTO950
1170 U(T)=U(T)+2:I=I+1:V=2
```

```
1180 GOTO950
1190 IF T>=11 THEN 1670
1195 M=0:GOTO970
1200 REM DATA TO CASSETTE
1210 PRINT@961,"PRESS ENTER AFTER VIEWI
     NG FILE";
1220 INPUT A$
1230 CLS:J=2
1240 PRINT
1250 PRINT"PLACE PLAYER IN RECORD MODE."
1260 PRINT"PRESS ENTER";
1270 INPUT A$
1280 PRINT#-1,F
1290 FOR I=1TOF:PRINT#-1,F$(I),D$(I),H$
     (I),R(I):NEXT
1300 I=1
1305 IF R(I)=0 THEN 1330
1310 PRINT#-1,C$(I)
1315 IF I<>F THEN 1325
1320 GOTO1330
1325 I=I+1:GOTO1300
1330 PRINT"DATA ON TAPE....."
1335 GOTO1700
1340 REM FROM CASSETTE
1350 CLS
1360 PRINT:J=1
1370 PRINT"PLACE PLAYER IN PLAY MODE."
1375 PRINT"ENTER FILE NAME (IF NO FILE
     NAME"
1380 PRINT"JUST PRESS ENTER)";
1390 INPUT A$
1400 INPUT#-1,F
1405 IF KL=1 KL=0
1410 FOR I=1TOF:INPUT#-1,F$(I),D$(I),H$
     (I),R(I):NEXT:GOTO1870
1415 I=1
1420 IF R(I)=0 THEN 1450
1425 INPUT#-1,C$(I)
1430 IF I<>F THEN 1440
1435 GOTO1450
1440 I=I+1:GOTO1420
1450 PRINT:IF KL=1 THEN 1400
```

```
1455 PRINT"FILE IN MEMORY, PRESS ENTER";
1460 INPUT A$
1470 F=I:I=1
1480 CLS
1490 GOTO870
1500 REM STRING TO LONG
1505 FOR X=1TO1000:NEXT
1510 PRINT
1520 PRINT"YOU HAVE EXCEEDED THE STRING
     LENGTH ";
1530 PRINTLEN(C$(I))
1540 PRINT"IF YOU WISH TO ADD MORE TO"
1545 PRINT"THE SAME PARAGRAPH (ADDED CO
     NTENTS)"
1550 PRINT"ENTER THE SAME DATE FOR THE"
1560 PRINT"NEXT ENTRY. WHEN IT IS PRINT
     ED"
1570 PRINT"OUT,THE ENTIRE CONTENTS OF T
     HE CLIP-"
1580 PRINT"PING WILL BE PRINTED TOGETHE
     R."
1590 PRINT"PRESS ENTER TO CONTINUE";
1600 INPUT A$
1610 GOTO720
1670 PRINT@961,"PRESS ENTER";
1680 INPUT A$
1682 RESTORE:FOR H=1TO10:READ U(H):NEXT
1685 CLS
1690 W=1:GOTO880
1700 PRINT:PRINT
1710 PRINT"PRESS ENTER";
1720 INPUT A$
1730 CLS
1735 IF J=2 THEN 1760
1740 PRINT
1750 PRINT"END OF FILE CONTENTS."
1760 PRINT
1770 PRINT"1) LOAD ANOTHER FILE INTO ME
     MORY"
1780 PRINT"2) START ANOTHER FILE"
1790 PRINT"3) END PROGRAM"
1800 PRINT
```

```
1810 PRINT"SELECT";
1820 INPUT A
1830 ON A GOTO 1340,1840,1950
1840 REM ANOTHER FILE
1850 FOR I=1TOF:R(I)=0:NEXT
1860 GOTO540
1870 REM RIGHT FILE ?
1880 FOR Y=1TOF
1890 IF A$=F$(Y) THEN 1930
1900 NEXT:PRINT
1910 PRINT"SEARCHING FOR FILE....."
1920 KL=1
1930 PRINT
1940 IF KL<>1 THEN PRINT"FILE LOCATED..
     ..."
1945 GOTO1415
1950 REM END OF PROGRAM
1960 CLS
1970 PRINT
1980 PRINT"END OF NEWSPAPER CLIPPINGS..
     ..."
1990 END
```

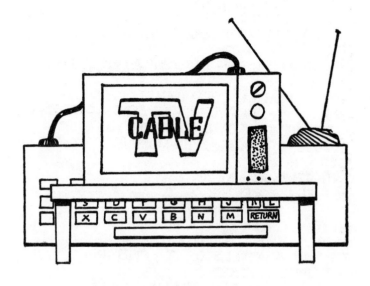

TV LISTINGS (DAILY)

Can't keep up with your TV listings booklet? Pages you wanted to see were turned into paper airplanes by your children? This program is just what you need. The time, title, channel, and program contents of all TV programs can be entered for a 24 hr. period, stored on cassette tape, and recalled whenever you wish. Inputting data will be a flash. The computer will print and run a clock for you. When the clock reaches a desired time slot, stop the clock and input your program!

SAMPLE RUN

* * * * TV LISTINGS (DAILY) * * * *

INSTRUCTIONS? <u>YES</u>
EVER GET TIRED OF LOOKING THROUGH A TV LISTING
BOOKLET WONDERING WHAT'S ON AT A CERTAIN TIME?
ONLY TO FIND OUT ONE OF YOUR CHILDREN DECIDED
THEY
WANTED TO USE THAT PAGE FOR A PAPER AIRPLANE!!

THIS PROGRAM WILL LET YOU ENTER TV PROGRAMS FOR
A 24 HOUR PERIOD, THEN THEY CAN BE STORED ON CAS-
SETTE TAPE TO RECALL WHENEVER YOU WISH.
(UP TO 25 PROGRAMS—EVEN MORE IF YOU ALTER THE
DIM
STATEMENTS AT LINE 20).
PRESS ENTER? <ENTER>

ENTRY OF THE PROGRAMS ARE SIMPLE:
A) COMPUTER WILL PRINT A TIME SCHEDULE,
WHEN YOU WANT TO STOP AT A CERTAIN
SLOT—PRESS ANY KEY
B) YOU ENTER NAME OF THE SHOW
C) YOU ENTER A BRIEF DESCRIPTION OF
THE SHOWS CONTENTS
D) COMPUTER WILL ASK CHANNEL SELECTION
(UHF/VHF/OTHER)

PRESS ENTER TO BEGIN STORAGE? <ENTER>
TIME SLOTS WILL BE PRINTED NOW
(30 MIN. INCREMENTS).
WHEN THE COMPUTER REACHES A TIME SLOT THAT YOU
WANT TO ENTER A SHOW IN PRESS ANY KEY TO STOP.
TIME WILL BEGIN WITH 12:00 A.M

DO YOU WANT TO LOAD DATA FROM TAPE (Y/N) ? <u>N</u>
ENTER THE DAY? <u>MON</u>
12:00 A.M. MON
12:30 A.M. MON

*

*

6:00 A.M. MON <SPACE BAR>

ENTER NAME OF PROGRAM FOR 6:00 A.M.
? <u>FARM REPORT</u>
ENTER A BRIEF DESCRIPTION OF "FARM REPORT"
? <u>OPENING ELEVATOR PRICES</u>
ENTER CHANNEL OF "FARM REPORT"
?<u>13</u>
CHANNEL 13—VHF (Y/N) ? <u>Y</u>

TIME OF PROGRAM: 6:00 A.M.
TITLE OF PROGRAM: "FARM REPORT"
CHANNEL OF PROGRAM: 13 (VHF)
BRIEF DESCRIPTION OF PROGRAM: "OPENING ELEVATOR
PRICES"

ARE THERE ANY OTHER SHOWS YOU WANT TO LIST FOR
6:00 A.M. ? <u>N</u>
DATA WILL NOW BE TRANSFERED TO TAPE.
PLACE CASSETTE PLAYER IN RECORD MODE.
THEN PRESS ENTER? <ENTER>
DATA NOW BEING TRANSFERED . . . .
PRESS ENTER TO CONTINUE TIME SLOTS? <ENTER>
6:30 A.M. MON
7:00 A.M. MON
.
.
.
12:00 P.M. MON
THAT CONCLUDES A 24 HOUR CLOCK CYCLE . . . . .
WOULD YOU LIKE TO SEE THE ENTIRE 24 HOUR
PROGRAM LISTING YOU'VE SELECTED? <u>N</u>
END OF TV LISTINGS . . . . . .
ALL OF YOUR MATERIAL IS NOW ON CASSETTE TAPE,
TO RECALL WHENEVER YOU LIKE.

Remember, if you plan on inputting more than 25 programs, change
the DIM statements, LINE 20 before you start any entrys.

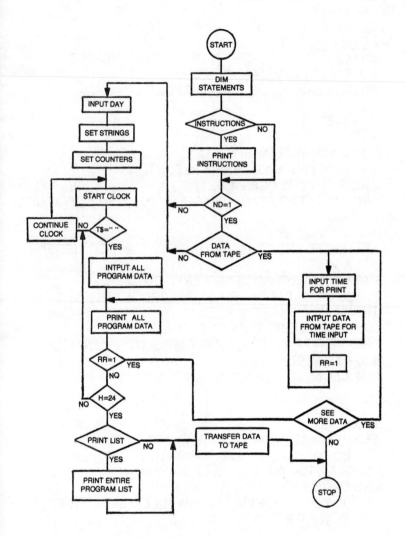

Flowchart for T V LISTINGS (DAILY)

Program Listing

```
10 REM PROGRAM TITLE: T V  LISTINGS (DAI
   LY)
20 CLS:CLEAR 1000:DIM T(25),C(25),MN$(25
   ),N$(25),D$(25),XX$(25)
30 PRINT@15,"**** T.V  LISTINGS (DAILY)
   ****"
40 PRINT
50 INPUT"INSTRUCTIONS (YES/NO)";A$
60 IF LEFT$(A$,1)="N" THEN ND=1:PRINT:PR
   INT:GOTO330
70 PRINT"EVER GET TIRED OF LOOKING THROU
   GH A T V  LISTING"
80 PRINT"BOOKLET WONDERING WHAT'S ON AT
   A CERTAIN TIME ?"
90 PRINT"ONLY TO FIND OUT ONE OF YOUR CH
   ILDREN DECIDED THEY"
100 PRINT"WANTED TO USE THAT PAGE FOR A P
    APER AIRPLANE !!"
110 PRINT
120 PRINT"THIS PROGRAM WILL LET YOU ENTER
    T V  PROGRAMS FOR"
130 PRINT"A 24 HOUR PERIOD, THEN THEY CAN
    BE STORED ON CASS-"
140 PRINT"ETTE TAPE TO RECALL WHENEVER YO
    U WISH."
145 PRINT"(UP TO 25 PROGRAMS -- EVEN MORE
    IF YOU ALTER THE DIM"
146 PRINT"STATEMENTS AT LINE 20)."
150 INPUT"PRESS ENTER";X:CLS
160 PRINT
170 PRINT"ENTRY OF THE PROGRAMS ARE SIMPL
    E:"
180 PRINT"A)  COMPUTER WILL PRINT A TIME
    SCHEDULE, WHEN YOU WANT"
185 PRINT"TO STOP AT A CERTAIN SLOT -- PR
    ESS ANY KEY"
190 PRINT"B)  YOU ENTER NAME OF THE SHOW"
200 PRINT"C)  YOU ENTER A BRIEF DESCRIPTI
    ON OF THE SHOWS CONTENTS"
205 PRINT"D)  COMPUTER WILL ASK CHANNEL S
    ELECTION (UHF/VHF/OTHER)"
```

```
210 PRINT
260 PRINT
270 INPUT"PRESS ENTER TO BEGIN STORAGE";X
    :CLS
280 PRINT
290 PRINT"TIME SLOTS WILL BE PRINTED NOW
    (30 MIN. INCREIMENTS)."
300 PRINT"WHEN THE COMPUTER REACHES A TIM
    E SLOT THAT YOU"
310 PRINT"WANT TO ENTER A SHOW IN PRESS A
    NY KEY TO STOP."
320 PRINT"TIME WILL BEGIN WITH 12:00 A.M."
330 PRINT:IF ND<>1 THEN340
335 INPUT"DO YOU WANT TO LOAD DATA FROM T
    APE (Y/N)";A$
338 IF A$="Y" THEN DD$="1":GOTO1400
340 INPUT"ENTER THE DAY";DD$:PRINT@38
    4,"                    "
350 CLS:A$="A.M.":P$="P.M.":Z$=A$
360 T=12:M=T:H=0:I=1:UU=7:LL=1:TS=1
370 IF T<=9 PRINT@385,T ELSE PRINT@384,T
375 PRINT@387,":00":PRINT@393,Z$:IF H=24
    THEN900
380 IF M-INT(M)=.5 PRINT@387,":30"
385 PRINT@399,DD$
390 FOR TI=1TO100:T$=INKEY$:IF T$<>""THEN
    460 ELSE NEXT
400 REM IF T=13 THEN T=1:M=T
410 M=M+.5
420 IF (M-INT(M))<>.5 THEN T=T+1:H=H+1:IF
    T=13 THEN T=1:M=T
430 IF H>=12 AND H<=24 THEN Z$=P$
450 GOTO370
460 PRINT
470 PRINT"ENTER NAME OF PROGRAM FOR ";T;
480 IF (M-INT(M))=.5 PRINT ":30 "; ELSE P
    RINT":00 ";
490 PRINTZ$
495 T(I)=T:Z$(I)=Z$
500 MN(I)=M-INT(M):IF MN(I)=.5 THEN MN$(I
    )="3" ELSE MN$(I)="0"
510 INPUT N$(I)
```

```
520 PRINT"ENTER A BRIEF DESCRIPTION OF ";
    CHR$(34);N$(I);CHR$(34)
530 INPUT D$(I)
540 PRINT"ENTER CHANNEL OF ";CHR$(34);N$(
    I);CHR$(34)
550 INPUT C(I)
560 IF C(I)>=2 AND C(I)<=13 THEN XX$(I)="
    VHF":GOTO590
570 IF C(I)>=14 AND C(I)<=83 THEN XX$(I)=
    "UHF":GOTO620
580 GOTO650
590 PRINT"CHANNEL ";C(I);" --- VHF (Y/N)";
600 INPUT Q$(I)
610 IF Q$(I)="Y" THEN665
620 PRINT"CHANNEL ";C(I);" --- UHF (Y/N)";
630 INPUT Q$(I)
640 IF Q$(I)="Y" THEN665
650 PRINT"ENTER FORM OF RECEPTION ";C$(I)
    ;" (CABLE, ETC.)";
660 INPUT Q$(I):XX$(I)=Q$(I)
665 IF RR=1 PRINT DD$:PRINT:ELSE PRINT
670 PRINT"TIME OF PROGRAM : ";
675 PRINT T(I);":";MN$(I);"0 ";Z$(I)
680 PRINT"TITLE OF PROGRAM: ";
685 PRINT CHR$(34);N$(I);CHR$(34)
690 PRINT"CHANNEL OF PROGRAM: ";
695 PRINTC(I);" (";XX$(I);")"
700 PRINT"BRIEF DESCRIPTION OF PROGRAM:"
710 PRINT CHR$(34);D$(I);CHR$(34)
715 IF RR=1 THEN PRINT:GOTO1520
720 LM=0
730 FOR XX=1TO50:NEXT
740 PRINT
750 LM=LM+1
760 IF LM<>UU THEN730
770 PRINT:IF RC=1 THEN FOR JK=1TO3000:NEX
    T:GOTO1000
780 PRINT"ARE THERE ANY OTHER SHOWS THAT"
790 PRINT"YOU WANT TO LIST FOR ";T;":";MN
    $(I);"0 ";Z$;" ";
800 INPUT YY$
810 U=I:I=I+1:TS=TS+1
```

43

```
820 IF YY$="YES" THEN LL=LL+1:PRINT:GOTO4
    60
830 CLS:GOSUB1200:TS=LL:LL=1:GOTO370
900 PRINT
910 PRINT"THAT CONCLUDES A";H;"HOUR CLOCK
     CYCLE....."
920 PRINT:U=I
930 PRINT"WOULD YOU LIKE TO SEE THE ENTIR
    E";H;"HOUR"
940 PRINT"PROGRAM LISTING YOU'VE SELECTED
    ";
950 INPUT YY$
960 IF YY$="YES" THEN980
970 GOTO1100
980 RC=1:I=1:UU=8
990 GOTO665
1000 I=I+1
1010 IF I<=TS THEN990
1020 FOR JK=1TO3000:NEXT
1030 GOTO1100
1100 PRINT
1110 PRINT"END OF T V  LISTINGS....."
1120 PRINT"ALL OF YOUR MATERIAL IS NOW ON
      CASSETTE TAPE,"
1130 PRINT"TO RECALL WHENEVER YOU LIKE."
1140 GOTO1700
1200 REM FOR TRANSFER OF DATA TO TAPE
1210 REM FOR JK=1TO3500:NEXT
1220 PRINT:I=1
1225 PRINT"DATA WILL NOW BE TRANSFERED TO
      TAPE."
1230 PRINT"PLACE CASSETTE PLAYER IN RECORD
      MODE."
1240 INPUT"THEN PRESS ENTER";ZZ
1260 PRINT"DATA NOW BEING TRANSFERED....."
1265 PRINT#-1,DD$
1270 PRINT#-1,LL
1280 PRINT#-1,T(I),MN$(I),Z$(I)
1290 PRINT#-1,N$(I),D$(I),C(I),XX$(I)
1295 IF I<=LL THEN I=I+1:GOTO1265
1310 INPUT"PRESS ENTER TO CONTINUE TIME SL
     OTS";Y
```

```
1320 I=U:CLS:RETURN
1400 REM LOAD DATA FROM TAPE
1405 PRINT"IF THE SHOW YOU WANT TO LOAD IS
     ON THE HOUR, (I.E."
1406 PRINT"12:00) FOR MINUTES, ENTER '0',
     ELSE ENTER"
1407 PRINT"A '3' FOR MINUTES (I.E. 12:30).
     ":PRINT
1410 PRINT"READY CASSETTE PLAYER."
1415 PRINT"THEN ENTER HOUR, MINUTE, A.M. O
     R P.M.";
1420 INPUT TT,MI,H$:I=1:L=1
1429 IF LEN(DD$)=0 GOTO1650:ELSE INPUT#-1,
     DD$
1430 INPUT#-1,LL
1440 INPUT#-1,T(I),MN$(I),Z$(I)
1445 IF T(I)<>TT OR VAL(MN$(I))<>MI OR Z$(
     I)<>H$ THEN GOSUB1600:DD$="":GOTO1429
1448 IF G<>1 PRINT:PRINT"DATA LOCATED...LO
     ADING INTO MEMORY."
1450 INPUT#-1,N$(I),D$(I),C(I),XX$(I)
1455 IF I+1<=LL THEN I=I+1:G=1:GOTO1429
1460 PRINT:PRINT"DATA NOW IN COMPUTER MEMO
     RY."
1470 PRINT:I=1
1480 PRINT"PRESS ENTER TO SEE SHOWS";
1490 INPUT Y
1500 CLS:PRINT:RR=1:TS=LL
1510 GOTO665
1520 I=I+1:IF I<=TS THEN FOR JK=1TO2550:NE
     XT:T(I)=T(I-1):MN$(I)=MN$(I-1):Z$(I)=
     Z$(I-1):PRINT:GOTO1510
1550 PRINT"TRANSFER MORE DATA (Y/N)";
1560 INPUT YY$
1570 IF YY$="Y" THEN PRINT:GOTO1410
1580 GOTO1580
1600 REM RIGHT DATA?
1610 IF G<>2 THEN PRINT:PRINT"SEARCHING FO
     R CORRECT DATA....."
1620 INPUT#-1,N$(I),D$(I),C(I),XX$(I)
1630 G=2:RETURN
1650 PRINT
```

```
1660 PRINT"NO TIME OF ";TT;":";MI;"0 ";H$;
     " CAN BE LOCATED."
1670 PRINT"TRY AGAIN...REVERSE THE TAPE AN
     D START OVER"
1680 PRINT"BUT MAKE SURE THE TIME SLOT YOU
      REQUEST IS ON TAPE."
1690 FOR JK=1TO5000:NEXT:CLS:DD$="1":GOTO1
     400
1700 PRINT
1710 PRINT"END OF PROGRAM.........."
1720 END
1730 REM YOU MIGHT NOTE FROM PRACTICE THAT
      AFTER YOU HAVE
1740 REM LOADED ALL THE T.V. PROGRAMS ON T
     APE AND YOU WANT
1750 REM TO RECALL A CERTAIN ONE, START TH
     E TAPE AT THE
1760 REM BEGINNING, AS THE COMPUTER WILL '
     SEARCH' UNTIL
1770 REM IT HAS LOCATED WHAT TIME YOU HAVE
      ENTERED.
```

TV LISTINGS (WEEKLY)

This program will take you one step further than the previous one. It will let you input and store all programs of your choice for 1 week, beginning with Saturday and ending with Friday.

Recalling TV data from tape will be a snap, all you need input is the day you want to view. The computer will 'search' through your file, until it reaches the day you've selected. Program requires 16K.

SAMPLE RUN

TV LISTINGS (WEEKLY)

SELECT:

1) BEGINNING FILE
2) RECEIVE DATA FROM RECORDER

<u>1</u>

THIS PROGRAM WILL RECEIVE ALL THE DATA YOU INPUT
FOR EACH AND EVERY TV PROGRAM YOU WANT, THEN
STORE EACH DAYS LISTING ON CASSETTE TAPE. WHEN
READY TO RETRIEVE THE DATA, YOU ENTER THE DAY
YOU WANT, THE COMPUTER WILL 'SEARCH' FOR THAT
DAY.
THEN LIST THE PROGRAMS ONE BY ONE.
NOTE: THIS PROGRAM IS DESIGNED TO ACCEPT UP TO
25 PROGRAMS FOR 1 DAY).
IF YOU ARE SHORT ON MEMORY SPACE, ENTER ONLY
BRIEF DESCRIPTIONS OF EACH PROGRAM.
ALL THIS . . . WITHOUT THE HASSLE OF ASKING, WHERE'S
THE TV LISTING BOOKLET?

PRESS ANY KEY <SPACE BAR>

AS WITH ANY ORDINARY TV LISTING BOOKLET, THE DAY
OF THE WEEK WILL BEGIN WITH SATURDAY AND END
WITH FRIDAY. THE DAY AND A CLOCK WILL BE PRINTED
(THE
CLOCK WILL ADVANCE 30 MINUTES, EVERY SECOND).
WHEN
YOU WANT TO STOP THE CLOCK AND ENTER THE PRO-
GRAM(S)
PRESS ANY KEY.

YOU WILL THEN ENTER THE CHANNEL OF THE SHOW,
THE
TITLE, AND A DESCRIPTION OF IT'S CONTENTS. AFTER
YOU HAVE FINISHED WITH THAT TIME SLOT, THE DATA
WILL BE PROCESSED TO CASSETTE TAPE, FOR FUTURE
REFERENCE, THEN THE CLOCK WILL CONTINUE.

PRESS ANY KEY <SPACE BAR>

At this point you will begin inputting all tv data information. The 'clock' will use the CHR$(23) function, making reading of time a little easier.

TO START CLOCK PRESS ANY KEY <SPACE BAR>
12:00 A.M. SATURDAY
12:30 A.M. SATURDAY
.
.
.
7:00 A.M. SATURDAY <SPACE BAR>

TIME: 7:00 A.M.

CHANNEL OF PROGRAM? 13
TITLE OF PROGRAM? CAPTAIN KANGAROO
DESCRIPTION OF CAPTAIN KANGAROO?
?NONE

CHANNEL: 13
TITLE: CAPTAIN KANGAROO
DESCRIPTION OF CAPTAIN KANGAROO:
NONE

ARE THERE ANY OTHER SHOWS YOU WANT TO LIST
FOR 7:00 A.M. SATURDAY
?NO
7:00 A.M. SATURDAY
7:30 A.M. SATURDAY
8:00 A.M. SATURDAY
.
.
.
12:00 P.M. SATURDAY

THE DATA WILL NOW BE STORED ON CASSETTE TAPE-
FOR BEGINNING OF WEEK.
PLACE PLAYER IN RECORD MODE, THEN PRESS ENTER?
<ENTER>
DATA NOW ON TAPE.
PRESS ANY KEY TO CONTINUE CLOCK FOR INPUT

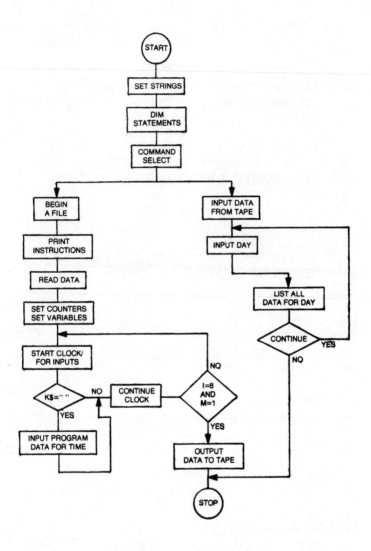

Flowchart for T V LISTINGS (WEEKLY)

50

Program Listing

```
5 REM PROGRAM TITLE: T V  LISTINGS (WEE
  KLY)
10 CLS
20 PRINT@15,"T V  LISTINGS (WEEKLY)"
30 CLEAR1000:PRINT:Q$=CHR$(143)
40 DIM C(25),M$(25),Z$(25),CH(25),T$(25)
  ,C$(25)
50 REM LINE 40 WILL LET USER INPUT 25 PR
  OGRAMS FOR 1 DAY
60 PRINT"SELECT:"
70 PRINT
80 PRINT"1) BEGINNING FILE"
90 PRINT"2) RECEIVE DATA FROM RECORDER"
100 Q=384
110 GOSUB25000
120 ON VAL(W$) GOTO 130,1500
130 CLS:PRINT
140 PRINT"THIS PROGRAM WILL RECEIVE ALL T
  HE DATA YOU INPUT"
150 PRINT"FOR EACH AND EVERY T V  PROGRAM
   YOU WANT, THEN"
160 PRINT"STORE EACH DAYS LISTING ON CASS
  ETTE TAPE. WHEN"
170 PRINT"READY TO RETRIEVE THE DATA, YOU
   ENTER THE DAY"
180 PRINT"YOU WANT, THE COMPUTER WILL 'SE
  ARCH' FOR THAT DAY."
210 PRINT"THEN LIST THE PROGRAMS ONE BY O
  NE."
220 PRINT"(NOTE: THIS PROGRAM IS DESIGNED
   TO ACCEPT UP TO"
230 PRINT"25 PROGRAMS FOR 1 DAY)."
235 PRINT"IF YOU ARE   SHORT ON MEMORY
   SPACE, ENTER ONLY BRIEF"
238 PRINT"DESCRIPTIONS OF EACH PROGRAM."
240 PRINT"ALL THIS...WITHOUT THE HASSLE O
  F ASKING, WHERE'S"
250 PRINT"THE T V  LISTING BOOKLET ?"
260 REM CONTINUE INSTRUCTIONS
270 GOSUB25070
280 Q=910:GOSUB25000
290 CLS:PRINT
```

```
300 PRINT"AS WITH ANY ORDINARY T V  LISTI
    NG BOOKLET, THE DAY"
310 PRINT"OF THE WEEK WILL BEGIN WITH SAT
    URDAY AND END WITH"
320 PRINT"FRIDAY. THE DAY AND A CLOCK WIL
    L BE PRINTED (THE"
330 PRINT"CLOCK WILL ADVANCE 30 MINUTES,
    EVERY SECOND). WHEN"
340 PRINT"YOU WANT TO STOP THE CLOCK AND
    ENTER THE PROGRAM(S)"
350 PRINT"PRESS ANY KEY."
360 PRINT
370 PRINT"YOU WILL THEN ENTER THE CHANNEL
     OF THE SHOW, THE"
380 PRINT"TITLE, AND A DESCRIPTION OF IT'
    S CONTENTS. AFTER"
390 PRINT"YOU HAVE FINISHED WITH THAT TIM
    E SLOT, THE DATA"
400 PRINT"WILL BE PROCESSED TO CASSETTE T
    APE, FOR FUTURE"
410 PRINT"REFERENCE, THEN THE CLOCK WILL
    CONTINUE."
415 REM SEE REM STATEMENTS - LINES 1300-
420 GOSUB25070
430 GOSUB25000
440 REM READ DAYS
450 FOR I=1TO7:READ D$(I):NEXT
460 DATA SATURDAY,SUNDAY,MONDAY,TUESDAY,W
    EDNESDAY
470 DATA THURSDAY,FRIDAY
480 REM SET COUNTERS
490 C=12:A$="A.M.":P$="P":I=1:M$="00":N=1
500 CLS:PRINTCHR$(23)
505 PRINT@0,"TO START CLOCK, PRESS ANY KE
    Y":Q=62:GOSUB25000
506 PRINT@0,"                            "
510 M=0:Z$=A$:YY=326
520 IF C=13 C=1
530 IF C<=9 PRINT@YY,C; ELSE PRINT@YY-2,C;
535 PRINT@YY+4,":";M$;"  ";Z$;"  ";D$(I);
    "        "
540 FOR L=1TO75:K$=INKEY$:IF K$<>""THEN 6
    10 ELSE NEXT
```

```
545 REM CHANGE SPEED OF CLOCK BY DECREASI
    NG
546 REM OR INCREASING LOOP AT LINE 540
550 IF C=13 C=1 ELSE IF MM<>0 THEN C=C+1
555 MM=M-INT(M):IF MM=.5 THEN M$="30" ELS
    E M$="00"
560 IF M>=12 Z$=P$+RIGHT$(A$,3)
570 IF M=24 THEN 790 ELSE M=M+.5
580 IF I=8 AND M=1 THEN600
585 IF M>=0 AND M<=12 THEN Z$=A$
590 GOTO520
600 PRINT@YY+128,"END OF WEEK....."
605 GOTO2090:REM END OF PROGRAM
610 REM STOP CLOCK FOR INPUT
615 VB=1
620 PRINT@YY+128+2,"TIME: ";C;":";M$;"   "
    ;Z$
630 FOR KJ=1TO1000:NEXT:CLS:PRINT
640 INPUT"CHANNEL OF PROGRAM";CH(N)
650 INPUT"TITLE OF PROGRAM";T$(N)
660 PRINT"DESCRIPTION OF ";T$(N)
670 INPUT C$(N)
680 PRINT
685 C(N)=C:M$(N)=M$:Z$(N)=Z$
690 PRINT"CHANNEL: ";CH(N)
700 PRINT"TITLE: ";T$(N)
710 PRINT"DESCRIPTION OF ";T$(N);":"
720 PRINTC$(N)
730 FOR KJ=1TO500:NEXT
740 PRINT
750 PRINT"ARE THEIR ANY OTHER SHOWS YOU W
    ANT TO LIST"
760 PRINT"FOR ";C;":";M$;"   ";Z$;"    ";D$
    (I);
770 INPUT ZZ$
780 IF ZZ$="YES" THEN N=N+1:GOTO630 ELSE8
    00
790 GOSUB1000:REM SAVE DATA ON TAPE
795 M=0:I=I+1:N=0:Z$=A$
800 CLS:PRINTCHR$(23)
820 N=N+1:GOTO520
1000 REM OUTPUT DATA TO CASSETTE TAPE
```

```
1005 Y=I:V=1
1010 CLS:PRINT:IF VB=1 THEN1020
1015 PRINT"IF YOU HAVE NO PROGRAMS TO TRAN
     SFER --"
1016 PRINT"PRESS <X> THEN <ENTER>."
1017 FOR KJ=1TO1500:NEXT
1018 CLS:PRINT
1020 PRINT"THE DATA WILL NOW BE STORED ON
     CASSETTE TAPE."
1025 IF E=1 THEN1035
1030 PRINT"START AT THE BEGINNING OF A TAP
     E -"
1032 PRINT"FOR BEGINNING OF WEEK."
1035 PRINT"PLACE PLAYER IN RECORD MODE, TH
     EN PRESS ENTER";
1040 INPUT ZZ
1060 REM DAY
1070 PRINT#-1,D$(Y)
1080 REM AMOUNT OF PROGRAMS PER TIME SLOT
     & TIME
1090 PRINT#-1,N,C(V),M$(V),Z$(V)
1100 REM CHANNEL
1120 REM TITLE
1140 REM DESCRIPTION
1150 PRINT#-1,CH(V),T$(V),C$(V)
1160 IF V<>N THEN V=V+1:GOTO1080
1180 PRINT:PRINT"DATA NOW ON TAPE."
1190 PRINT"PRESS ANY KEY TO CONTINUE CLOCK
      FOR INPUT"
1200 IF E=0 THEN Q=490 ELSE Q=362
1205 GOSUB25000
1210 E=1
1220 VB=0
1230 RETURN
1300 REM WHEN ENTERING DATA FOR PROGRAMS
1310 REM START WITH LOWEST CHANNEL, THAT
1320 REM IS IF YOU ARE GOING TO ENTER DATA
1330 REM FOR CHANNELS 4 & 5, START WITH
1340 REM CHANNEL 4 THEN GO TO CHANNEL 5
1350 REM THIS WILL SAVE TIME WHEN YOU WANT
1360 REM TO 'SEARCH' FOR A GIVEN PROGRAM
1370 REM THAT YOU HAVE PUT ON TAPE
```

```
1380 REM ALSO, START WITH THE BEGINNING DA
     Y WHEN
1390 REM HAVING THE COMPUTER 'SEARCH' FOR
     THE DATA
1400 REM YOU REQUEST -- OR YOU'LL BE REVER
     SING
1410 REM THE TAPE ALOT
1500 CLS
1510 PRINT
1520 PRINT"YOU CAN NOW RECEIVE DATA FROM T
     APE."
1530 PRINT"PLACE RECORDER IN THE PLAY MODE."
1540 DY=1:K=1:PRINT
1550 PRINT"THEN ENTER THE DAY";
1560 INPUT DD$
1570 INPUT#-1,D$(DY)
1580 IF LEFT$(D$(DY),2)<>LEFT$(DD$,2) GOSU
     B2200:GOTO1570
1590 PRINT DD$;"  LOCATED....."
1600 PRINT
1610 PRINT"RECEIVING DATA FROM RECORDER."
1680 INPUT#-1,N,C(K),M$(K),Z$(K)
1700 INPUT#-1,CH(K),T$(K),C$(K)
1720 IF K<>N THEN K=K+1:GOTO1680
1800 REM PRINT DAY, TIME, CHANNEL, TITLE
1810 REM AND DESCRIPTION OF PROGRAM
1815 K=K-1
1816 TL=1:CLS:PRINT
1820 PRINT"DAY:   ";D$(DY)
1830 PRINT"TIME: ";C(TL);":";M$(TL);"   ";Z
     $(TL)
1840 PRINT"CHANNEL: ";CH(TL)
1850 PRINT"TITLE: ";T$(TL)
1860 PRINT"DESCRIPTION OF ";T$(TL);":"
1870 PRINTC$(TL)
1880 IF TL<>K THEN 1900
1890 GOTO2000
1900 PRINT
1910 PRINT"PRESS ENTER WHEN READY TO CONTI
     NUE LISTING";
1920 INPUT YY
1930 TL=TL+1
```

```
1940 CLS:PRINT:GOTO1820
2000 PRINT
2010 PRINT"DO YOU WANT THE LISTING AGAIN (
     Y/N)";
2020 INPUT I$
2030 IF LEFT$(I$,1)<>"N" THEN1816
2040 PRINT
2050 PRINT"ARE THEIR ANY OTHER LISTINGS (D
     AY)"
2060 PRINT"THAT YOU WISH TO SEE (Y/N)";
2070 INPUT I$
2080 IF LEFT$(I$,1)<>"N" THEN K=1:CLS:GOTO
     1550
2090 PRINT
2100 PRINT"END OF PROGRAM....."
2110 PRINT"FILE CLOSED."
2120 END
2200 REM SEARCHING FOR DAY
2210 IF DY<=1 PRINT:PRINT"SEARCHING FOR ";
     DD$
2220 INPUT #-1,N,C(K),M$(K),Z$(K)
2230 INPUT#-1,CH(K),T$(K),C$(K)
2250 IF K<>N THEN K=K+1:GOTO2220
2260 DY=DY+1:K=1:N=0
2270 RETURN
25000 PRINT@Q,Q$
25010 FOR J=1TO75:NEXT
25020 PRINT@Q," "
25030 FOR KJ=1TO25:NEXT
25040 FOR JK=1TO100:NEXT
25050 W$=INKEY$:IF W$="" THEN25000
25060 RETURN
25070 PRINT:PRINT"PRESS ANY KEY"
25080 RETURN
```

RADIO PROGRAMS

There's more to life than just TV, right? That is where this program
comes in. It will let you enter and store all radio programs of your
choice. So if you haven't noticed, turn on your radio once in awhile,
there are some interesting programs on the air!

SAMPLE RUN

** RADIO PROGRAMS **

RECALL PROGRAMS FROM TAPE? <u>N</u>
SEE INSTRUCTIONS? <u>Y</u>

SO YOU THINK THAT EVERYTHING WORTH
ANYTHING IS ON TELEVISION?
TRY YOUR RADIO ONCE IN A WHILE,
YOU'LL FIND SOME VERY INTERESTING
PROGRAMS THERE. THIS PROGRAM USED
PROPERLY WILL LET YOU KNOW WHEN
ALL THOSE RADIO PROGRAMS ARE AIRED.
FOLLOW ALL INSTRUCTIONS FOR
INPUTTING THE DESIRED INFORMATION
YOU WANT TO SAVE ON TAPE,
THEN RECALL THE DATA ITEMS DAILY TO
FIND OUT THE PROGRAMS THAT ARE TO
BE AIRED THAT EVENING.
PRESS A KEY <SPACE BAR>

THIS PROGRAM WILL CARRY YOU
THROUGH ONE (1) WEEK, WHATEVER
DAY YOU START WITH, YOU WILL
HAVE 7 DAYS WITH WHICH TO
INPUT DATA.
IF YOU HAVE NO RADIO PROGRAM TO
INPUT FOR A GIVEN DAY, JUST
PRESS ENTER FOR <TITLE OF BROADCAST>.

INPUT DAY YOU WISH TO START WITH? MONDAY

*** MONDAY ***

TITLE OF BROADCAST? <u>OUTER SPACE</u>
STATION (CALL LETTERS)? <u>WAXX</u>
DATE OF BROADCAST? <u>01/01/81</u>
TIME OF BROADCAST? <u>9 P.M.</u>

PRESS ENTER TO INPUT TUESDAY'S
RADIO BROADCASTS? <ENTER>

TITLE OF BROADCAST? <u>OUTER SPACE (PART II)</u>
STATION (CALL LETTERS)? <u>WAXX</u>
DATE OF BROADCAST? <u>01/02/81</u>
TIME OF BROADCAST? <u>9 P.M.</u>

PRESS ENTER TO INPUT WEDNESDAY'S
RADIO BROADCASTS? <ENTER>

*** WEDNESDAY ***

TITLE OF BROADCAST? <u>OUTER SPACE (CONCLUSION)</u>
STATION (CALL LETTERS) ?<u>WAXX</u>
DATE OF BROADCAST? <u>01/03/81</u>
TIME OF BROADCAST? <u>9:30 P.M.</u>

PRESS ENTER TO INPUT THURSDAY'S
RADIO BROADCASTS? <ENTER>

*** THURSDAY ***

TITLE OF BROADCAST? <u>YESTERDAY'S RADIO</u>
STATION (CALL LETTERS) ?<u>WLMX</u>
DATE OF BROADCAST <u>01/04/81</u>
TIME OF BROADCAST? <u>10:15 P.M.</u>

PRESS ENTER TO INPUT FRIDAY'S
RADIO BROADCASTS? <ENTER>

*** FRIDAY ***

TITLE OF BROADCAST? <u>LEGENDS OF MONSTERS</u>
STATION (CALL LETTERS)? <u>WWXX</u>
DATE OF BROADCAST? <u>01/05/81</u>
TIME OF BROADCAST? <u>11 P.M.</u>

PRESS ENTER TO INPUT SATURDAY'S
RADIO BROADCASTS? <ENTER>

*** SATURDAY ***

TITLE OF BROADCAST? <u>LEGENDS OF MONSTERS (PART 2)</u>
STATION (CALL LETTERS)? <u>WWXX</u>
DATE OF BROADCAST? <u>01/06/81</u>
TIME OF BROADCAST? <u>11 P.M.</u>

PRESS ENTER TO INPUT SUNDAY'S
RADIO BROADCASTS? <ENTER>

*** SUNDAY ***

TITLE OF BROADCAST? <u>WESTERN DRAMAS</u>
STATION (CALL LETTERS)?<u>WSWS</u>
DATE OF BROADCAST? <u>01/07/81</u>
TIME OF BROADCAST? <u>8:30 P.M.</u>

END OF WEEK . . . . .

DO YOU WANT THE ENTIRE WEEK
OF BROADCASTS PRINTED BEFORE
SAVING THEM ON TAPE (Y/N)? <u>Y</u>

*** MONDAY ***

TITLE OF BROADCAST: <u>OUTER SPACE</u>
STATION (CALL LETTERS): <u>WAXX</u>
DATE OF BROADCAST: <u>01/01/81</u>
TIME OF BROADCAST: <u>9 P.M.</u>

*** TUESDAY ***

TITLE OF BROADCAST: <u>OUTER SPACE (PART II)</u>
STATION (CALL LETTERS): <u>WAXX</u>
DATE OF BROADCAST: <u>01/02/81</u>
TIME OF BROADCAST: <u>9 P.M.</u>

*** WEDNESDAY ***

TITLE OF BROADCAST: <u>OUTER SPACE (CONCLUSION)</u>
STATION (CALL LETTERS): <u>WAXX</u>
DATE OF BROADCAST: <u>9:30 P.M</u>

.
.
.

*** SUNDAY ***
TITLE OF BROADCAST: <u>WESTERN DRAMAS</u>
STATION (CALL LETTERS): <u>WSWS</u>
DATE OF BROADCAST: <u>01/07/81</u>
TIME OF BROADCAST: <u>8:30 P.M.</u>

READY PLAYER, PRESS RECORD & PLAY
BUTTONS, THEN PRESS ENTER?

You can see that from the sample run you will only be able to input one radio program per day, if you feel you'll need more, change the program and add more PRINT statements to ask if there are more radio programs to input for that same day. If yes, branch the program to save the current data on tape, then have it return back to the same day. Of course you will have to set the counters if adding more data to the same day.

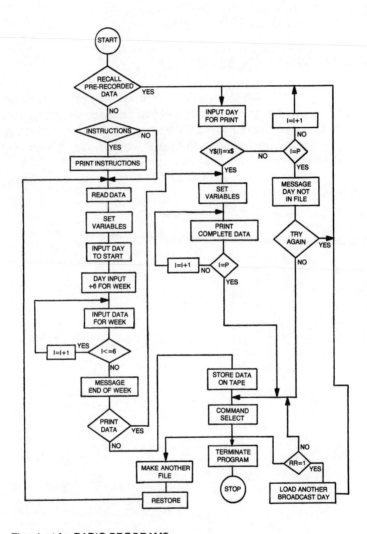

Flowchart for RADIO PROGRAMS

Program Listing


```
10 REM PROGRAM TITLE: RADIO PROGRAMS
20 CLEAR1000
30 CLS
100 PRINTTAB(15);"** RADIO PROGRAMS **
    "
110 PRINT
120 PRINT"RECALL PROGRAMS FROM TAPE";
130 INPUT X$
140 IF X$="Y" THEN 1200
150 PRINT"SEE INSTRUCTIONS";
160 INPUT X$
170 IF X$="N" THEN 440
180 PRINT
190 PRINT"SO YOU THINK THAT EVERYTHING
     WORTH"
200 PRINT"ANYTHING IS ON TELEVISION ?"
210 PRINT"TRY YOUR RADIO ONCE IN A WHI
    LE,"
220 PRINT"YOU'LL FIND SOME VERY INTERE
    STING"
230 PRINT"PROGRAMS THERE. THIS PROGRAM
     USED"
240 PRINT"PROPERLY WILL LET YOU KNOW W
    HEN"
250 PRINT"ALL THOSE RADIO PROGRAMS ARE
     AIRED."
260 PRINT"FOLLOW ALL INSTRUCTIONS FOR"
270 PRINT"INPUTTING THE DESIRED INFORM
    ATION"
280 PRINT"YOU WANT TO SAVE ON TAPE,"
290 PRINT"THEN RECALL THE DATA ITEMS D
    AILY TO"
300 PRINT"FIND OUT THE PROGRAMS THAT A
    RE TO"
310 PRINT"BE AIRED THAT EVENING."
320 PRINT:GOTO360
330 PRINT"PRESS A KEY"
340 X$=INKEY$:IF X$="" THEN 340
350 RETURN
360 GOSUB330
```

```
370 CLS
380 PRINT
390 PRINT"THIS PROGRAM WILL CARRY YOU"
400 PRINT"THROUGH ONE (1) WEEK, WHATEV
    ER"
410 PRINT"DAY YOU START WITH, YOU WILL
    "
420 PRINT"HAVE 7 DAYS WITH WHICH TO"
430 PRINT"INPUT DATA."
432 PRINT"IF YOU HAVE NO RADIO PROGRAM
     TO"
433 PRINT"INPUT FOR A GIVEN DAY, JUST"
434 PRINT"PRESS ENTER FOR <TITLE OF BR
    OADCAST>."
440 REM DAYS OF WEEK
450 FOR I=1TO7:READ D$(I):NEXT
460 I=1:D1=1:PRINT
470 PRINT"INPUT DAY YOU WISH TO START
    WITH";
480 INPUT Y$
485 FOR I=1TO7:IF D$(I)=Y$ THEN D1=I:N
    EXT:GOTO495 ELSE NEXT:GOTO495
490 PRINT"CORRECT SPELLING, THEN TRY A
    GAIN.":GOTO460
495 REM GET 7 DAYS
500 IF D$(D1)<>Y$ THEN 490
505 D=1
510 IF D1>=8 THEN D1=1
520 Y$(D)=D$(D1)
530 D=D+1
540 D1=D1+1
550 IF D<=7 THEN 510
560 REM INPUT DATA FOR DAYS
570 CLS
580 I=1:PRINT
590 PRINT TAB(15);"*** ";Y$(I);" ***"
600 PRINT
610 PRINT"TITLE OF BROADCAST";
620 INPUT T$(I)
625 IF T$(I)="" THEN 690
630 PRINT"STATION (CALL LETTERS)";
640 INPUT L$(I)
```

```
650 PRINT"DATE OF BROADCAST";
660 INPUT M$(I)
670 PRINT"TIME OF BROADCAST";
680 INPUT Q$(I)
690 IF I<=6 THEN 710
700 P=I:GOTO800
710 I=I+1
720 PRINT"PRESS ENTER TO INPUT ";Y$(I)
    ;"'S"
730 PRINT"RADIO BROADCASTS";
740 INPUT X
750 CLS
760 PRINT
770 GOTO590
800 PRINT
810 PRINT"END OF WEEK....."
820 PRINT:GOSUB330
830 CLS
840 PRINT
850 PRINT"DO YOU WANT THE ENTIRE WEEK"
860 PRINT"OF BROADCASTS PRINTED BEFORE
    "
870 PRINT"SAVING THEM ON TAPE (Y/N)";
880 INPUT A$
890 IF A$="N" THEN 1600
900 REM PRINT RADIO BROADCAST DATA
905 I=1
910 CLS:PRINT
920 PRINT TAB(15);"*** ";Y$(I);" ***"
930 PRINT
940 IF T$(I)="" THEN 1050
950 PRINT"TITLE OF BROADCAST: ";T$(I)
960 PRINT"STATION (CALL LETTERS): ";L$
    (I)
970 PRINT"DATE OF BROADCAST: ";M$(I)
980 PRINT"TIME OF BROADCAST: ";Q$(I)
985 IF RR=1 THEN M=1:GOTO1000
990 IF I<>P THEN 1010
1000 PRINT:GOSUB330
1005 IF M<>1 GOTO1600
1006 M=0:GOTO1730
1010 I=I+1
```

65

```
1015 PRINT:GOSUB330
1020 CLS
1030 PRINT
1040 GOTO920
1050 PRINT
1060 PRINT"YOU HAVE NO BROADCASTS LISTE
     D"
1070 PRINT"FOR ";Y$(I);"....."
1075 IF RR=1 PRINT"OR YOU HAVE PASSED I
     T ON TAPE."
1080 PRINT
1090 GOSUB330
1100 GOTO990
1200 REM RECALL DATA
1210 CLS:M=1
1220 PRINT
1230 PRINT"1) LOAD ENTIRE FILE"
1240 PRINT"2) LOAD A CERTAIN DAY"
1250 PRINT
1260 PRINT"SELECT";
1270 INPUT X
1280 ON X GOTO 1290,1420
1290 PRINT"PLACE TAPE IN CASSETTE MACHI
     NE,"
1300 PRINT"PRESS 'PLAY' BUTTON, THEN EN
     TER";
1310 INPUT X
1320 INPUT#-1,P
1325 IF J=1 THEN 1350
1330 PRINT"LOADING RADIO BROADCAST DATA
     ....."
1340 FOR I=1TOP
1350 INPUT#-1,Y$(I),T$(I),L$(I),M$(I),Q
     $(I)
1355 IF J=1 THEN 1470
1360 NEXT
1370 PRINT
1380 PRINT"DATA IN MEMORY."
1390 PRINT
1400 GOSUB330
1410 GOTO905
1420 PRINT"INPUT DAY YOU WISH TO LOAD"
```

```
1425 IF RR=1 PRINT"MUST BE LATER THAN "
     ;Y$(I):I=I+1
1430 INPUT X$
1440 J=1
1445 IF RR=1 THEN 1350
1450 I=1
1460 GOTO1320
1470 IF Y$(I)<>X$ THEN 1486
1480 PRINT"DATA LOCATED...IN MEMORY."
1485 PRINT:GOSUB330:RR=1:GOTO910
1486 IF I=1 PRINT"SEARCHING FOR ";X$
1490 IF I<>P THEN 1560
1500 PRINT"DAY CANNOT BE LOCATED IN FIL
     E....."
1510 PRINT"TRY AGAIN (Y/N)";
1520 INPUT A$
1530 IF A$="N" THEN RR=0:GOTO1730
1540 PRINT"REWIND TAPE....."
1550 GOTO1420
1560 I=I+1
1570 GOTO1350
1600 REM BROADCAST DATA TO TAPE
1610 CLS
1620 PRINT
1630 PRINT"READY PLAYER, PRESS RECORD &
      PLAY"
1640 PRINT"BUTTONS, THEN PRESS ENTER";
1650 INPUT X
1660 PRINT#-1,P
1670 PRINT"SAVING BROADCASTS DATA....."
1680 FOR I=1TOP
1690 PRINT#-1,Y$(I),T$(I),L$(I),M$(I),Q
     $(I)
1700 NEXT
1710 PRINT
1720 PRINT"DATA NOW ON TAPE....."
1730 PRINT
1740 PRINT"1) MAKE ANOTHER BROADCAST FI
     LE"
1750 PRINT"2) TERMINATE PROGRAM"
1755 IF RR=1 PRINT"3) LOAD ANOTHER BROA
     DCAST DAY"
```

```
1760 PRINT
1770 PRINT"SELECT";
1780 INPUT X
1790 ON X GOTO 1800,1900,1420
1800 RESTORE
1810 IF J=1 J=0
1820 GOTO440
1900 REM PROGRAM TERMINATE
1910 CLS
1920 PRINT
1930 PRINT"PROGRAM TERMINATED....."
1940 END
5000 DATA SATURDAY,SUNDAY,MONDAY
5010 DATA TUESDAY,WEDNESDAY,THURSDAY
5020 DATA FRIDAY
```

MESSAGE CENTER

Sure you could use your computer as is for a message center, but, if someone's in a hurry they won't squint to read the message you've left for them!

This program takes your message (up to 7 words), tears it apart letter-by-letter and assigns each of them to SET statements, making ¾ inches high! Messages can be stored on cassette tape, to be recalled by anyone expecting a message. Other characters you can use include the period (.) and the question mark (?).

** MESSAGE CENTER **

LOAD A MESSAGE FROM TAPE? <u>NO</u>

INSTRUCTIONS? <u>YES</u>

THIS PROGRAM WILL LET YOU
ENTER A MESSAGE OF UP TO
7 WORDS (7 CHARACTERS PER
WORD). THE CHARACTERS WILL
BE ABOUT ¾ INCHES HIGH, SO
YOUR MESSAGE WILL GET ACROSS.

PRESS ENTER? <ENTER>

AFTER YOU ENTER YOUR MESSAGE
(1 WORD AT A TIME), PRESS ENTER
AGAIN, THEN YOUR MESSAGE WILL <PRINT>.
AFTER YOU HAVE SEEN IT YOU CAN THEN
STORE IN ON TAPE, THIS
WAY WHEN SOMEONE COMES IN
ALL THEY HAVE TO DO IS BOOT-UP
THE SYSTEM AND LOAD YOUR
MESSAGE FROM TAPE.

PRESS ENTER? <ENTER>

BESIDES THE LETTERS A-Z, THE
NUMERALS 0-9 CAN ALSO BE
ENTERED. THE OTHER CHARACTERS
YOU CAN USE ARE, THE! ? .
AND THE '
SO PRESS ENTER, AND GET YOUR
MESSAGE ACROSS!!

ENTER YOUR MESSAGE? <u>PLACE   </u>

NO BLANK SPACES ALLOWED...START OVER.

ENTER YOUR MESSAGE? <u>PLACE</u>

ENTER YOUR MESSAGE? <u>YOUR</u>

ENTER YOUR MESSAGE? <u>MESSAGE</u>

ENTER YOUR MESSAGE? <u>IN</u>

ENTER YOUR MESSAGE? <u>LARGE</u>

ENTER YOUR MESSAGE? <u>LETTERS</u>

PLACE
YOUR
MESSAGE
IN
LARGE
LETTERS

ANOTHER MESSAGE? <u>YES</u>

ENTER YOUR MESSAGE? <u>CALL</u>

ENTER YOUR MESSAGE? <u>THE</u>

ENTER YOUR MESSAGE? <u>PLANT</u>

ENTER YOUR MESSAGE? <u>AT</u>

ENTER YOUR MESSAGE? <u>3</u>

ENTER YOUR MESSAGE? <u>P.M.</u>

CALL
THE
PLANT
AT
3
P.M.

ANOTHER MESSAGE? <u>YES</u>

ENTER YOUR MESSAGE? <u>YOUR MESSAGE</u>

TOO MANY LETTERS...START OVER.
ENTER YOUR MESSAGE? <u>YOUR</u>

ENTER YOUR MESSAGE? <u>WORDS</u>

ENTER YOUR MESSAGE? <u>MUST</u>

ENTER YOUR MESSAGE? <u>BE</u>

ENTER YOUR MESSAGE? <u>LESS</u>

ENTER YOUR MESSAGE? <u>THAN</u>

ENTER YOUR MESSAGE? <u>SEVEN</u>

ENTER YOUR MESSAGE? <u>EIGHT</u>

TOO MANY WORDS, ONLY 7 ALLOWED...START OVER.

The message is then wiped out. You will note from the beginning of the sample run a message was printed, NO BLANK SPACES ALLOWED...START OVER. The blank space was entered right after the word. Remember that you can INPUT no more than 7 words and no more than 7 characters per word.

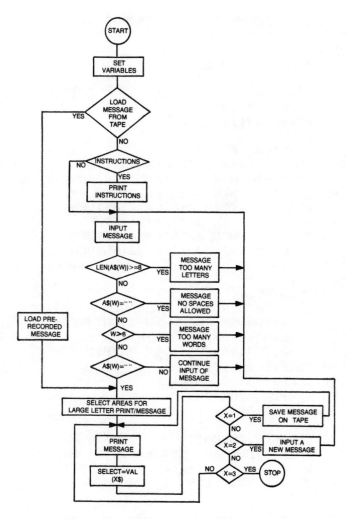

Flowchart for MESSAGE CENTER

Program Listing

```
10 CLS
15 REM PROGRAM TITLE: MESSAGE CENTER
20 L=0:M=2:N=5:I=1:Q=1
30 F=192
40 IF RR=1 THEN 290
45 IF RR=2 THEN 200
50 GOTO3000
55 IF K>=120 THEN80
60 J=K+6:K=J+12
70 RETURN
80 M=M+7:L=L+7:N=N+7
90 IF LT=3 THEN J=26:K=38:RETURN
100 IF LT=2 THEN J=38:K=50:RETURN
105 IF LT=1 THEN J=45:K=57:RETURN
110 IF LT>=7 THEN J=0:K=12:RETURN
115 IF LT=6 THEN J=5:K=17:RETURN
120 IF LT=5 THEN J=14:K=26:RETURN
130 IF LT=4 THEN J=20:K=32:RETURN
140 RETURN
200 W=1
210 PRINT@F,;
220 INPUT"ENTER YOUR MESSAGE";A$(W)
225 IF A$(W)="" THEN W=W-1:GOTO260
230 IF LEN(A$(W))>=8 THEN 300
235 IF RIGHT$(A$(W),1)=" " THEN 340
240 PRINT@F+20,"            "
245 IF W>=8 THEN 360
250 W=W+1:GOTO210
260 LT=LEN(A$(Q))
280 CLS
290 GOSUB90:GOTO400
300 PRINT"TOO MANY LETTERS...START OVE
    R."
310 FOR T=1TO1500:NEXT
320 CLS
330 GOTO200
340 PRINT"NO BLANK SPACES ALLOWED...ST
    ART OVER."
350 GOTO310
360 PRINT"TO MANY WORDS, ONLY 7 ALLOWE
    D...START OVER."
```

74

```
370 GOTO310
400 REM LETTER SELECT
410 U=ASC(MID$(A$(Q),I,1))-64
420 IF U=-31 THEN 1700
425 IF U=-25 THEN 1800
430 IF U=-18 THEN 1710
440 IF U=-1  THEN 1750
450 GOTO1900
500 REM LETTER SELECT
510 ON U GOTO 520,550,600,630,660,690,
    730,780,810,840,880,930,960,1000,1
     030,1060,1090,1110,1130,1170,1200
    ,1230,1260,1310,1340,1380
520 FOR X=JTOK:SET(X,L):SET(X,M):NEXT
530 FOR Y=LTON:SET(J,Y):SET(K,Y):NEXT
540 GOSUB55:GOTO1500
550 FOR X=JTOK:SET(X,L):SET(X,M):SET(X
    ,M+3):NEXT
560 FOR Y=LTON:SET(J,Y):NEXT:SET(K+1,M
    -1)
570 SET(K+1,M+1):SET(K+1,M+2)
580 GOSUB55:GOTO1500
600 FOR X=JTOK:SET(X,L):SET(X,N):NEXT
610 FOR Y=LTON:SET(J,Y):NEXT
620 GOSUB55:GOTO1500
630 FOR X=JTOK-1:SET(X,L):SET(X,N):NEX
    T
635 FOR Y=LTON:SET(J,Y):NEXT
640 SET(K,M-1):SET(K+1,M):SET(K+1,M+1)
    :SET(K,M+2)
650 GOSUB55:GOTO1500
660 FOR X=JTOK:SET(X,L):SET(X,M):SET(X
    ,N):NEXT
670 FOR Y=LTON:SET(J,Y):NEXT
680 GOSUB55:GOTO1500
690 FOR X=JTOK-2:SET(X,L):NEXT
700 FOR X=JTOK-4:SET(X,M):NEXT
710 FOR Y=LTON:SET(J,Y):NEXT
720 GOSUB55:GOTO1500
730 FOR X=JTOK:SET(X,L):SET(X,N):NEXT
740 FOR Y=LTON:SET(J,Y):NEXT
750 FOR Y=M+1TON:SET(K,Y):NEXT
```

```
760 FOR X=J+5TOK:SET(X,M+1):NEXT
770 GOSUB55:GOTO1500
780 FOR Y=LTON:SET(J,Y):SET(J+1,Y)
785 SET(K,Y):SET(K-1,Y):NEXT
790 FOR X=JTOK:SET(X,M):NEXT
800 GOSUB55:GOTO1500
810 FOR Y=LTON:SET(J+5,Y):SET(J+6,Y):N
    EXT
815 IF J=0 K=12
820 FOR X=J+3TOK-4:SET(X,L):SET(X,N):N
    EXT
830 GOSUB55:GOTO1500
840 FOR Y=LTON:SET(K-1,Y):SET(K,Y):NEX
    T
850 FOR X=J+3TOK:SET(X,N):NEXT
860 FOR Y=L+3TON:SET(J+3,Y):NEXT
870 GOSUB55:GOTO1500
880 FOR Y=LTON:SET(J+3,Y):SET(J+4,Y):N
    EXT
885 IF K=10 K=12
890 FOR X=J+3TOK-5:SET(X,M):NEXT
900 SET(K-4,M-1):SET(K-3,M-2):SET(K-4,
    M+1)
905 SET(K-3,M-1):SET(K-2,M-2)
910 SET(K-3,M+2):SET(K-2,M+3)
915 SET(K-4,M+2):SET(K-3,M+3)
920 GOSUB55:GOTO1500
930 FOR Y=LTON:SET(J+4,Y):SET(J+5,Y):N
    EXT
940 FOR X=J+4TOK:SET(X,N):NEXT
950 GOSUB55:GOTO1500
960 FOR Y=LTON:SET(J+1,Y):SET(J+2,Y)
965 SET(K-1,Y):SET(K-2,Y):NEXT
970 FOR Y=LTOL+3:SET(J+2,Y):J=J+1:NEXT
980 FOR Y=LTOL+3:SET(K-2,Y):K=K-1:NEXT
985 J=J+2:K=K+2
990 GOSUB55:GOTO1500
1000 FOR Y=LTON:SET(J+1,Y):SET(J+2,Y)
1005 SET(K-1,Y):SET(K-2,Y):NEXT
1010 FOR Y=LTON:SET(J+3,Y):SET(J+4,Y):J
     =J+1:NEXT
1015 SET(K-3,N)
```

```
1020 GOSUB55:GOTO1500
1030 FOR Y=LTON:SET(J+1,Y):SET(K-1,Y):N
     EXT
1040 FOR X=J+2TOK-2:SET(X,L):SET(X,N):N
     EXT
1045 IF G=1 G=0:SET(K-3,N-1):SET(K-4,N-
     1)
1050 GOSUB55:GOTO1500
1060 FOR Y=LTON:SET(J+1,Y):SET(J+2,Y):N
     EXT
1070 FOR X=J+3TOK-1:SET(X,L):SET(X,M):N
     EXT
1075 FOR Y=LTOM:SET(K-1,Y):NEXT
1080 IF G=2 G=0:FOR Y=M+1TON:SET(J+8,Y)
     :SET(J+9,Y):J=J+1:NEXT
1085 GOSUB55:GOTO1500
1090 G=1
1100 GOTO1030
1110 G=2
1120 GOTO1060
1130 FOR X=JTOK-2:SET(X,L):SET(X,M):SET
     (X,N):NEXT
1140 FOR Y=LTOM:SET(J,Y):NEXT
1150 FOR Y=MTON:SET(K-2,Y):NEXT
1160 GOSUB55:GOTO1500
1170 FOR X=JTOK-3:SET(X,L):NEXT
1180 FOR Y=L+1TON:SET(J+4,Y):SET(J+5,Y)
     :NEXT
1190 GOTO1160
1200 FOR Y=LTON:SET(J+1,Y):SET(J+2,Y)
1205 SET(K-1,Y):SET(K-2,Y):NEXT
1210 FOR X=J+1TOK-1:SET(X,N):NEXT
1220 GOTO1160
1230 FOR Y=LTON:SET(J-1,Y):SET(J,Y):J=J
     +1:NEXT
1240 FOR Y=LTON:SET(K-2,Y):SET(K-1,Y):K
     =K-1:NEXT
1250 GOTO1160:J=J+4:K=K+4:GOTO1160
1260 FOR Y=LTON:SET(J+1,Y):SET(J+2,Y)
1270 SET(K,Y):SET(K-1,Y):NEXT
1280 FOR X=J+7TOK-2:SET(X,M):M=M+1:NEXT
1285 M=M-4
```

```
1290 FOR Y=MTON:SET(J+6,Y):J=J-1:NEXT
1300 GOTO1160
1310 FOR Y=LTON:SET(J+3,Y):SET(J+4,Y):J
     =J+1:NEXT
1320 FOR Y=LTON:SET(K-3,Y):SET(K-4,Y):K
     =K-1:NEXT
1330 GOTO1160
1340 FOR Y=LTOM:SET(J,Y):SET(J+1,Y):SET
     (J+2,Y):J=J+1:NEXT
1350 FOR Y=LTOM:SET(K,Y):SET(K-1,Y):SET
     (K-2,Y):K=K-1:NEXT
1360 FOR Y=MTON:SET(J+2,Y):SET(J+3,Y):S
     ET(J+4,Y):NEXT
1370 GOTO1160
1380 FOR X=J+1TOK-1:SET(X,L):SET(X,N):N
     EXT
1390 FOR Y=LTON:SET(K-1,Y):SET(K-2,Y):S
     ET(K-3,Y):K=K-2:NEXT
1400 K=K+8:GOTO1160
1500 REM LETTERS PER WORD
1510 IF I<>LT THEN 1550
1520 GOTO1600
1550 I=I+1
1570 GOTO400
1600 IF Q<>W THEN 1620
1610 FOR XX=1TO3500:NEXT:GOTO3500
1620 Q=Q+1:LT=LEN(A$(Q))
1630 GOSUB80:I=1
1640 GOTO400
1700 FOR Y=LTON-2:SET(J+2,Y):SET(J+3,Y)
     :NEXT
1710 SET(J+2,N):SET(J+3,N)
1720 J=J-3:K=K-3:GOSUB55:GOTO1500
1750 FOR X=J+2TOK-1:SET(X,L):SET(X,M):N
     EXT
1760 FOR Y=LTOM:SET(K,Y):NEXT
1770 FOR Y=M+1TON-2:SET(J+2,Y):NEXT
1780 GOTO1710
1800 SET(J+2,L):SET(J+3,L):SET(J+3,M-1)
1810 GOTO1720
1900 REM NUMBERS
1910 IF U=-16 THEN 2020
```

```
1920 IF U=-15 THEN 2050
1930 IF U=-14 THEN 2080
1940 IF U=-13 THEN 2130
1950 IF U=-12 THEN 2170
1960 IF U=-11 THEN 1130
1970 IF U=-10 THEN 2210
1980 IF U=-9 THEN 2250
1990 IF U=-8 THEN 2290
2000 IF U=-7 THEN 2340
2010 GOTO500
2020 FOR X=J+2TOK-2:SET(X,L):SET(X,N):N
     EXT
2030 FOR Y=LTON:SET(J+2,Y):SET(K-2,Y):N
     EXT
2040 GOSUB55:GOTO1500
2050 FOR Y=LTON:SET(J+4,Y):SET(J+5,Y):N
     EXT
2060 SET(J+3,L):SET(J+3,N):SET(J+6,N)
2070 GOTO2040
2080 FOR X=J+2TOK-1:SET(X,L):SET(X,M)
2090 SET(X,N):NEXT
2100 FOR Y=LTOM:SET(K-1,Y):NEXT
2110 FOR Y=MTON:SET(J+2,Y):NEXT
2120 GOTO2040
2130 FOR X=J+2TOK-1:SET(X,L):SET(X,M)
2140 SET(X,N):NEXT
2150 FOR Y=LTON:SET(K-1,Y):NEXT
2160 GOTO2040
2170 FOR Y=LTOM:SET(J+2,Y):NEXT
2180 FOR Y=LTON:SET(K-1,Y):NEXT
2190 FOR X=J+3TOK-2:SET(X,M):NEXT
2200 GOTO2040
2210 FOR Y=LTON:SET(J+1,Y):SET(J+2,Y):N
     EXT
2220 FOR Y=M+1TON:SET(K-1,Y):NEXT
2230 FOR X=J+3TOK-2:SET(X,M+1):SET(X,N)
     :NEXT
2240 GOTO2040
2250 FOR Y=LTON:SET(K,Y):SET(K-1,Y):NEX
     T
2260 FOR X=J+2TOK-1:SET(X,L):NEXT
2270 SET(J+2,M-1):SET(J+3,M-1)
```

```
2280  GOTO2040
2290  FOR Y=LTOM-1:SET(J+2,Y):SET(K-1,Y)
      :NEXT
2300  FOR Y=MTON:SET(J+1,Y):SET(K,Y):NEX
      T
2310  FOR X=J+2TOK-1:SET(X,L):SET(X,M)
2320  SET(X,N):NEXT
2330  GOTO2040
2340  FOR Y=LTOM:SET(J+2,Y):NEXT
2350  FOR Y=LTON:SET(K-1,Y):NEXT
2360  FOR X=J+3TOK-2:SET(X,L):SET(X,M):N
      EXT
2370  GOTO2040
3000  CLS
3020  PRINT"** MESSAGE CENTER **"
3030  PRINT
3040  PRINT"LOAD A MESSAGE FROM TAPE";
3050  INPUT A$
3060  IF A$="YES" THEN 3640
3070  PRINT"INSTRUCTIONS";
3080  INPUT A$
3090  IF A$<>"YES" THEN CLS:GOTO200
3100  PRINT
3110  PRINT"THIS PROGRAM WILL LET YOU"
3120  PRINT"ENTER A MESSAGE OF UP TO"
3130  PRINT"7 WORDS (7 CHARACTERS PER"
3140  PRINT"WORD). THE CHARACTERS WILL"
3150  PRINT"BE ABOUT 3/4 INCHES HIGH, SO
      "
3160  PRINT"YOUR MESSAGE WILL GET ACROSS
      ."
3165  PRINT
3170  PRINT"PRESS ENTER";
3180  INPUT X$
3190  CLS
3200  PRINT
3210  PRINT"AFTER YOU ENTER YOUR MESSAGE
      "
3220  PRINT"(1 WORD AT A TIME), PRESS EN
      TER"
3225  PRINT"AGAIN, THEN YOUR MESSAGE WIL
      L <PRINT>."
```

```
3226 PRINT"AFTER YOU HAVE SEEN IT YOU C
     AN THEN"
3230 PRINT"THEN STORE IT ON TAPE, THIS"
3240 PRINT"WAY WHEN SOMEONE COMES IN"
3250 PRINT"ALL THEY HAVE TO DO IS BOOT-
     UP"
3260 PRINT"THE SYSTEM AND LOAD YOUR"
3270 PRINT"MESSAGE FROM TAPE."
3280 PRINT
3290 PRINT"PRESS ENTER";
3300 INPUT X$
3310 CLS
3320 PRINT
3330 PRINT"BESIDES THE LETTERS A-Z, THE
     "
3340 PRINT"NUMERALS 0-9 CAN ALSO BE"
3350 PRINT"ENTERED. THE OTHER CHARACTER
     S"
3360 PRINT"YOU CAN USE ARE, THE ! ? ,"
3370 PRINT"AND THE  '"
3380 PRINT"SO PRESS ENTER, AND GET YOUR
     "
3390 PRINT"MESSAGE ACROSS !!"
3400 INPUT X$
3410 CLS
3420 GOTO200
3500 FOR X=0TO127:SET(X,44):NEXT
3510 PRINT@960,"1) MESSAGE TO TAPE";
3520 PRINT@982,"2) NEW MESSAGE";
3525 PRINT@1000,"3) CANCEL PROGRAM";
3530 X$=INKEY$:IF X$="" THEN3530
3540 ON VAL(X$) GOTO 3550,3780,3800
3550 CLS:PRINT
3560 PRINT"READY TAPE PLAYER, THEN PRES
     S ENTER";
3570 INPUT X$
3580 PRINT"PRINTING MESSAGE ON TAPE....
     ."
3590 PRINT#-1,W
3600 FOR I=1TOW
3610 PRINT#-1,A$(I):NEXT
3620 PRINT"MESSAGE ON TAPE....."
```

```
3630 FOR XX=1TO2500:NEXT:GOTO3800
3640 PRINT"PLACE TAPE PLAYER IN PLAY MO
     DE"
3650 PRINT"THEN PRESS ENTER";
3660 INPUT X$
3670 INPUT#-1,W
3690 PRINT"INPUTTING A MESSAGE....."
3700 FOR I=1TOW
3710 INPUT#-1,A$(I):NEXT
3720 PRINT
3730 PRINT"MESSAGE IN MEMORY....."
3740 PRINT"PRESS ENTER TO SEE";
3750 INPUT X$
3760 RR=1:Q=1
3770 LT=LEN(A$(Q)):GOTO 10
3780 FOR I=1TOW:A$(W)="":NEXT
3790 RR=2:GOTO10
3800 CLS
3810 PRINT
3820 PRINT"END OF MESSAGE CENTER....."
3830 END
```

ARRANGING YOUR FURNITURE

It is agonizing to move furniture around only to find out that where you've moved it, it doesn't look right. You can use the drawing abilities of your computer so you can see how the room will look before you lug the furniture around.

The second part to the program Computer Draw will let your computer draw what 'it' wants randomly. Follow the applicable REM statements and remove the necessary REM commands from these lines. Then watch it draw.

SAMPLE RUN

<><>ARRANGING YOUR FURNITURE<><>

INSTRUCTIONS? <u>YES</u>

NO DOUBT YOU HAVE STRUGGLED TO MOVE
YOUR FURNITURE AROUND TO DIFFERENT AREAS
TO FIND THE MOST IMPRESSIVE AND MOST
FUNCTIONAL WAY TO ARRANGE THE PIECES.
YOU CAN DO ALL THAT WITH THIS PROGRAM
TO SEE WHAT THE ROOM WILL LOOK LIKE
BEFORE YOU STRAIN YOUR BACK MOVING ANY
OF THE PIECES.
DRAWING OF THE PIECES OF YOUR FURNITURE
WILL BE QUITE SIMPLE, USING THE
FOLLOWING KEYS:

PRESS ENTER? <ENTER>

LEFT ARROW KEY—TO DRAW LEFT
RIGHT ARROW KEY—TO DRAW RIGHT
UP ARROW KEY—TO DRAW UP
DOWN ARROW KEY—TO DRAW DOWN
HOLD DOWN THE <SHIFT> KEY AND
ONE OF THE 4 ABOVE KEYS TO MOVE
THE LIGHTED BLOCK TO A CERTAIN AREA
ON THE VIDEO, OR ERASE LINES.
TO DRAW DIAGONAL LINES:
PRESS THE UP + RIGHT ARROW KEYS
PRESS THE UP + LEFT ARROW KEYS
PRESS THE DOWN + RIGHT ARROW KEYS
PRESS THE DOWN + LEFT ARROW KEYS

PRESS ENTER? <ENTER>

TO CLEAR THE ENTIRE VIDEO AND
START OVER PRESS THE <CLEAR> KEY.
TO CANCEL PROGRAM PRESS THE <SHIFT>
KEY + THE <CLEAR> KEY.

PRESS ENTER NOW TO BEGIN?

At this point you'll start drawing a room with the different pieces of furniture added to it. A unique feature to this program is that when you tire of arranging your furniture, you can let your computer draw for you. To do this, follow the REM instructions in the final lines of program listing.

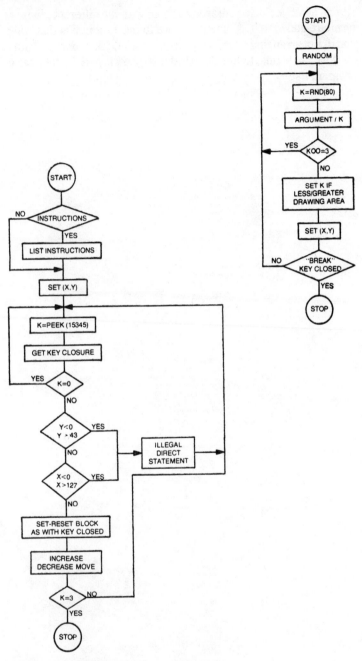

Flowchart for ARRANGING YOUR FURNITURE

Program Listing

```
10 REM PROGRAM TITLE: ARRANGING YOUR
   FURNITURE
12 REM AND ** COMPUTER DRAWING **
13 REM SEE REM STATEMENTS STARTING AT
   LINE 1200
15 CLS
20 PRINTTAB(10);"<><> ARRANGING YOUR
   FURNITURE <><>"
30 PRINT
40 PRINT"INSTRUCTIONS";
50 INPUT A$
60 IF A$="NO" THEN 400
70 PRINT
80 PRINT"NO DOUBT YOU HAVE STRUGGLED
   TO MOVE"
90 PRINT"YOUR FURNITURE AROUND TO DIFF
   ERENT AREAS"
100 PRINT"TO FIND THE MOST IMPRESSIVE
    AND MOST"
110 PRINT"FUNCTIONAL WAY TO ARRANGE TH
    E PIECES."
120 PRINT"YOU CAN DO ALL THAT WITH THI
    S PROGRAM"
130 PRINT"TO SEE WHAT THE ROOM WILL LO
    OK LIKE"
140 PRINT"BEFORE YOU STRAIN YOUR BACK
    MOVING ANY"
150 PRINT"OF THE PIECES."
160 PRINT"DRAWING OF THE PIECES OF YOU
    R FURNITURE"
170 PRINT"WILL BE QUITE SIMPLE, USING
    THE"
180 PRINT"FOLLOWING KEYS:"
190 PRINT
200 PRINT"PRESS ENTER";
210 INPUT A$
220 CLS
230 PRINT
240 PRINT"LEFT ARROW KEY -- TO DRAW LE
    FT"
```

```
250 PRINT"RIGHT ARROW KEY -- TO DRAW R
    IGHT"
260 PRINT"UP ARROW KEY -- TO DRAW UP"
270 PRINT"DOWN ARROW KEY -- TO DRAW DO
    WN"
280 PRINT"HOLD DOWN THE <SHIFT> KEY AN
    D"
290 PRINT"ONE OF THE 4 ABOVE KEYS TO M
    OVE"
300 PRINT"THE LIGHTED BLOCK TO A CERTA
    IN AREA"
310 PRINT"ON THE VIDEO, OR ERASE LINES
    ."
315 PRINT"TO DRAW DIAGONAL LINES:"
320 PRINT"PRESS THE UP + RIGHT ARROW K
    EYS"
325 PRINT"PRESS THE UP + LEFT ARROW KE
    YS"
330 PRINT"PRESS THE DOWN + RIGHT ARROW
     KEYS"
335 PRINT"PRESS THE DOWN + LEFT ARROW
    KEYS"
340 PRINT
345 PRINT"PRESS ENTER";
350 INPUT A$
355 CLS
360 PRINT
365 PRINT"TO CLEAR THE ENTIRE VIDEO AN
    D"
370 PRINT"START OVER PRESS THE <CLEAR>
     KEY."
375 PRINT"TO CANCEL PROGRAM PRESS THE
    <SHIFT>"
380 PRINT"KEY + THE <CLEAR> KEY."
385 PRINT
390 PRINT"PRESS ENTER NOW TO BEGIN";
395 INPUT A$
400 X=0:Y=0
410 CLS
420 SET(X,Y)
422 REM RANDOM:JJ=1
425 REM K=RND(80)
```

```
430 REM IF K<=3 THEN 425
435 REM IF K>=4 AND K<=8 K=8:GOTO495
440 REM IF K>=4 AND K<=9 K=9:GOTO495
445 REM IF K>=4 AND K<=16 K=16:GOTO495
450 REM IF K>=4 AND K<=17 K=17:GOTO495
455 REM IF K>=4 AND K<=32 K=32:GOTO495
460 REM IF K>=4 AND K<=33 K=33:GOTO495
465 REM IF K>=4 AND K<=40 K=40:GOTO495
470 REM IF K>=4 AND K<=48 K=48:GOTO495
475 REM IF K>=4 AND K<=64 K=64:GOTO495
480 REM IF K>=4 AND K<=65 K=65:GOTO495
485 REM IF K>=4 AND K<=72 K=72:GOTO495
490 REM IF K>=4 AND K<=80 K=80
495 REM GOTO510
500 K=PEEK(15345)
501 IF K=3 THEN 1100
505 IF K=2 THEN CLS:GOTO400
510 IF K=8 THEN 570
515 IF K=9 THEN 575
520 IF K=16 THEN 580
525 IF K=17 THEN 585
530 IF K=32 THEN 590
535 IF K=33 THEN 595
536 IF K=40 THEN 596
537 IF K=48 THEN 597
540 IF K=64 THEN 600
545 IF K=65 THEN 605
546 IF K=72 THEN 610
548 IF K=80 THEN 615
550 X=X:Y=Y
555 REM IF JJ=1 THEN 425
560 GOTO500
570 Y=Y-1:GOTO800
575 Y=Y-1:RESET(X,Y+1):GOTO800
580 Y=Y+1:GOTO800
585 Y=Y+1:RESET(X,Y-1):GOTO800
590 X=X-1:GOTO800
595 X=X-1:RESET(X+1,Y):GOTO800
596 Y=Y-1:X=X-1:GOTO800
597 Y=Y+1:X=X-1:GOTO800
600 X=X+1:GOTO800
605 X=X+1:RESET(X-1,Y):GOTO800
```

```
610 Y=Y-1:X=X+1:GOTO800
615 Y=Y+1:X=X+1
800 REM LEGAL ?
810 IF Y<0 THEN Y=0:GOSUB1000
820 IF Y>43 THEN Y=43:GOSUB1000
830 IF X<0 THEN X=0:GOSUB1000
840 IF X>127 THEN X=127:GOSUB1000
850 REM IF JJ=1 AND MM=1 THEN MM=0:GOT
    O940
860 SET(X,Y)
870 REM IF JJ=1 THEN 920
910 GOTO500
920 REM D=D+1
930 REM IF D<=30 THEN K=K:GOTO510
940 REM D=0
950 REM GOTO425
1000 REM NOT LEGAL STATEMENT
1005 REM IF JJ=1 MM=1:RETURN
1010 PRINT@960,"END OF VIDEO CAPABILITI
     ES";
1020 FOR J=1TO1000:NEXT
1030 PRINT@960,"SELECT ANOTHER ROUTE
        ";
1040 FOR J=1TO1000:NEXT
1050 PRINT@960,"                        ";
1060 RETURN
1100 REM END OF PROGRAM
1110 CLS
1120 PRINT
1130 PRINT"END OF PROGRAM....."
1140 END
1310 REM AT LINE 422 THEIR ARE <REM>
1320 REM STATEMENTS. DELETE <REM> FROM
1330 REM THE FOLLOWING LINES AND YOUR
1340 REM COMPUTER WILL DRAW FOR YOU:
1350 REM LINES <422-495>
1360 REM LINES <555, 850 & 870>
1370 REM LINES <920-950>
1380 REM AND AT LINE <1005>
1390 REM TO STOP * COMPUTER DRAWING *
1400 REM PRESS THE <BREAK> KEY
```

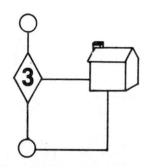

Programs for the Den or Living Room

Monthly Money Budget. Lets you know how much money you will or won't have at the end of a month.

Monthly Bill Organizer. Input all of your bill data, including names, addresses, due dates and balances. Throw away that old filing cabinet!

Extra Income. Have a hobby on the side that earns you money? You can enter all data about it, with this program.

Checkbook Balance. Keep up with all those checks you have written—deposits and balances too. Recall only one at a time or the entire file.

Warranties On Purchased Items. For anyone who has bought something and couldn't find their warranty information sheet, when the item 'broke down' and had to be returned for repairs.

Vehicle Maintenance and Repair. Lets you know everything about your vehicle, in or out of warranty.

Home Inventory. Keep tabs on everything you own with this in-depth storage program.

Medicine Log. Prescription dates, types of medicine and doctor's name are just a few items you'll be able to keep on file using this program.

Setting Up a Yardsale. Get rid of all that old 'junk' using your home computer!

MONTHLY MONEY BUDGET

This program will let you input all your income and your bills. All data will be printed out in a 'neat' fashion to let you see where your money has gone or will go, also printing what you'll have left (if any).

You can store the completed data to cassette tape for future reference or to add to it, when you choose.

SAMPLE RUN

MONTHLY MONEY BUDGET

INPUT STORED DATA? <u>NO</u>

INSTRUCTIONS FOR BEGINNING
THE MONTHLY FILE? <u>YES</u>

THIS PROGRAM CALLED 'MONTHLY MONEY
BUDGET' WILL HELP YOU PLAN
YOUR OWN BUDGET MORE PROFICIENTLY
THAN YOU THOUGHT IMAGINABLE.
YOU WILL ENTER ALL NECESSARY
DATA (WHEN ASKED TO DO SO), THE
COMPUTER WILL DO ALL THE ARITH-
METIC, DRAW A CHART AND PROCESS
ALL APPLICABLE DATA TO THE CASS-
ETTE RECORDER FOR FUTURE REFER-
ENCE.

PRESS ANY KEY . . . . . <SPACE BAR>

THERE ARE 2 CATAGORIES CONTAINED
WITHIN THIS MONTHLY MONEY
BUDGET ORGANIZER:

A) CONTROLLABLE MONTHLY EXPENSES
B) FIXED MONTHLY EXPENSES

NATURALLY, EVERYONE SHOULD AND
HAS THEIR OWN PERSONAL LIFE STYLE,
THIS IS MERELY AN ORGANIZER PROGRAM
TO MAKE THE MONTHLY PROCESSING OF
A BUDGET MORE SIMPLER FOR YOU.

PRESS ANY KEY . . . . . <SPACE BAR>

THE DIFFERENT CATAGORIES CONTAINED
WITHIN (A) AS YOU JUST READ ARE:

1) CLEANING
2) CLOTHING PURCHASES
3) RECREATION
4) EDUCATION/BOOKS

5) SAVINGS
6) MAINTENANCE/REPAIRS

PRESS ANY KEY . . . . . <SPACE BAR>

THE DIFFERENT CATAGORIES CONTAINED
WITHIN (B) ARE:

1) CHARGE ACCOUNT PAYMENTS
2) INSURANCE
3) TRANSPORTATION
4) FOOD
5) UTILITIES/FUEL
6) MORTAGE/RENT

PRESS ANY KEY . . . . . <SPACE BAR>

YOU PROBABLY HAVE OTHER MONTHLY
ITEMS YOU'LL WANT TO LIST TOO.

ENTER MONTH FOR THIS FILE
(ENTER BY NUMBER, I.E., 1
FOR JANUARY, 2 FOR FEBRUARY,
AND SO FOURTH)? 2
ENTER YEAR? 1981

ENTER NOW, ALL OF YOUR
TOTAL TAKE HOME PAY (WITH
THIS AND ALL OTHER AMOUNTS ENTERED
DO NOT USE THE ($) DOLLAR SIGN, JUST
ENTER THE AMOUNT)? 1200
ENTER NOW ANY OTHER MONTHLY INCOME
YOU RECEIVE? 0

NOW FOR THE DEDUCTIONS.

ENTER TOTAL AMOUNTS FOR THE
NEXT 12 ITEMS, IF 0 (ZERO)
ENTER 0.

CLEANING? 5
CLOTHING PURCHASES? 25
RECREATION? 15
EDUCATION/BOOKS? 35
SAVINGS? 50

MAINTENANCE/REPAIRS? <u>200</u>
CHARGE ACCOUNT PAYMENTS? <u>200</u>
INSURANCE? <u>75</u>
TRANSPORTATION? <u>75</u>
FOOD? <u>300</u>
UTILITIES/FUEL? <u>200</u>
MORTAGE/RENT? <u>200</u>

ARE THEIR ANY OTHER DEDUCTIONS
YOU WANT TO LIST (YES/NO)? <u>NO</u>

PRESS ANY KEY . . . . . <SPACE BAR>

IF YOUR ITEMS ARE GREATER
THAN 12, HOLD DOWN THE
<SHIFT> KEY AND PRESS THE
<@> TO FREEZE DISPLAY.

AFTER YOU HAVE FINISHED LOOKING
AT THE ITEMS, PRESS ANY KEY.

PRESS ANY KEY . . . . . <SPACE BAR>

FEBRUARY 1981

TOTAL MONEY AVAILABLE	x xx$1,200.00
CLEANING	xxxxxxx$5.00
CLOTHING PURCHASES	xxxxxx$25.00
RECREATION	xxxxxx$15.00
EDUCATION/BOOKS	xxxxxx$35.00
SAVINGS	xxxxxx$50.00
MAINTENANCE/REPAIRS	xxxxx$200.00
CHARGE ACCOUNT PAYMENTS	xxxxx$200.00
INSURANCE	xxxxxx$75.00
TRANSPORTATION	xxxxxx$75.00
FOOD	xxxxx$300.00
UTILITIES/FUEL	xxxxx$200.00
MORTAGE/RENT	xxxxx$200.00

TOTAL DEDUCTIONS: x xx$1,380.00

YOU ARE IN THE RED FOR: FEBRUARY 1981
HAVING A MINUS BALANCE OF: ****-$180.00

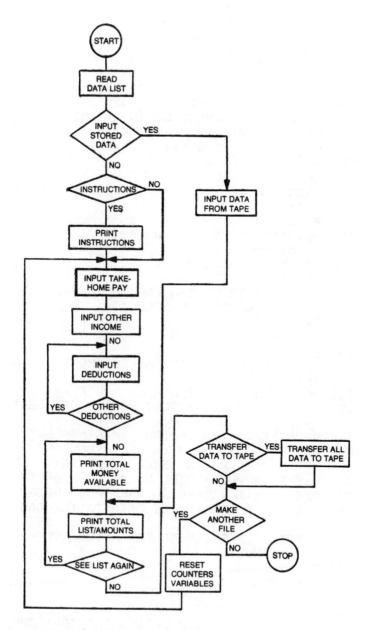

Flowchart for MONTHLY MONEY BUDGET

Program Listing

```
10 REM PROGRAM TITLE: MONTHLY MONEY BUDG
   ET
20 CLEAR1000:DIM D$(30),Y$(12),D(30)
30 REM DIM STATEMENT - LINE 20 WILL
40 REM LET USER INPUT UP TO 30 ITEMS
50 FOR I=1TO12:READ D$(I):NEXT
60 FOR I=1TO12:READ Y$(I):NEXT
80 M$="**$###,##.##"
90 CLS
100 PRINTTAB(12);"*** MONTHLY MONEY BUDGE
    T ***"
110 PRINT
120 PRINT"INPUT STORED DATA";
130 INPUT A$
140 IF A$="YES" THEN1570
145 PRINT
150 PRINT"INSTRUCTIONS FOR BEGINNING"
160 PRINT"THE MONTHLY FILE";
170 INPUT A$
180 IF A$="NO" THEN755
190 PRINT
200 PRINT"THIS PROGRAM CALLED 'MONTHLY MO
    NEY"
210 PRINT"BUDGET' WILL HELP YOU PLAN"
220 PRINT"YOUR OWN BUDGET MORE PROFICIENT
    LY"
230 PRINT"THAN YOU THOUGHT IMAGINABLE."
240 PRINT"YOU WILL ENTER ALL NECESSARY"
250 PRINT"DATA (WHEN ASKED TO DO SO), THE"
260 PRINT"COMPUTER WILL DO ALL THE ARITH-"
270 PRINT"METIC, DRAW A CHART AND PROCESS"
280 PRINT"ALL APPLICABLE DATA TO THE CASS
    -"
290 PRINT"ETTE RECORDER FOR FUTURE REFER-"
300 PRINT"ENCE.
310 PRINT
330 GOSUB2500
340 CLS
350 PRINT
360 PRINT"THEIR ARE 2 CATEGORIES CONTAINE
    D"
```

```
370 PRINT"WITHIN THIS MONTHLY MONEY"
380 PRINT"BUDGET ORGANIZER:"
390 PRINT"A) CONTROLLABLE MONTHLY EXPENSE
    S"
400 PRINT"B) FIXED MONTHLY EXPENSES"
410 PRINT
420 PRINT"NATURALLY, EVERYONE SHOULD AND"
430 PRINT"HAS THEIR OWN PERSONAL LIFE STY
    LE,"
440 PRINT"THIS IS MERELY AN ORGANIZER PRO
    GRAM"
450 PRINT"TO MAKE THE MONTHLY PROCESSING
    OF"
460 PRINT"A BUDGET MORE SIMPLER FOR YOU."
470 PRINT
490 GOSUB2500
500 CLS
510 PRINT
520 PRINT"THE DIFFERENT CATEGORIES CONTAI
    NED"
530 PRINT"WITHIN (A) AS YOU JUST READ ARE
    :"
535 PRINT
540 PRINT"1) ";D$(1)
550 PRINT"2) ";D$(2)
560 PRINT"3) ";D$(3)
570 PRINT"4) ";D$(4)
580 PRINT"5) ";D$(5)
590 PRINT"6) ";D$(6)
595 PRINT:GOSUB2500:CLS:PRINT
610 PRINT"THE DIFFERENT CATEGORIES CONTAI
    NED"
620 PRINT"WITHIN (B) ARE:"
625 PRINT
630 PRINT"1) ";D$(7)
640 PRINT"2) ";D$(8)
650 PRINT"3) ";D$(9)
660 PRINT"4) ";D$(10)
670 PRINT"5) ";D$(11)
680 PRINT"6) ";D$(12)
690 PRINT
710 GOSUB2500
```

```
720 CLS
730 PRINT
740 PRINT"YOU PROBABLY HAVE OTHER MONTHLY"
750 PRINT"ITEMS YOU'LL WANT TO LIST TOO."
755 PRINT
760 PRINT"ENTER MONTH FOR THIS FILE"
762 PRINT"(ENTER BY NUMBER, I.E., 1"
763 PRINT"FOR JANUARY, 2 FOR FEBURARY,"
764 PRINT"AND SO FOURTH)";
765 INPUT Y
766 PRINT"ENTER YEAR";
767 INPUT Q$
768 PRINT
770 PRINT"ENTER NOW, ALL OF YOUR"
780 PRINT"TOTAL TAKE HOME PAY (WITH"
790 PRINT"THIS AND ALL OTHER AMOUNTS ENTE
    RED"
800 PRINT"DO NOT USE THE <$> DOLLAR SIGN,
     JUST"
810 PRINT"ENTER THE AMOUNT)";
820 INPUT T
830 PRINT"ENTER NOW ANY OTHER MONTHLY INC
    OME"
840 PRINT"YOU RECEIVE";
850 INPUT T1
855 CLS:PRINT
860 T2=(T+T1)
865 PRINT
870 PRINT"NOW FOR THE DEDUCTIONS."
880 PRINT
890 PRINT"ENTER TOTAL AMOUNTS FOR THE"
900 PRINT"NEXT 12 ITEMS, IF 0 (ZERO)"
910 PRINT"ENTER 0."
915 PRINT
920 FOR I=1TO12
930 PRINT@512,D$(I);
940 INPUT D(I)
950 PRINT@512,"                          "
960 D=(D(I)+D)
970 NEXT:I=I-1
980 PRINT
990 PRINT"ARE THEIR ANY OTHER DEDUCTIONS"
```

```
1000 PRINT"YOU WANT TO LIST (YES / NO)";
1010 INPUT A$
1020 IF A$="YES" THEN 1035
1030 U=I+1:GOTO1105
1035 I=I+1
1040 PRINT"ENTER NAME OF ITEM";
1050 INPUT D$(I)
1060 PRINT"ENTER TOTAL AMOUNT OF ";
1070 PRINT D$(I);
1080 INPUT D(I)
1090 D=(D(I)+D)
1100 GOTO980
1105 YY$=Y$(Y)
1110 PRINT
1120 GOSUB2500:CLS:GOSUB2800
1130 I=1:K=1:J=50
1140 PRINTTAB(J-33);YY$ TAB(J-20);Q$
1145 FOR X=0TO127:SET(X,5):NEXT
1150 PRINT@128,"TOTAL MONEY AVAILABLE" TAB
     (J);USING M$;T2
1160 PRINTTAB(K);D$(I) TAB(J);USING M$;D(I)
1170 I=I+1
1190 IF I<>U THEN1160
1200 GOTO1270
1210 REM PRINT LIST AGAIN?
1220 PRINT
1230 PRINT"SEE LIST AGAIN (YES / NO)";
1240 INPUT A$
1250 IF A$="YES" THEN CLS:GOTO1130
1260 RETURN
1270 REM INCOME - DEDUCTIONS
1280 T3=(T2-D):IF T3<0 THEN KK=1
1285 FOR X=0TO127:SET(X,45):NEXT
1286 PRINT:PRINT"TOTAL DEDUCTIONS:"TAB(J);
     USING M$;D
1288 GOSUB1800
1289 IF KK=1 THEN1350
1290 PRINT"TOTAL BALANCE FOR: ";YY$;" ";Q$
1295 PRINT"AFTER DEDUCTIONS: "TAB(J);
1300 PRINT USING M$;T3
1310 Z$=INKEY$:IF Z$="" THEN1310
1320 GOSUB1210
```

```
1330 GOTO1400
1350 REM IN THE RED
1360 PRINT"YOU ARE IN THE RED FOR: ";Y$(Y)
     ;" ";Q$
1370 PRINT"HAVING A MINUS BALANCE OF: "TAB
     (J);
1380 PRINT USING M$;T3
1390 GOTO1310
1400 REM TRANSFER DATA TO TAPE?
1410 CLS
1420 PRINT
1425 IF DD=1 THEN1900
1430 PRINT"DO YOU WANT ALL DATA TRANSFERRE
     D"
1440 PRINT"TO CASSETTE TAPE (YES / NO)";
1450 INPUT A$
1460 IF LEFT$(A$,1)="N" THEN1900
1470 PRINT
1480 PRINT"READY CASSETTE PLAYER, PLACE"
1490 PRINT"IN RECORD MODE, THEN PRESS ENTE
     R";
1500 INPUT A$
1510 PRINT"DATA BEING TRANSFERRED....."
1520 PRINT#-1,YY$,Q$
1530 PRINT#-1,T2,D,U
1540 FOR J=1TOU:PRINT#-1,D(J):NEXT
1545 PRINT
1550 PRINT"TRANSFER COMPLETE....."
1560 GOTO1900
1570 PRINT
1580 PRINT"ENTER MONTH YOU WISH TO INPUT"
1590 PRINT"FROM CASSETTE PLAYER";
1600 INPUT A$
1610 PRINT"PLACE CASSETTE PLAYER IN PLAY"
1620 PRINT"MODE, AND PRESS ENTER";
1630 INPUT X$
1640 INPUT #-1,YY$,Q$
1650 IF YY$<>A$ THEN PRINT:PRINT"SEARCHING
      FOR ";A$:INPUT #-1,T2,D,U:FOR J=1TOU
     :INPUT#-1,D(J):NEXT:GOTO1640
1655 PRINT
1660 PRINTA$;" LOCATED....."
```

```
1670 INPUT#-1,T2,D,U
1680 FOR J=1TOU:INPUT#-1,D(J):NEXT
1690 DD=1
1700 GOTO1110
1800 REM TIME LOOP
1810 FOR H=1TO(I*300):NEXT
1820 RETURN
1900 REM ANOTHER FILE
1910 PRINT
1920 PRINT"WOULD YOU LIKE TO MAKE"
1930 PRINT"ANOTHER FILE NOW";
1940 INPUT A$
1950 IF RIGHT$(A$,1)="S" THEN1970
1960 GOTO1990
1970 T=0:T1=0:T3=0:D=0:KK=0:DD=0
1980 CLS
1985 GOTO755
1990 PRINT
2000 PRINT"END OF PROGRAM....."
2010 END
2500 REM GET KEY CLOSURE
2505 PRINT"PRESS ANY KEY....."
2510 A$=INKEY$
2520 IF A$="" THEN2510
2530 RETURN
2600 REM DATA FOR D$
2610 DATA CLEANING,CLOTHING PURCHASES,RECR
     EATION
2620 DATA EDUCATION / BOOKS,SAVINGS
2630 DATA MAINTENANCE / REPAIRS
2640 DATA CHARGE ACCOUNT PAYMENTS,INSURANCE
2650 DATA TRANSPORTATION,FOOD
2660 DATA UTILITIES / FUEL
2670 DATA MORTGAGE / RENT
2680 DATA JANUARY,FEBRUARY,MARCH
2690 DATA APRIL,MAY,JUNE,JULY
2700 DATA AUGUST,SEPTEMBER,OCTOBER
2710 DATA NOVEMBER,DECEMBER
2800 PRINT
2810 PRINT"IF YOUR ITEMS ARE GREATER"
2820 PRINT"THAN 12, HOLD DOWN THE"
2830 PRINT"<SHIFT> KEY AND PRESS THE"
```

```
2840 PRINT"<@> TO FREEZE DISPLAY."
2850 PRINT
2860 PRINT"AFTER YOU HAVE FINISHED LOOKING"
2870 PRINT"AT THE ITEMS, PRESS ANY KEY."
2880 PRINT
2890 GOSUB2500
2900 CLS
2910 RETURN
```

MONTHLY BILL ORGANIZER

Can't remember the doctor's office address, but you need to send some money for a past due bill? How about all those 'little' payments that are due every month? Do you find it a hassle to dig out the addresses and amount of payment?

This program will take away that cluttered filing cabinet problem. With it you can input all your bills, due dates, and current addresses. You can then transfer the data to cassette tape for storage.

SAMPLE RUN

MONTHLY BILL ORGANIZER

1) INSTRUCTIONS
2) INPUT DATA FROM RECORDER
3) SAVE DATA ON TAPE
4) START A BILL FILE
5) PRINTOUT BILL FILE
6) CANCEL PROGRAM

SELECT? 1

ALMOST EVERYONE HAS RACKED THEIR
BRAINS TRYING TO REMEMBER WHICH
BILLS ARE DUE WHEN. THIS PROGRAM
WILL LET YOUR COMPUTER REMEMBER
FOR YOU. ALL AREAS WILL BE COVERED
FROM THE CURRENT DATE TO THE AMOUNT
OF THE BILL TO THE WITHSTANDING BAL-
ANCE.

AFTER ENTERING ALL DATA YOU CAN THEN
TRANSFER ALL THE COMPLETED DATA
TO YOUR RECORDER, TO REVIEW AS YOU
FIND NECESSARY.

PRESS ENTER? <ENTER>

LET'S START BY ENTERING THE
CURRENT MONTH? JANUARY
NOW ENTER THE YEAR? 1981

ENTERING ANY MONEY AMOUNTS: DO
NOT ENTER WITH THE <$> SIGN
ONLY ENTER THE AMOUNT.
YOU'LL FIND IT MUCH EASIER IF
YOU ENTER THE BILLS IN THE
ORDER THEY ARE DUE (ORDER AS
PER DAY DUE IN MONTH).

AFTER YOU HAVE FINISHED ENTERING
ALL THE INFORMATION AND WANT TO

RETURN TO THE COMMAND LIST, ENTER
XX FOR A TITLE OF FIRM.

TITLE OF FIRM (TO WHOM YOU OWE)?
TELSTAR FURNITURE
ADDRESS OF FIRM?
2223 S. SECOND
MONTHLY PAYMENT? 45
DUE DATE? 2
BALANCE OF BILL? 450

TITLE OF FIRM (TO WHOM YOU OWE)?
LEFTY'S AUTO
ADDRESS OF FIRM?
8990 N. MAIN
MONTHLY PAYMENT? 199
DUE DATE? 3
BALANCE OF BIL? 4400

TITLE OF FIRM (TO WHOM YOU OWE)?
MAIN T.V.
ADDRESS OF FIRM?
19 WEST MAIN
MONTHLY PAYMENT? 35
DUE DATE? 3
BALANCE OF BILL? 300

TITLE OF FIRM (TO WHOM YOU OWE)?
ED'S MUSIC STORE
ADDRESS OF FIRM?
1215 EAST MAIN ST.
MONTHLY PAYMENT? 15
DUE DATE? 10
BALANCE OF BILL? 90

TITLE OF FIRM (TO WHOM YOU OWE)?
THE CARPET SHOP
ADDRESS OF FIRM?
3412 E. MAIN - SOUTH SEAS CALIF. 00001
MONTHLY PAYMENT? 45
DUE DATE? 19
BALANCE OF BILL? 1200

TITLE OF FIRM (TO WHOM YOU OWE)?
XX

1) INSTRUCTIONS
2) INPUT DATA FROM RECORDER
3) SAVE DATA ON TAPE
4) START A BILL FILE
5) PRINTOUT BILL FILE
6) CANCEL PROGRAM

SELECT? 5

TITLE	MONTHLY PMT.	DATE DUE	BALANCE
TELSTAR T.V.	$45.00	2	$450.00
LEFTY'S AUTO	$199.00	3	$4400.00
MAIN T.V.	$35.00	3	$300.00
ED'S MUSIC STORE	$15.00	10	$90.00
THE CARPET SHOP	$45.00	19	$1200.00

(1) SEE AN ADDRESS (2) MAKE CHANGES (3) COMMAND
LIST? 1
ENTER TITLE OF FIRM (BY NUMBER)? 9

NO SUCH TITLE.. . .. . ..

(1) SEE AN ADDRESS (2) MAKE CHANGES (3) COMMAND
LIST? 1

ENTER TITLE OF FIRM (BY NUMBER)? 5

3412 E. MAIN-SOUTH SEAS CALIF. 00001

(1) SEE AN ADDRESS (2) MAKE CHANGES (3) COMMAND
LIST? 2

ENTER TITLE OF FIRM (BY NUMBER)? 5

EACH PART OF THE BILL WILL BE LISTED
WHEN A PART IS REACHED YOU WANT TO CHANGE
HOLD DOWN THE SPACE BAR
TITLE: THE CARPET SHOP
ADDRESS OF FIRM: 3412 E. MAIN-SOUTH SEAS CALIF 00001
<SPACE BAR>
ENTER THE CORRECTED LINE? 3412 E. MAIN-SOUTH SEAS
CALIF 00010

108

TITLE	MONTHLY PMT.	DATE DUE	BALANCE
TELSTAR T.V.	$45.00	2	$450.00
LEFTY'S AUTO	$199.00	3	$4400.00
MAIN T.V.	$35.00	3	$300.00
ED'S MUSIC STORE	$15.00	10	$90.00
THE CARPET SHOP	$45.00	19	$1200.00

(1) SEE AN ADDRESS (2) MAKE CHANGES (3) COMMAND LIST? 3

1) INSTRUCTIONS
2) INPUT DATA FROM RECORDER
3) SAVE DATA ON TAPE
4) START A BILL FILE
5) PRINTOUT BILL FILE
6) CANCEL PROGRAM

SELECT? 3
DATA WILL NOW BE TRANSFERRED
TO CASSETTE TAPE, SET PLAYER
IN RECORD MODE, AND PRESS ENTER? ENTER
RECORDING DATA . . . . . .
TRANSFER COMPLETE . . . .

1) INSTRUCTIONS
2) INPUT DATA FROM RECORDER
3) SAVE DATA ON TAPE
4) START A BILL FILE
5) PRINTOUT BILL FILE
6) CANCEL PROGRAM

SELECT? 6

END OF FILE PROGRAM . . . . .

Just a slight sample of what you can do with this program. If your bill payment requires you to send it out-of-town you should enter the city, state and zip code (as in sample run input # 5), otherwise you need enter only the street address.

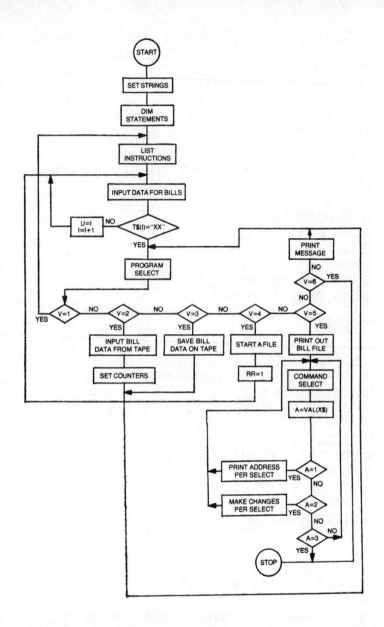

Flowchart for MONTHLY BILL ORGANIZER

110

Program Listing

```
100 REM PROGRAM TITLE: MONTHLY BILL OR
    GANIZER
110 CLEAR1000
150 CLS:R=1
160 D$="$$######.##"
170 DIM T$(30),A$(30),MP(30),D(30),B(3
    0)
200 PRINTTAB(15);"MONTHLY BILL ORGANIZ
    ER"
300 PRINT
305 GOTO10000
340 PRINT
345 PRINT"ALMOST EVERYONE HAS RACKED T
    HEIR"
350 PRINT"BRAINS TRYING TO REMEMBER WH
    ICH"
355 PRINT"BILLS ARE DUE WHEN. THIS PRO
    GRAM"
360 PRINT"WILL LET YOUR COMPUTER REMEM
    BER"
365 PRINT"FOR YOU. ALL AREAS WILL BE C
    OVERED"
370 PRINT"FROM THE CURRENT DATE TO THE
     AMOUNT"
375 PRINT"OF THE BILL TO THE WITHSTAND
    ING BAL-"
380 PRINT"ANCE."
385 PRINT
390 PRINT"AFTER ENTERING ALL DATA YOU
    CAN THEN"
395 PRINT"TRANSFER ALL THE COMPLETED D
    ATA"
400 PRINT"TO YOUR RECORDER, TO REVIEW
    AS YOU"
405 PRINT"FIND NECESSARY."
410 PRINT
415 PRINT"PRESS ENTER";
420 INPUT Q$
425 CLS
430 PRINT
```

```
435 PRINT"LET'S START BY ENTERING THE"
440 PRINT"CURRENT MONTH";
445 INPUT M$
450 PRINT"NOW ENTER THE YEAR";
455 INPUT Y$
460 PRINT
465 IF RR=1 THEN540
470 PRINT"ENTERING ANY MONEY AMOUNTS:
    DO"
475 PRINT"NOT ENTER WITH THE <$> SIGN"
480 PRINT"ONLY ENTER THE AMOUNT."
490 PRINT"YOU'LL FIND IT MUCH EASIER I
    F"
495 PRINT"YOU ENTER THE BILLS IN THE"
500 PRINT"ORDER THEY ARE DUE (ORDER AS
    "
505 PRINT"PER DAY DUE IN MONTH)."
510 PRINT
515 PRINT"AFTER YOU HAVE FINISHED ENTE
    RING"
520 PRINT"ALL THE INFORMATION AND WANT
     TO"
525 PRINT"RETURN TO THE COMMAND LIST,
    ENTER"
530 PRINT"XX FOR A TITLE OF FIRM."
535 FOR X=1TO3500:NEXT
540 CLS
545 PRINT
550 I=1
555 PRINT"TITLE OF FIRM (TO WHOM YOU O
    WE)";
560 INPUT T$(I)
562 IF T$(I)="XX" THEN I=I-1:CLS:PRINT
    :PRINT:GOTO10000
565 PRINT"ADDRESS OF FIRM";
570 INPUT A$(I)
575 PRINT"MONTHLY PAYMENT";
580 INPUT MF(I)
585 PRINT"DATE DUE";
590 INPUT D(I)
595 PRINT"BALANCE OF BILL";
600 INPUT B(I)
```

```
605 U=I:I=I+1
610 CLS
615 PRINT
620 GOTO555
700 REM DATA TO RECORDER
710 CLS
720 PRINT
730 PRINT"DATA WILL NOW BE TRANSFERRED
    "
740 PRINT"TO CASSETTE TAPE, SET PLAYER
    "
750 PRINT"IN RECORD MODE, AND PRESS EN
    TER";
760 INPUT XX$
770 PRINT
780 PRINT"RECORDING DATA....."
790 PRINT#-1,M$,Y$,U
800 FOR I=1TOU
810 PRINT#-1,T$(I),A$(I),MP(I),D(I),B(
    I)
820 NEXT
830 PRINT
840 PRINT"TRANSFER COMPLETE....."
850 FOR XX=1TO1500:NEXT
860 CLS
870 PRINT:PRINT
880 GOTO10000
1000 REM PRINTOUT LIST OF BILLS
1010 CLS
1020 FOR X=0TO127:SET(X,0):NEXT
1040 PRINT@15,M$;:PRINT@40,Y$
1045 FOR X=0TO127:SET(X,3):NEXT:PRINT
1050 PRINTTAB(0);"TITLE";TAB(15);"MONTH
     LY PMT.";
1060 PRINTTAB(35);"DATE DUE";TAB(55);"B
     ALANCE"
1070 PRINT
1080 U=1
1085 IF T$(U)="XX" THEN1150
1090 PRINTTAB(0);T$(U);TAB(15);USING D$
     ;MP(U);
1100 PRINTTAB(37);D(U);TAB(53);USING D$
     ;B(U)
```

113

```
1110 IF U<>I THEN 1130
1120 GOTO1150
1130 U=U+1
1140 GOTO1085
1150 FOR X=0TO127:SET(X,44):NEXT
1160 GOTO1200
1170 PRINT@965,"
                                        ";
1180 PRINT@965,;
1190 RETURN
1200 GOSUB1170
1210 PRINT"(1) SEE AN ADDRESS   (2) MAKE
      CHANGES   (3) COMMAND LIST";
1220 X$=INKEY$:IF X$="" THEN1220
1230 ON VAL(X$) GOTO 1300,1400,10180
1300 REM PRINT ADDRESS
1310 GOSUB1170
1320 PRINT"ENTER TITLE OF FIRM (BY NUMB
      ER)";
1330 X$=INKEY$:IF X$="" THEN1330
1340 A=VAL(X$)
1350 GOSUB1170
1360 IF A$(A)="" PRINT"NO ADDRESS IN FI
      LE.....";:GOTO1380
1370 PRINT A$(A);
1380 FOR X=1TO3000:NEXT
1390 GOTO1200
1400 REM CHANGES
1410 GOSUB1170
1420 PRINT"ENTER TITLE OF FIRM (BY NUMB
      ER)";
1430 X$=INKEY$:IF X$="" THEN1430
1440 A=VAL(X$)
1450 IF T$(A)="" PRINT"NO SUCH TITLE...
      ..";:GOTO1380
1460 GOSUB1170
1470 PRINT"EACH PART OF THE BILL WILL B
      E LISTED";
1480 GOSUB1700:GOSUB1170
1490 PRINT"WHEN A PART IS REACHED YOU W
      ANT TO CHANGE";
1500 GOSUB1700:GOSUB1170
```

```
1510 PRINT"HOLD DOWN THE <SPACE BAR>";
1520 GOSUB1700:GOSUB1170
1530 PRINT"TITLE: ";T$(A);
1540 GOSUB1800
1550 GOSUB1170
1560 PRINT"ADDRESS OF FIRM: ";A$(A);
1570 GOSUB1800
1580 GOSUB1170
1590 PRINT"MONTHLY PAYMENT: ";MP(A);
1600 GOSUB1800
1610 GOSUB1170
1620 PRINT"DATE DUE: ";D(A);
1630 GOSUB1800
1640 GOSUB1170
1650 PRINT"BALANCE: ";B(A);
1660 GOSUB1800
1670 GOSUB1170
1680 GOTO1200
1700 FOR X=1TO2500:NEXT
1710 RETURN
1800 REM CHANGES
1810 FOR X=1TO1000:NEXT
1820 X$=INKEY$
1830 IF X$<>" " THEN R=R+1:RETURN
1840 GOSUB1170
1850 PRINT"ENTER THE CORRECTED LINE";
1870 ON R GOTO1880,1890,1900,1910,1920
1880 INPUT T$(A):GOTO1930
1890 INPUT A$(A):GOTO1930
1900 INPUT MP(A):GOTO1930
1910 INPUT D(A):GOTO1930
1920 INPUT B(A)
1930 R=1
1940 GOTO1000
2000 REM DATA FROM RECORDER
2010 CLS
2020 PRINT
2030 PRINT"PLACE UNIT IN PLAY MODE,"
2040 PRINT"AND PRESS ENTER";
2050 INPUT XX$
2060 INPUT#-1,M$,Y$,U
2070 FOR I=1TOU
```

115

```
2080 INPUT#-1,T$(I),A$(I),MP(I),D(I),B(
     I)
2090 NEXT
2100 PRINT
2110 PRINT"DATA NOW IN COMPUTER MEMORY.
     ....."
2120 FOR XX=1TO1500:NEXT
2130 CLS
2140 PRINT:PRINT
2150 GOTO10000
2200 REM CANCEL PROGRAM
2210 PRINT
2220 PRINT"END OF FILE PROGRAM....."
2230 FOR XX=1TO3000:NEXT
2240 END
10000 PRINT
10010 PRINT"1) INSTRUCTIONS"
10020 PRINT"2) INPUT DATA FROM RECORDER"
10030 PRINT"3) SAVE DATA ON TAPE"
10040 PRINT"4) START A BILL FILE"
10050 PRINT"5) PRINTOUT BILL FILE"
10055 PRINT"6) CANCEL PROGRAM"
10060 PRINT
10070 PRINT"SELECT"
10080 A$=INKEY$
10090 PRINT@647,CHR$(143)
10100 FOR L=1TO100:NEXT
10110 PRINT@647," "
10120 FOR L=1TO25:NEXT
10130 IF A$="" THEN10080
10140 V=VAL(A$):CLS:PRINT
10150 ON V GOTO 340,2000,700,10160,1000,
     2200
10160 RR=1
10170 GOTO425
10180 CLS
10190 PRINT:PRINT
10200 GOTO10000
```

EXTRA INCOME

Have a hobby where you purchase numerous items to produce a certain item, sold for extra income? Perhaps you have some other source of extra income that you want to keep a complete file on. In this program data entrys can be all items purchased for and sold from your hobby. They can be transferred to tape for storage, to review, or add to at any time.

Printout, includes items purchased, items sold, amounts, and totals. The program also gives a summary of gains and losses.

SAMPLE RUN

EXTRA INCOME

NEED INSTRUCTIONS? <u>YES</u>

IF YOU HAVE A HOBBY THAT PAYS
YOU EXTRA INCOME OR SOME OTHER
SOURCE OTHER THAN A HOBBY THAT
BRINGS YOU EXTRA INCOME AND NEED
SOME WAY TO FILE IT, THIS PROGRAM
IS JUST THE TICKET.
IF YOU HAVE MORE THAN ONE SOURCE
OF EXTRA INCOME ALL DATA CAN
BE ENTERED.

PRESS A KEY <SPACE BAR>

YOU CAN ENTER ITEMS PURCHASED FOR
THE HOBBY AND AMOUNT OF MONEY
THAT YOU'VE BROUGHT IN, FROM
ALL THE ITEMS THAT YOU'VE SOLD.
IF YOU ENTER ALL ITEMS PURCHASED
PLUS ALL ITEMS SOLD CORRECTLY,
THE COMPUTER CAN PRINT YOUR
GAINS OR LOSSES. IF YOUR
LOSSES ARE TOO GREAT, THE COMPUTER
WILL HAVE A MESSAGE FOR YOU!!
IF AMOUNT OF <ITEM PURCHASED>
IS EQUAL TO 0 (ZERO), ENTER 0.
DO THE SAME FOR AMOUNT OF <ITEM SOLD>.

PRESS A KEY <SPACE BAR>

COMMAND LIST

(1) START EXTRA INCOME FILE
(2) RECALL ITEMS PURCHASED
(3) RECALL ITEMS SOLD
(4) RECALL GAINS/LOSSES
(5) SAVE FILE ON TAPE
(6) INPUT FILE FROM TAPE

118

(7) ADD DATA TO FILE
(8) TERMINATE PROGRAM

SELECT ONLY ONE? 1

SOURCE OF EXTRA INCOME (TITLE)? WOOD PICTURES
AMOUNT OF ITEM PURCHASED FOR WOOD PICTURES? 25
ENTER THAT ITEM? CLEAR PINE
DATE PURCHASED? 01/01/80
AMOUNT OF ITEM SOLD FROM WOOD PICTURES? 0
CONTINUE ENTRYS (Y/N)? Y

STARTING DATE OF FILE (M/D/Y)? 01/01/80

AMOUNT OF ITEM PURCHASED FOR WOOD PICTURES? 5
ENTER THAT ITEM? BRUSHES (3)
DATE PURCHASED? 01/01/80
AMOUNT OF ITEM SOLD FROM WOOD PICTURES? 0
CONTINUE ENTRYS (Y/N)? Y

AMOUNT OF ITEM PURCHASED FOR WOOD PICTURES? 15
ENTER THAT ITEM? PICTURE HANGERS
DATE PURCHASED? 01/02/80
AMOUNT OF ITEM SOLD FROM WOOD PICTURES? 0
CONTINUE ENTRYS (Y/N)? Y

AMOUNT OF ITEM PURCHASED FOR WOOD PICTURES? 10
ENTER THAT ITEM? STAIN
DATE PURCHASED? 01/03/80
AMOUNT OF ITEM SOLD FROM WOOD PICTURES? 75
ENTER THAT ITEM? SOLID WOOD PICTURE
DATE SOLD? 01/03/80
CONTINUE ENTRYS (Y/N)? N

CLOSING DATE OF FILE (M/D/Y)? 01/03/80

TOTAL DAYS IN FILE: 3

PRESS ENTER? <ENTER>

COMMAND LIST

(1) START EXTRA INCOME FILE

119

(2) RECALL ITEMS PURCHASED
(3) RECALL ITEMS SOLD
(4) RECALL GAINS/LOSSES
(5) SAVE FILE ON TAPE
(6) INPUT FILE FROM TAPE
(7) ADD DATA TO FILE
(8) TERMINATE PROGRAM

SELECT ONLY ONE? <u>2</u>

ITEM PURCHASED	AMOUNT OF ITEM	DATE PURCHASED
(1) CLEAR PINE	$25.00	01/01/80
(2) BRUSHES (3)	$5.00	01/01/80
(3) PICTURE HANGERS	$15.00	01/02/80
(4) STAIN	$10.00	01/03/80

TOTAL OF ITEMS PURCHASED: $55.00

PRESS ENTER? <ENTER>

COMMAND LIST

(1) START EXTRA INCOME FILE
(2) RECALL ITEMS PURCHASED
(3) RECALL ITEMS SOLD
(4) RECALL GAINS/LOSSES
(5) SAVE FILE ON TAPE
(6) INPUT FILE FROM TAPE
(7) ADD DATA TO FILE
(8) TERMINATE PROGRAM

SELECT ONLY ONE? <u>3</u>

WOOD PICTURES

ITEM SOLD	AMOUNT RECEIVED	DATE SOLD
(1) N/A	$0.00	N/A
(2) N/A	$0.00	N/A
(3) N/A	$0.00	N/A
(4) SOLID WOOD PICTURE	$75.00	01/03/80

TOTAL OF ITEMS SOLD: $75.00

PRESS ENTER? <ENTER>

* COMMAND LIST *

(1) START EXTRA INCOME FILE
(2) RECALL ITEMS PURCHASED
(3) RECALL ITEMS SOLD
(4) RECALL GAINS/LOSSES
(5) SAVE FILE ON TAPE
(6) INPUT FILE FROM TAPE
(7) ADD DATA TO FILE
(8) TERMINATE PROGRAM

SELECT ONLY ONE? 8

PROGRAM TERMINATED, ALL DATA
CLEARED FROM MEMORY.

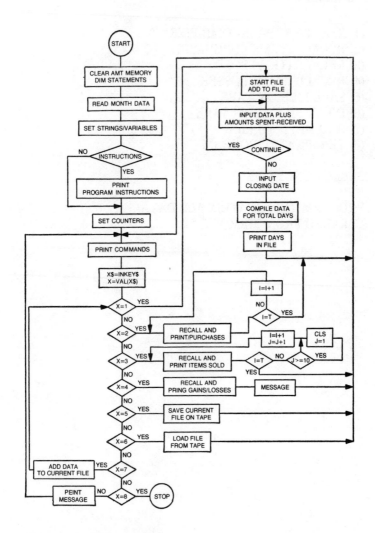

Flowchart for EXTRA INCOME

122

```
Program Listing
10 REM PROGRAM TITLE: EXTRA INCOME
20 CLEAR 1000
30 DIM M(12),P(40),P$(40),S(40),S$(40)
35 DIM DP$(40),DS$(40)
40 FOR I=1TO12:READ M(I):NEXT
50 DATA 31,28,31,30,31,30
60 DATA 31,31,30,31,30,31
70 D$="$$####.##"
80 P1=0:S2=0:CLS
100 PRINTTAB(15);"*** EXTRA INCOME ***"
110 PRINT
150 PRINT"NEED INSTRUCTIONS";
160 INPUT I$
170 IF I$="YES" GOTO2500
180 CLS
190 PRINT
200 GOTO2730
205 I=1:P=0:PRINT
210 PRINT"SOURCE OF EXTRA INCOME (TITL
    E)";
220 INPUT T$
230 PRINT"AMOUNT OF ITEM PURCHASED FOR
    ";T$;
240 INPUT P(I)
242 P1=P(I)+P1
243 IF P(I)=0 THEN P$(I)="N/A":DP$(I)=
    P$(I):GOTO250
245 INPUT"ENTER THAT ITEM";P$(I)
246 INPUT"DATE PURCHASED";DP$(I)
250 PRINT"AMOUNT OF ITEM SOLD FROM ";T
    $;
260 INPUT S(I)
262 S2=S(I)+S2
263 IF S(I)=0 THEN S$(I)="N/A":DS$(I)=
    S$(I):GOTO275
265 INPUT"ENTER THAT ITEM";S$(I)
270 INPUT"DATE SOLD";DS$(I)
275 PRINT
280 IF I=1 INPUT"STARTING DATE OF FILE
    (M/D/Y)";S$:Z$=S$:GOTO400
290 PRINT"CONTINUE ENTRYS (Y/N)";
300 INPUT I$
310 IF I$="N" THEN 340
320 I=I+1
330 PRINT:GOTO230
```

123

```
340 PRINT:P=1
350 PRINT"ENTER CLOSING DATE OF FILE (
    M/D/Y)";
360 INPUT C$
370 Z$=C$:GOTO400
380 T=I:I=1
390 GOTO500
400 REM LEADING ZERO'S
410 IF VAL(LEFT$(Z$,2))>=10 AND VAL(LE
    FT$(Z$,2))<=12 THEN 430
420 IF LEN(Z$)<=6 THEN 450 ELSE IF P=1
    THEN 380 ELSE 290
430 IF LEN(Z$)<=7 THEN 450
440 IF P=1 THEN 380 ELSE 290
450 PRINT"ENTER AGAIN, USE LEADING ZER
    O'S WHERE NECESSARY."
460 Z$="":IF P=1 THEN 340 ELSE 275
500 REM COMPILE DATA
510 S=VAL(LEFT$(S$,2))
520 S1=VAL(MID$(S$,4,2))
530 C=VAL(LEFT$(C$,2))
540 C1=VAL(MID$(C$,4,2))
550 IF ABS(S-C)>=2 THEN 572
560 IF S<>C THEN C2=M(S)+C1:GOTO580
570 C2=ABS(S1-C1)+1:GOTO 580
572 IF S>=1 AND C<=11 THEN C=C-1
575 FOR I=STOC:C2=M(I)+C2:NEXT
580 IF S1>1 THEN C2=C2-S1
600 PRINT"TOTAL DAYS IN FILE:";C2
610 PRINT
620 PRINT"PRESS ENTER";
630 INPUT X
640 CLS
650 PRINT:GOTO2730
660 REM ITEMS PURCHASED
670 IF T=0 THEN 690
680 I=1:J=1:GOTO710
690 PRINT"NO DATA IN FILE....RETURN TO
    COMMAND LIST."
700 GOTO610
710 CLS:PRINT TAB(20);T$
730 PRINT"ITEM PURCHASED" TAB(25);"AMO
    UNT OF ITEM";
735 PRINT TAB(50);"DATE PURCHASED"
740 PRINT
750 PRINTCHR$(40);I;CHR$(41);"  ";P$(I
    );
```

```
760 PRINT TAB(25);USING D$;P(I);
765 PRINT TAB(52);DP$(I)
770 IF I<>T THEN 790
780 GOTO830
790 IF J>=10 THEN 810
800 J=J+1:I=I+1:GOTO750
810 PRINTTAB(20);"PRESS ENTER";
815 INPUT X
820 CLS:J=1:I=I+1:GOTO710
830 PRINTTAB(15);"TOTAL OF ITEMS PURCH
    ASED:";
835 PRINTUSING D$;P1
840 GOTO620
850 REM ITEMS SOLD
860 IF T=0 THEN 690
870 I=1:J=1
880 CLS:PRINT TAB(20);T$
890 PRINT"ITEM SOLD" TAB(25);"AMOUNT R
    ECEIVED";
900 PRINT TAB(50);"DATE SOLD"
910 PRINT
920 PRINTCHR$(40);I;CHR$(41);"  ";S$(I
    );
930 PRINT TAB(25);USING D$;S(I);
940 PRINT TAB(52);DS$(I)
950 IF I<>T THEN 970
960 GOTO1020
970 IF J>=10 THEN 990
980 J=J+1:I=I+1:GOTO920
990 PRINT TAB(15);"PRESS ENTER";
1000 INPUT X
1010 J=1:I=I+1:GOTO880
1020 PRINT TAB(15);"TOTAL OF ITEMS SOLD
     :";
1030 PRINTUSING D$;S2
1040 GOTO620
1050 REM GAINS / LOSSES
1060 CLS
1070 PRINT
1080 PRINT"FOR THE";C2;"DAYS IN FILE:"
1090 PRINT
1100 IF P1=S2 THEN 1130
1110 IF P1>S2 THEN 1170
1120 IF P1<S2 THEN 1210
1130 PRINT"YOU BROKE EVEN:"
1140 PRINT"ITEMS PURCHASED =";
```

```
1145 PRINTUSING D$;P1
1150 PRINT"AMOUNT RECEIVED ON ITEMS SOL
     D =";
1155 PRINTUSING D$;S2
1160 GOTO610
1170 PRINT"YOU PURCHASED MORE ITEMS THA
     N YOU SOLD."
1180 PRINT"YOU SHOULD BETTER YOUR SELLI
     NG POWER."
1190 PRINT
1200 GOTO1140
1210 PRINT"YOU'VE DONE VERY WELL."
1220 PRINT"ITEMS SOLD (AMOUNT RECEIVED)
     IS GREATER"
1230 PRINT"THAN ITEMS PURCHASED."
1240 PRINT
1250 GOTO1140
1260 REM FILE <TO> CASSETTE
1270 CLS
1280 PRINT
1290 PRINT"PLACE PLAYER IN RECORD MODE
     --"
1300 PRINT"THEN PRESS ENTER";
1310 INPUT X
1320 PRINT#-1,T$
1330 PRINT"SAVING ON TAPE....."
1340 PRINT#-1,T
1350 FOR I=1TOT:PRINT#-1,P(I),P$(I),DP$
     (I)
1360 PRINT#-1,S(I),S$(I),DS$(I):NEXT
1370 PRINT#-1,S$,C$,C2
1380 PRINT#-1,P1,S2
1390 PRINT"TRANSFER COMPLETED....."
1400 GOTO610
1410 REM <FROM> CASSETTE
1420 CLS
1430 PRINT
1440 PRINT"PLACE PLAYER IN PLAY MODE --"
1450 PRINT"THEN PRESS ENTER";
1460 INPUT X
1470 INPUT#-1,T$
1480 PRINT"LOADING FILE INTO MEMORY..."
1490 INPUT#-1,T
1500 FOR I=1TOT:INPUT#-1,P(I),P$(I),DP$
     (I)
1510 INPUT#-1,S(I),S$(I),DS$(I):NEXT
1520 INPUT#-1,S$,C$,C2
```

```
1530 INPUT#-1,P1,S2
1540 PRINT"FILE IN MEMORY....."
1550 GOTO610
1560 REM ADD TO FILE
1570 CLS
1580 PRINT
1590 PRINT"COMPUTER READY TO RECEIVE"
1600 PRINT"ADDITIONAL DATA INTO CURRENT
     FILE."
1610 PRINT"PRESS ENTER TO CONTINUE";
1620 INPUT X
1630 I=I+1
1640 CLS
1650 PRINT
1660 GOTO230
1700 REM <TERMINATE> PROGRAM
1710 CLS
1720 PRINT
1730 PRINT"PROGRAM TERMINATED, ALL DATA"
1740 PRINT"CLEARED FROM MEMORY."
1750 CLEAR
1760 END
2500 REM INSTRUCTIONS
2510 PRINT
2520 PRINT"IF YOU HAVE A HOBBY THAT PAY
     S"
2530 PRINT"YOU EXTRA INCOME OR SOME OTH
     ER"
2540 PRINT"SOURCE OTHER THAN A HOBBY TH
     AT"
2550 PRINT"BRINGS YOU EXTRA INCOME AND
     NEED"
2560 PRINT"SOME WAY TO FILE IT, THIS PR
     OGRAM"
2570 PRINT"IS JUST THE TICKET."
2580 PRINT"IF YOU HAVE MORE THAN ONE SO
     URCE"
2590 PRINT"OF EXTRA INCOME ALL DATA CAN'
2600 PRINT"BE ENTERED."
2610 GOSUB3000
2620 PRINT"YOU CAN ENTER ITEMS PURCHASE
     D FOR"
2630 PRINT"THE HOBBY AND AMOUNT OF MONE
     Y"
2640 PRINT"THAT YOU'VE BROUGHT IN, FROM'
2650 PRINT"ALL THE ITEMS THAT YOU'VE SO
     LD."
```

```
2670 PRINT"IF YOU ENTER ALL ITEMS PURCH
     ASED"
2675 PRINT"PLUS ALL ITEMS SOLD CORRECTL
     Y,"
2680 PRINT"THE COMPUTER CAN PRINT YOUR"
2690 PRINT"GAINS OR LOSSES. IF YOUR"
2700 PRINT"LOSSES ARE TO GREAT, THE COM
     PUTER"
2701 PRINT"WILL HAVE A MESSAGE FOR YOU
     !!"
2705 PRINT"IF AMOUNT OF <ITEM PURCHASED
     >"
2706 PRINT"IS EQUAL TO 0 (ZERO), ENTER
     0."
2708 PRINT"DO THE SAME FOR AMOUNT OF <I
     TEM SOLD>."
2720 GOSUB3000
2730 PRINTTAB(15);"* COMMAND LIST *"
2740 PRINT
2750 PRINT"(1) START EXTRA INCOME FILE"
2760 PRINT"(2) RECALL ITEMS PURCHASED"
2770 PRINT"(3) RECALL ITEMS SOLD"
2780 PRINT"(4) RECALL GAINS / LOSSES"
2790 PRINT"(5) SAVE FILE ON TAPE"
2800 PRINT"(6) INPUT FILE FROM TAPE"
2810 PRINT"(7) ADD DATA TO FILE"
2815 PRINT"(8) TERMINATE PROGRAM"
2850 PRINT
2860 PRINT"SELECT ONLY ONE ?"
2870 GOSUB3020
2880 X=VAL(X$)
2890 ON X GOTO 205,660,850,1050,1260,14
     10,1560,1700
2895 PRINT"TRY AGAIN...SELECT 1-7"
2900 FOR T=1TO1000:NEXT
2910 CLS
2920 PRINT
2930 GOTO2730
3000 REM KEY CLOSURE
3010 PRINT@896,"PRESS A KEY"
3020 X$=INKEY$
3030 IF X$="" THEN 3020
3040 CLS
3050 PRINT
3060 RETURN
```

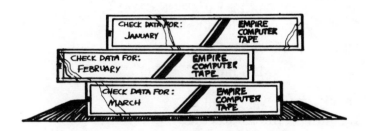

CHECKBOOK BALANCE (WITH FILING)

Almost everyone uses a checkbook, and almost everyone at one time or another has to go through their checkbook to find out necessary information about a certain check.

This program will list all of your checks, deposits, and balances. Individual checks can be recalled by number or the entire check file can be listed, including amounts of checks, dates written, etc. Deposits (including dates) can also be recalled and listed on command.

SAMPLE RUN

THIS CHECKBOOK PROGRAM WILL
LET YOU ENTER ALL DATA FOR
CHECKS WRITTEN IN A ONE MONTH PERIOD.
AFTERWHICH YOU CAN SAVE THE
ENTIRE FILE ON TAPE.
CHECKS CAN BE RECALLED ONE
AT A TIME BY THEIR CHECK NUMBER,
DEPOSITS AND BALANCES CAN ALSO
BE RECALLED (BY DATE), UP TO 100
CHECKS CAN BE ENTERED, THEN THE
ENTIRE FILE CAN BE SAVED ON CASSETTE
TAPE FOR FUTURE REFERENCE.

PRESS ENTER <ENTER>

ENTER BEGINNING BALANCE? 500

SELECT BY NUMBER ONLY:
1) MAKE A CHECKBOOK FILE
2) SEE A CHECK (RECALL)
3) DEPOSITS AND BALANCES (RECALL)
4) SAVE FILE ON TAPE
5) LOAD FILE FROM TAPE
6) TERMINATE PROGRAM
1
ENTER THE FOLLOWING INFORMATION.
(NOTE: ENTERING CHECK DATES -- EXAMPLE: 10/10/80)

TO RETURN TO COMMAND LIST -- PRESS 'ENTER'.
CHECK NUMBER? 100
CHECK DATE? 10/10/80
CHECK AMOUNT? 25.5
DEPOSIT? 125.75

CHECK NUMBER? 101
CHECK DATE? 10/10/80
CHECK AMOUNT? 14.75
DEPOSIT? 0

CHECK NUMBER? 102
CHECK DATE? 10/15/80

CHECK AMOUNT? <u>12</u>
DEPOSIT? <u>0</u>

CHECK NUMBER? <u>103</u>
CHECK DATE? <u>10/16/80</u>
CHECK AMOUNT? <u>35.65</u>
DEPOSIT? <u>300</u>

CHECK NUMBER? <u>104</u>
CHECK DATE? <u>10/20/80</u>
CHECK AMOUNT? <u>100</u>
DEPOSIT? <u>0</u>

CHECK NUMBER? <u>105</u>
CHECK DATE? <u>10/29/80</u>
CHECK AMOUNT? <u>44.87</u>
DEPOSIT? <u>100</u>

CHECK NUMBER? <u>106</u>
CHECK DATE? <u>10/30/80</u>
CHECK AMOUNT? <u>200</u>
DEPOSIT? <u>0</u>

CHECK NUMBER? <u>107</u>
CHECK DATE? <u>11/02/80</u>
CHECK AMOUNT? <u>14.27</u>
DEPOSIT? <u>0</u>

CHECK NUMBER? <ENTER>

SELECT BY NUMBER ONLY:
1) MAKE A CHECKBOOK FILE
2) SEE A CHECK (RECALL)
3) DEPOSITS AND BALANCES (RECALL)
4) SAVE FILE ON TAPE
5) LOAD FILE FROM TAPE
6) TERMINATE PROGRAM
<u>2</u>

TO RETURN TO COMMAND LIST -- ENTER 00.
ENTER 1 TO SEE ENTIRE CHECK FILE -- ELSE ENTER 0? <u>0</u>
ENTER CHECK NUMBER? <u>100</u>

CHECK #	DATE OF CHECK	AMOUNT
100	10/10/80	$25.50

SELECT BY NUMBER ONLY:
1) MAKE A CHECKBOOK FILE
2) SEE A CHECK (RECALL)
3) DEPOSITS AND BALANCES (RECALL)
4) SAVE FILE ON TAPE
5) LOAD FILE FROM TAPE
6) TERMINATE PROGRAM
<u>3</u>

SELECT ONLY ONE:
1) DEPOSITS
2) ENDING BALANCE
3) BALANCE ON A CERTAIN DATE
<u>1</u>

DATE OF DEPOSIT	AMOUNT OF DEPOSIT
10/10/80	$125.75
10/16/80	$300.00
10/29/80	$100.00

PRESS ENTER? <ENTER>

SELECT BY NUMBER ONLY:
1) MAKE A CHECKBOOK FILE
2) SEE A CHECK (RECALL)
3) DEPOSITS AND BALANCES (RECALL)
4) SAVE FILE ON TAPE
5) LOAD FILE FROM TAPE
6) TERMINATE PROGRAM
? <u>3</u>

SELECT ONLY ONE:
1) DEPOSITS
2) ENDING BALANCE
3) BALANCE ON A CERTAIN DATE
? <u>2</u>

YOUR ENDING BALANCE IS: $578.71

PRESS ENTER? <ENTER>

SELECT BY NUMBER ONLY:
1) MAKE A CHECKBOOK FILE
2) SEE A CHECK (RECALL)
3) DEPOSITS AND BALANCES (RECALL)
4) SAVE FILE ON TAPE
5) LOAD FILE FROM TAPE
6) TERMINATE PROGRAM
<u>2</u>

TO RETURN TO COMMAND LIST -- ENTER 00.
ENTER 1 TO SEE ENTIRE CHECK FILE -- ELSE ENTER 0? <u>1</u>

CHECK #	DATE OF CHECK	AMOUNT
100	10/10/80	$25.50
101	10/10/80	$14.75
102	10/15/80	$12.00
103	10/16/80	$35.65
104	10/20/80	$100.00
105	10/29/80	$44.87
106	10/30/80	$200.00
107	11/02/80	$14.27

PRESS ENTER? <ENTER>

SELECT BY NUMBER ONLY:
1) MAKE A CHECKBOOK FILE
2) SEE A CHECK (RECALL)
3) DEPOSITS AND BALANCES (RECALL)
4) SAVE FILE ON TAPE
5) LOAD FILE FROM TAPE
6) TERMINATE PROGRAM
<u>6</u>

TERMINATION OF PROGRAM . . .

Of course the check data should be transferred to tape before terminating the program, but you can see from the sample run that this program can be very useful for keeping an accurate checkbook. You can take the program further by adding more lines such as checks that are cancelled or whom the checks were paid to.

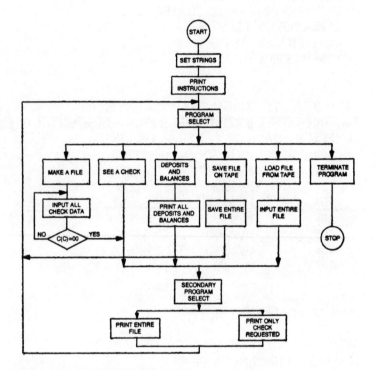

Flowchart for CHECKBOOK BALANCE

134

Program Listing

```
5 REM CHECKBOOK BALANCE (WITH FILING)
10 CLEAR1000:DIM C(100),A(100),D(100)
   ,B(100)
20 D$="$$###,###.##"
100 CLS:PRINT:P=588
110 PRINT"THIS CHECKBOOK PROGRAM WILL
    LET YOU ENTER ALL"
120 PRINT"DATA FOR CHECKS WRITTEN IN A
    ONE MONTH PERIOD."
130 PRINT"AFTERWHICH YOU CAN SAVE THE
    ENTIRE FILE ON TAPE."
140 PRINT"CHECKS CAN BE RECALLED ONE A
    T A TIME BY THEIR"
150 PRINT"CHECK NUMBER, DEPOSITS AND B
    ALANCES CAN ALSO"
160 PRINT"BE RECALLED (BY DATE). UP TO
    100 CHECKS"
170 PRINT"CAN BE ENTERED, THEN THE ENT
    IRE FILE CAN BE"
180 PRINT"SAVED ON CASSETTE TAPE FOR F
    UTURE REFERENCE."
190 PRINT"PRESS ENTER"
200 GOSUB10000
210 CLS:PRINT:IF C>0 THEN220
215 INPUT"ENTER BEGINNING BALANCE";B:CLS
220 PRINT:PRINT"SELECT BY NUMBER ONLY:"
230 PRINT"1)    MAKE A CHECKBOOK FILE"
240 PRINT"2)    SEE A CHECK (RECALL)"
250 PRINT"3)    DEPOSITS AND BALANCES (
    RECALL)"
260 PRINT"4)    SAVE FILE ON TAPE"
270 PRINT"5)    LOAD FILE FROM TAPE"
280 PRINT"6)    TERMINATE PROGRAM"
290 P=512:GOSUB10000
300 ON VAL(K$) GOTO310,430,610,900,105
    0,1200
310 C=1:CLS:PRINT
320 PRINT"ENTER THE FOLLOWING INFORMAT
    ION."
330 PRINT"(NOTE: ENTERING CHECK DATES
    -- EXAMPLE: 10/10/80)"
```

```
340 PRINT
350 PRINT"TO RETURN TO COMMAND LIST -- PR
    ESS 'ENTER'.'
370 INPUT"CHECK NUMBER";C(C):IF C(C)=00 T
    HEN FOR KK=1TO250:NEXT:CLS:GOTO220
380 INPUT"CHECK DATE";D$(C)
390 INPUT"CHECK AMOUNT";A(C)
400 INPUT"DEPOSIT";D(C)
405 FOR KK=1TO250:NEXT
410 B=B+(D(C)-A(C)):B(C)=B:C=C+1
420 PRINT:GOTO370
430 CLS:PRINT
440 PRINT"TO RETURN TO COMMAND LIST -- EN
    TER 00.'
450 PRINT:INPUT"ENTER 1 TO SEE ENTIRE CHE
    CK FILE -- ELSE ENTER 0";N:IF N=1 THE
    N550
460 INPUT"ENTER CHECK NUMBER";CN:IF CN=00
     THEN210
470 FOR I=1TOC
480 IF CN=C(I) THEN520
490 NEXT
500 PRINT"CHECK NUMBER REQUESTED --";CN;"
    -- NOT IN FILE.'
510 FOR KK=1TO1500:NEXT:GOTO430
520 PRINTTAB(5);"CHECK #" TAB(23);"DATE O
    F CHECK" TAB(49);"AMOUNT"
530 PRINTTAB(5);C(I) TAB(26);D$(I) TAB(45
    );USING D$;A(I)
540 P=525:PRINT:PRINT"PRESS ENTER":GOSUB1
    0000:CLS:GOTO220
550 I=1
560 PRINTTAB(5);"CHECK #" TAB(23);"DATE O
    F CHECK" TAB(48);"AMOUNT"
570 PRINTTAB(5);C(I) TAB(25);D$(I) TAB(45
    );USING D$;A(I)
580 I=I+1
590 IF I<>C THEN570
600 GOSUB9000:GOTO220
610 CLS:PRINT
620 PRINT"SELECT ONLY ONE:'
630 PRINT"1) DEPOSITS"
```

```
640 PRINT"2) ENDING BALANCE"
650 PRINT"3) BALANCE ON A CERTAIN DATE"
660 P=320
670 GOSUB10000
680 ON VAL(K$) GOTO 690,760,810
690 FOR DP=1TOC:IF D(DP)<>0 THEN GOTO700:
    ELSE NEXT:PRINT"YOUR FILE SHOWS NO DE
    POSITS....":PRINT:GOTO750
700 I=1
710 PRINTTAB(5);"DATE OF DEPOSIT" TAB(32)
    ;"AMOUNT OF DEPOSIT"
720 IF D(I)<>0 PRINTTAB(7);D$(I) TAB(33);
    USING D$;D(I)
730 I=I+1
740 IF I<>C THEN720
750 GOSUB9000:GOTO220
760 REM ENDING BALANCE
780 PRINT
790 PRINT"YOUR ENDING BALANCE IS: ";USING
    D$;B
800 PRINT:PRINT"PRESS ENTER":P=588:GOSUB1
    0000:CLS:GOTO220
810 PRINT:PRINT"ENTER DATE ON WHICH YOU W
    ANT TO SEE THE BALANCE";
820 INPUT DT$
830 DB$=MID$(DT$,3,1):DB=VAL(DB$)
840 IF DB=C THEN DB=DB-1
860 PRINT"ON ";DT$;" YOUR FILE SHOWS A BA
    LANCE OF: "USING D$;B(DB)
870 PRINT:PRINT"PRESS ENTER":P=652
880 GOSUB10000:CLS:GOTO220
900 CLS:PRINT
910 PRINT"PLACE CASSETTE IN RECORD MODE,
    NOTE TAPE LOCATION FOR FILE."
920 PRINT
930 PRINT"WHEN READY, PRESS ENTER"
940 P=216:GOSUB10000
950 PRINT#-1,C
960 FOR I=1TOC-1:PRINT#-1,C(I),D$(I),A(I)
    ,D(I),B(I):NEXT
970 PRINT#-1,B
980 PRINT
```

```
990 PRINT"CHECK FILE NOW LOCATED ON TA
    PE."
1000 PRINT"PRESS ENTER TO RETURN TO COM
     MAND LIST"
1010 P=423:GOSUB10000:CLS:GOTO220
1050 CLS:PRINT
1060 PRINT"PLACE CASSETTE PLAYER IN PLA
     Y MODE."
1070 PRINT"THEN PRESS ENTER"
1080 P=145:GOSUB10000
1090 INPUT#-1,C
1100 FOR I=1TOC-1:INPUT#-1,C(I),D$(I),A
     (I),D(I),B(I):NEXT
1110 INPUT#-1,B
1120 PRINT
1130 PRINT"FILE NOW IN COMPUTER MEMORY."
1140 PRINT"PRESS ENTER TO RETURN TO COM
     MAND LIST"
1150 P=358:GOSUB10000:CLS:GOTO220
1200 REM PROGRAM TERMINATE
1210 CLS
1220 PRINT
1230 PRINT"TERMINATION OF PROGRAM..."
1240 END
9000 INPUT"PRESS ENTER";X
9010 CLS
9020 RETURN
10000 PRINT@P,CHR$(143)
10010 FOR I=1TO50:NEXT
10020 PRINT@P," "
10030 FOR I=1TO75:NEXT
10040 K$=INKEY$:IF K$=""THEN10000
10050 RETURN
```

WARRANTIES ON PURCHASED ITEMS

Anyone who purchases items that have guarantees and/or warranties will find this program useful. It will let your computer 'dig out' any warranty information you might need. You can input, store, and receive any of the warranty data at any time.

INPUT DATA? <u>NO</u>

WARRANTIES (LOG)

THIS PROGRAM WILL LET YOU KEEP
A MUCH MORE EFFICIENT LOG OF
WARRANTIES YOU HAVE ON PURCHASED
ITEMS. YOU CAN ENTER THE COMPLETE
DATA FOR THE WARRANTY HERE, WHILE
YOU KEEP THE ACTUAL WARRANTY IN
AN ALPHABETICAL FILE BOX. WHEN
YOU WANT TO REVIEW A WARRANTY, RECALL
THIS PROGRAM, FEED THE DATA FROM
YOUR CASSETTE PLAYER AND GET A
PRINTOUT OF THAT WARRANTY.

PRESS ANY KEY..... <SPACE BAR>

YOU WILL INPUT THE FOLLOWING:

A) ITEM PURCHASED
B) DATE OF PURCHASE
C) WHERE PURCHASED (STORE NAME)
D) SHORT LENGTH OF WARRANTY
E) ACTUAL LENGTH OF WARRANTY

(NOTE: ITEM (D) IS FOR DAYS OF WARRANTY
30, 90 DAYS, ETC. WHILE ITEM (E) IS
FOR AMOUNT OF YEAR(S) ITEM IS UNDER
WARRANTY, 1, 2, 3 YEARS, ETC.)

PRESS ANY KEY TO BEGIN LOG..... <SPACE BAR>

TO CANCEL INPUTS INTO LOG...
PRESS ENTER FOR <ITEM PURCHASED>

ITEM PURCHASED? <u>COLOR T.V.</u>
DATE OF PURCHASE <u>01/01/81</u>
WHERE PURCHASED? <u>FRED'S T.V.</u>
LENGTH OF WARRANTY (SHORT)? <u>90</u>
ACTUAL LENGTH? <u>1</u>

ITEM PURCHASED? <u>COMPUTER</u>
DATE OF PURCHASE? <u>01/30/81</u>
WHERE PURCHASED? <u>FRED'S COMPUTER</u>
LENGTH OF WARRANTY (SHORT)? <u>90</u>
ACTUAL LENGTH? <u>1</u>

ITEM PURCHASED? <u>WASHER</u>
DATE OF PURCHASE? <u>02/01/81</u>
WHERE PURCHASED? <u>FRED'S APPLIANCE</u>
LENGTH OF WARRANTY (SHORT)? <u>90</u>
ACTUAL LENGTH? <u>5</u>

ITEM PURCHASED? <u>CLOTHES DRYER</u>
DATE OF PURCHASE? <u>02/01/81</u>
WHERE PURCHASED? <u>FRED'S APPLIANCE</u>
LENGTH OF WARRANTY (SHORT)? <u>90</u>
ACTUAL LENGTH? <u>5</u>

ITEM PURCHASED? <u>MICROWAVE</u>
DATE OF PURCHASE? <u>02/20/81</u>
WHERE PURCHASED? <u>FRED'S APPLIANCE</u>
LENGTH OF WARRANTY (SHORT)? <u>90</u>
ACTUAL LENGTH? <u>1</u>

ALL DATA WILL BE PRINTED NOW.....

You will find the data print done in a very unique way, that's why the sample run was stopped at this point. You can add more data to the actual list, it's a very handy way for storing and recalling warranty data.

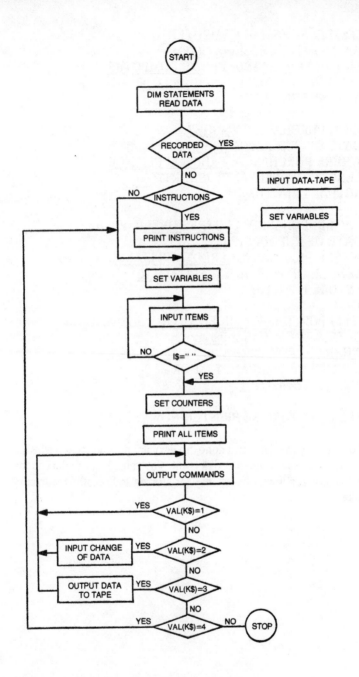

Flowchart for WARRANTIES ON PURCHASED ITEMS

142

Program Listing


```
10 REM PROGRAM TITLE: WARRANTIES ON
20 REM PURCHASED ITEMS (LOG)
30 CLEAR 1000
40 DIM M$(12),I$(20),D$(20),Y(13),Z(3
   1)
50 DIM W$(20),L(20),L1(20),T$(20)
60 FOR I=1TO12:READ M$(I):NEXT
65 CLS:PRINT
70 PRINT"INPUT DATA";
80 INPUT A$
85 IF A$="YES" THEN 1420
90 CLS
100 PRINTTAB(15);"WARRANTIES (LOG)"
110 PRINT
120 PRINT"THIS PROGRAM WILL LET YOU KE
    EP"
130 PRINT"A MUCH MORE EFFICENT LOG OF"
140 PRINT"WARRANTIES YOU HAVE ON PURCH
    ASED"
150 PRINT"ITEMS. YOU CAN ENTER THE COM
    PLETE"
160 PRINT"DATA FOR THE WARRANTY HERE,
    WHILE"
170 PRINT"YOU KEEP THE ACTUAL WARRANTY
     IN"
180 PRINT"AN ALPHABETICAL FILE BOX. WH
    EN"
190 PRINT"YOU WANT TO REVIEW A WARRANT
    Y, RECALL"
200 PRINT"THIS PROGRAM, FEED THE DATA
    FROM"
210 PRINT"YOUR CASSETTE PLAYER AND GET
     A"
220 PRINT"PRINTOUT OF THAT WARRANTY."
230 PRINT
240 PRINT"PRESS ANY KEY....."
250 GOSUB3000
260 CLS
270 PRINT
280 PRINT"YOU WILL INPUT THE FOLLOWING
    :"
```

```
290 PRINT
300 PRINT"A) ITEM PURCHASED"
310 PRINT"B) DATE OF PURCHASE"
320 PRINT"C) WHERE PURCHASED (STORE NA
    ME)"
330 PRINT"D) SHORT LENGTH OF WARRANTY"
340 PRINT"E) ACTUAL LENGTH OF WARRANTY"
350 PRINT
360 PRINT"(NOTE: ITEM (D) IS FOR DAYS
    OF WARRANTY"
370 PRINT"30, 90 DAYS, ETC. WHILE ITEM
    (E) IS"
380 PRINT"FOR AMOUNT OF YEAR(S) ITEM I
    S UNDER"
390 PRINT"WARRANTY, 1, 2, 3 YEARS, ETC
    .)"
400 PRINT
410 PRINT"PRESS ANY KEY TO BEGIN LOG..
    ..."
420 GOSUB3000
430 CLS
440 PRINT
450 PRINT"TO CANCEL INPUTS INTO LOG..."
460 PRINT"PRESS ENTER FOR <ITEM PURCHA
    SED>"
470 I=1
480 PRINT"ITEM PURCHASED";
490 INPUT I$(I)
495 IF I$(I)="" THEN 600
500 PRINT"DATE OF PURCHASE (M/D/Y)";
510 INPUT D$(I)
520 PRINT"WHERE PURCHASED";
530 INPUT W$(I)
540 PRINT"LENGTH OF WARRANTY (SHORT)";
550 INPUT L(I)
560 PRINT"ACTUAL LENGTH";
570 INPUT L1(I)
580 I=I+1
585 PRINT
590 GOTO480
600 I=I-1
610 T=I
```

```
620 Q=129:Q1=143:Q2=155:Q3=168
630 CLS
640 PRINT
650 PRINT"ALL DATA WILL BE PRINTED NOW
    ....."
660 FOR X=1TO1200:NEXT:I=1
670 FOR X=0TO127:SET(X,5):SET(X,9):NEXT
680 FOR Y=6TO8:SET(0,Y):SET(127,Y):NEXT
690 PRINT@Q,"ITEM";
700 PRINT@Q1,"DATE";
710 PRINT@Q2,"WHERE";
720 PRINT@Q3,"WARRANTY(SHORT/ACTUAL)";
730 Q=Q+128:Q1=Q1+128:Q2=Q2+128:Q3=Q3+
    128
735 IF LEN(I$(I))>=7 GOSUB3100:GOTO750
740 PRINT@Q,I$(I);
750 PRINT@Q1-2,D$(I);
755 IF LEN(W$(I))>=7 THEN RR=1:GOSUB31
    00:GOTO770
760 PRINT@Q2,W$(I);
770 PRINT@Q3,L(I);:PRINT@Q3+5,"DAYS";
780 PRINT@Q3+12,L1(I);:PRINT@Q3+16,"YE
    AR(S)";
800 GOSUB1700
810 FOR X=0TO127:SET(X,38):NEXT
820 PRINT@832,"(1) CONT. LIST";
830 PRINT@850,"(2) CHANGE DATA";
840 PRINT@870,"(3) STORE ON TAPE";
845 IF JJ=1 PRINT@914,"(4) END PROGRAM"
850 GOSUB3000
870 ON VAL(K$) GOTO 880,900,1200,2000
880 IF I=T THEN 1930 ELSE I=I+1
885 FOR X=0TO127:SET(X,12):RESET(X,12)
    :NEXT
886 FOR X=0TO70:SET(X,15):RESET(X,15):
    NEXT
887 FOR X=0TO127:SET(X,27):RESET(X,27)
    :NEXT
890 GOTO735
900 FOR X=0TO127:SET(X,39):RESET(X,39)
    :NEXT
905 FOR X=33TO70:SET(X,42):RESET(X,42)
    :NEXT
```

145

```
920  PRINT@832,"(1) ITEM";
930  PRINT@843,"(2) DATE";
940  PRINT@854,"(3) WHERE";
950  PRINT@865,"(4) WARRANTIES";
960  GOSUB3000
980  FOR X=0TO127:SET(X,39):RESET(X,39)
     :NEXT
990  ON VAL(K$) GOTO 1000,1030,1060,1090
1000 PRINT@832,"ENTER CORRECTED ITEM";
1010 INPUT I$(I)
1020 GOTO620:REM PRINTOUT
1030 PRINT@832,"ENTER CORRECTED DATE";
1040 INPUT D$(I)
1050 GOTO1020
1060 PRINT@832,"ENTER CORRECTED PLACE O
     F PURCHASE";
1070 INPUT W$(I)
1080 GOTO1020
1090 PRINT@832,"(1) SHORT  (2) ACTUAL";
1100 GOSUB3000
1120 FOR X=0TO127:SET(X,39):RESET(X,39)
     :NEXT
1130 ON VAL(K$) GOTO 1140,1170
1140 PRINT@832,"ENTER SHORT WARRANTY";
1150 INPUT L(I)
1160 GOTO1020
1170 PRINT@832,"ENTER ACTUAL WARRANTY";
1180 INPUT L1(I)
1190 GOTO1020
1200 REM TO TAPE
1210 CLS
1220 PRINT
1230 PRINT"PLACE PLAYER IN RECORD MODE.
     ...."
1240 PRINT"AND PRESS A KEY....."
1245 GOSUB3000
1250 PRINT
1260 PRINT"SAVING WARRANTY DATA....."
1270 PRINT#-1,T
1280 FOR I=1TOT
1290 PRINT#-1,I$(I),D$(I),W$(I)
1300 PRINT#-1,L(I),L1(I)
```

```
1310 NEXT
1320 PRINT
1330 PRINT"DATA ON TAPE....."
1340 PRINT"PRESS A KEY....."
1350 GOSUB3000:PRINT
1360 PRINT"WOULD YOU LIKE TO MAKE"
1370 PRINT"ANOTHER FILE (Y/N)";
1380 INPUT Q$
1390 IF Q$="Y" THEN 430
1400 GOTO2000:REM TO END
1410 REM FROM RECORDER
1420 CLS
1430 PRINT
1440 PRINT"PLACE PLAYER IN PLAY MODE...
     .."
1450 PRINT"AND PRESS A KEY....."
1460 GOSUB3000
1470 PRINT
1480 PRINT"INPUTTING DATA....."
1490 INPUT#-1,T
1500 FOR I=1TOT
1510 INPUT#-1,I$(I),D$(I),W$(I)
1520 INPUT#-1,L(I),L1(I)
1530 NEXT
1540 PRINT
1550 PRINT"DATA IN MEMORY....."
1560 PRINT
1570 PRINT"PRESS A KEY....."
1580 GOSUB3000
1590 JJ=1
1600 GOTO620:REM PRINTOUT
1700 REM WARRANTY EXPIRES
1710 H=VAL(MID$(D$(I),1,2))
1720 H1=VAL(MID$(D$(I),4,2))
1800 F=H1:F1=1:V=H
1810 IF F1<>L(I) THEN 1830
1820 GOTO1860
1830 IF V=13 V=1
1840 IF F=VAL(RIGHT$(M$(V),2)) THEN V=V
     +1:F=0:GOTO1810
1850 F=F+1:F1=F1+1:GOTO1810
1860 M$=LEFT$(M$(V),4)
```

```
1870 PRINT@Q+330,"THE SHORT TERM WARRAN
     TY EXPIRES ";
1880 PRINT LEFT$(M$(V),4);F
1890 IF I=T THEN 1910
1900 RETURN
1910 PRINT@Q+463,"** ALL WARRANTIES LIS
     TED **";
1920 RETURN
1930 FOR X=33TO91:SET(X,33)
1940 RESET(X,33):NEXT
1950 GOSUB1910
1960 GOTO810
2000 REM END OF PROGRAM
2010 CLS
2020 PRINT
2030 PRINT"END OF WARRANTY PROGRAM..."
2040 END
3000 REM KEY CLOSED ?
3010 K$=INKEY$
3020 IF K$="" THEN 3010
3030 RETURN
3100 REM LETTER LENGTH
3110 U=1:QQ=Q:T$(I)=""
3115 IF RR=1 THEN T$(I)=I$(I):I$(I)=W$(
     I):QQ=Q2
3120 IF MID$(I$(I),U,1)<>" " AND MID$(I
     $(I),U,1)<>"-" THEN 3130 ELSE 3145
3130 PRINT@QQ,MID$(I$(I),U,1);
3134 IF U>=LEN(I$(I)) THEN RETURN
3135 U=U+1:QQ=QQ+1:GOTO3120
3140 U=U+1
3145 IF RR=1 QQ=280 ELSE QQ=256
3150 PRINT@QQ+64,MID$(I$(I),U,1);
3160 IF U<>LEN(I$(I)) THEN 3180
3170 GOTO3200
3180 U=U+1:QQ=QQ+1
3190 GOTO3150
3200 REM RESET STRINGS & VARIABLES
3210 IF RR=1 RR=0:I$(I)=T$(I)
3220 RETURN
3300 DATA JAN. 31,FEB. 28,MAR. 31,APR.
     30
3310 DATA MAY 31,JUNE 30,JULY 31,AUG. 31
3320 DATA SEPT. 30,OCT. 31,NOV. 30,DEC.
     31
```

VEHICLE MAINTENANCE AND REPAIR

You can't remember when you had your vehicle greased or the oil changed? The mechanic didn't place a sticker on it for maintenance performed? This program is specifically designed to let you input all your vehicle information from owners name, to vehicle I.D., to maintenance due or maintenance performed. Individual lists can be recalled whenever you choose. Names and addresses of where you had maintenance or repairs performed can also be entered and recalled. The program will even let you know how much warranty time you have remaining on your vehicle.

SAMPLE RUN

VEHICLE MAINTENANCE & REPAIR

INPUT VEHICLE DATA FROM TAPE? <u>NO</u>

PRINT INSTRUCTIONS? <u>YES</u>

SO YOU'VE HAD YOUR VEHICLE GREASED
BUT YOU CAN'T REMEMBER THE DATE
BECAUSE THE MECHANIC DIDN'T PLACE A
STICKER ON THE VEHICLE SPECIFING THAT
DATE? OR YOU'VE HAD SOME REPAIR WORK
DONE, BUT CAN'T LOCATE THE SALES RECEIPT
OUTLINING THE DETAILS OF THE REPAIR
AND THE ACTUAL COST?

ENTER? <ENTER>

PERHAPS YOU'VE HAD SOME NEW TIRES
INSTALLED, THEY'VE WORN-OUT IN NO
TIME AT ALL, YOU CAN'T REMEMBER THE
PURCHASE DATE OR HOW MANY MILES THEY
WERE SUPPOSED TO LAST. THE DEALER CAN'T
HELP YOU, BECAUSE HE HAS DISCONTINUED
THAT BRAND.
WORRY OR WONDER NO MORE.
THIS PROGRAM IS DESIGNED TO LET YOU
ENTER ALL THE REQUIRED DATA YOU'LL
NEED TO REMEMBER ABOUT YOUR VEHICLE.
YOU CAN THEN STORE THE ENTIRE FILE
ON TAPE, RECALL IT AT ANY TIME AND
ADD MORE DATA TO IT IF YOU WISH.
ENTER? <ENTER>

THE PROGRAM WILL BEGIN WITH A
MAINTENANCE RECORD FOR YOUR VEHICLE.
THIS PART IS FOR MAINTENANCE & REPAIR
THAT <HAS NOT> BEEN PERFORMED, THAT IS,
IT IS A MAINTENANCE & REPAIR SERVICE
INTERVAL LOG, WHEN EACH ARE SUPPOSED
TO BE PERFORMED - MONTH(S) OR MILES.

OWNERS NAME? D. CHANCE
VEHICLE I.D. NUMBER? ADE1233U80
WARRANTY START DATE (M/D/Y)? 09/01/80
LENGTH OF WARRANTY (MONTHS)? 12
LENGTH OF WARRANTY (MILES)? 12000
MAKE AND MODEL OF VEHICLE?
FORD F-100 CUSTOM PKUP
YEAR VEHICLE WAS MANUFACTURED? 1980
ENGINE DISPLACEMENT (SIZE)? 302 C.I.

** MAINTENANCE & REPAIR SERVICE INTERVAL **

ANSWER EACH OF THE FOLLOWING
WITH <MONTHS OR MILES> THAT EACH
ARE SUPPOSED TO BE PERFORMED.
IF THERE ARE OTHER ITEMS THAT ARE
NOT COVERED HERE YOU CAN ENTER
THEM LATER.
(ENTER ONLY NUMERICAL CONTENT, THAT
IS, 12 MONTHS, ENTER <12> ONLY)

CHANGE ENGINE OIL? 12
REPLACE ENGINE OIL FILTER? 24
REPLACE SPARK PLUGS? 12
REPLACE ENGINE COOLANT? 12
LUBRICATION (GENERAL)? 5

** EMISSION CONTROL DEVICES **

CHECK DRIVE BELT CONDITION & TENSION? 2
CHECK & ADJUST IDLE SPEEDS? 10
CHECK & ADJUST CHOKE SYSTEM? 10

THAT IS THE PARTIAL LIST OF ITEMS.
DO YOU NEED TO ENTER MORE (Y/N)? Y

TO EXIT... JUST PRESS ENTER.
ENTER ITEM? VALVE ADJUSTMENT
MONTHS OR MILES TO BE PERFORMED? 6
ENTER ITEM? REPLACE WINDSHIELD WIPERS
MONTHS OR MILES TO BE PERFORMED? 12
ENTER ITEM? CHECK AIR IN TIRES

MONTHS OR MILES TO BE PERFORMED? 1
ENTER ITEM? <ENTER>

** SERVICE & REPAIR RECORD **

THIS PART OF THE PROGRAM WILL
LET YOU ENTER ALL SERVICE &
REPAIRS THAT HAVE BEEN PERFORMED
ON YOUR 1980 FORD F-100 CUSTOM PKUP

DO YOU HAVE SERVICE OR REPAIRS
THAT NEED TO BE ENTERED NOW (Y/N)? Y
TO EXIT ENTRIES . . . JUST PRESS ENTER.

SERVICE/REPAIRS COMPLETED?
FRONT BRAKES ADJUSTED
DATE OF SERVICE? 10/01/80
MILEAGE AT SERVICE? 5500
SERVICE SHOP (NAME & ADDRESS)?
JAKES AUTO 12 MAIN ST.
TOTAL COST OF SERVICE
(IF COVERED BY WARRANTY, ENTER 0 (ZERO))?
0

SERVICE/REPAIRS COMPLETED?
REAR BRAKES ADJUSTED
DATE OF SERVICE? 10/30/80
MILEAGE AT SERVICE? 5900
SERVICE SHOP (NAME & ADDRESS)?
JAKES AUTO 12 MAIN ST.
TOTAL COST OF SERVICE
(IF COVERED BY WARRANTY, ENTER 0 (ZERO))?
0

SERVICE/REPAIRS COMPLETED?
IDLE SPEED ADJUSTED
DATE OF SERVICE? 12/01/80
MILEAGE AT SERVICE? 7723.8
SERVICE SHOP (NAME & ADDRESS)?
JAKES AUTO 12 MAIN ST.
TOTAL COST OF SERVICE
(IF COVERED BY WARRANTY, ENTER 0 (ZERO))?
10

SERVICE/REPAIRS COMPLETED?
SET TACK AND DWELL
DATE OF SERVICE? 12/01/80
MILEAGE AT SERVICE? 7723.8
SERVICE SHOP (NAME & ADDRESS)?
JAKES AUTO 12 MAIN ST.
TOTAL COST OF SERVICE
(IF COVERED BY WARRANTY, ENTER 0 (ZERO))?
10

SERVICE/REPAIRS COMPLETED? <ENTER>

SEE DATA BEFORE SAVING ON TAPE (Y/N)? Y

1) LIST MAINTENANCE INTERVALS
2) LIST MAINTENANCE THAT IS DUE
   (PLUS WARRANTY INFORMATION)
3) LIST SERVICE/REPAIRS COMPLETED
4) ADD MORE DATA TO PRESENT LIST
5) END PROGRAM

ENTER CHOICE? 1

REQUIRED MAINTENANCE/SERVICE   INTERVAL
(MONTHS/MILES)

CHANGE ENGINE OIL	12 MONTHS
REPLACE ENGINE OIL FILTER	24 MONTHS
REPLACE SPARK PLUGS	12 MONTHS
REPLACE ENGINE COOLANT	12 MONTHS
LUBRICATION (GENERAL)	5 MONTHS
CHECK DRIVE BELT CONDITION & TENSION	2 MONTHS
CHECK & ADJUST IDLE SPEEDS	10 MONTHS
CHECK & ADJUST CHOKE SYSTEM	10 MONTHS
VALVE ADJUSTMENT	6 MONTHS
REPLACE WINDSHIELD WIPERS	12 MONTHS
CHECK AIR IN TIRES	1 MONTHS

PRESS ENTER TO EXIT? <ENTER>

WARRANTY INFORMATION (CONTINUED)

OWNER: D. CHANCE
VEHICLE I.D. NUMBER: ADE1233U80
WARRANTY START DATE: 09/01/80
LENGTH OF WARRANTY (MONTHS): 12
LENGTH OF WARRANTY (MILES): 12000
MAKE & MODEL: FORD F-100 CUSTOM PKUP
YEAR OF MANUFACTURE: 1980
ENGINE SIZE: 302 C.I.

PRESS ENTER TO EXIT? <ENTER>

ALL COMPLETED DATA WILL NOW BE
LOADED ON CASSETTE TAPE.
READY TAPE PLAYER, THEN PRESS ENTER?

You will probably have much more data to enter. This sample run was just to show a few things that can be covered, using this program. Be sure to follow all instructions when inputting data information for your file. Instead of typing in the additional maintenance each time, those items can be added to the program by putting them in DATA statements at the end of the program, and adjusting the loop in line 6 .

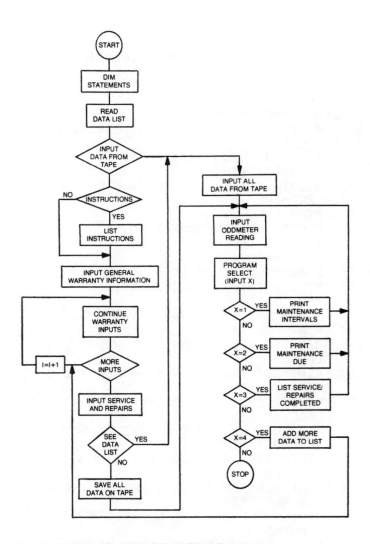

Flowchart for VEHICLE MAINTENANCE AND REPAIR

155

Program Listing

```
10 REM PROGRAM TITLE: VEHICLE MAINTEN
   ANCE & REPAIR
20 CLS
30 CLEAR1200
40 DIM A$(25),M(25)
50 DIM R$(25),R1$(25),R2(25),R3$(25),
   R4(25)
60 FOR I=1TO9:READ A$(I):NEXT
70 G$="$$#####.##"
100 PRINTTAB(15);"VEHICLE MAINTENANCE
    & REPAIR"
110 PRINT
120 PRINT"INPUT VEHICLE DATA FROM TAPE
    ";
130 INPUT A$
140 IF A$="YES" THEN 1600
150 PRINT"PRINT INSTRUCTIONS";
160 INPUT A$
170 IF A$="NO" THEN 530
180 PRINT
190 PRINT"SO YOU'VE HAD YOUR VEHICLE G
    REASED"
200 PRINT"BUT YOU CAN'T REMEMBER THE D
    ATE"
210 PRINT"BECAUSE THE MECHANIC DIDN'T
    PLACE A"
220 PRINT"STICKER ON THE VEHICLE SPECI
    FING THAT"
230 PRINT"DATE ? OR YOU'VE HAD SOME RE
    PAIR WORK"
240 PRINT"DONE, BUT CAN'T LOCATE THE S
    ALES RECEIPT"
250 PRINT"OUTLINING THE DETAILS OF THE
     REPAIR"
260 PRINT"AND THE ACTUAL COST ?"
265 PRINT"ENTER";:INPUT X:CLS:PRINT
270 PRINT"PERHAPS YOU'VE HAD SOME NEW
    TIRES"
280 PRINT"INSTALLED, THEY'VE WORN-OUT
    IN NO"
```

```
290 PRINT"TIME AT ALL, YOU CAN'T REMEM
    BER THE"
300 PRINT"PURCHASE DATE OR HOW MANY MI
    LES THEY"
310 PRINT "WERE SUPPOSED TO LAST.  THE
    DEALER CAN'T"
320 PRINT"HELP YOU, BECAUSE HE HAS DIS
    CONTINUED"
330 PRINT"THAT BRAND."
340 PRINT"WORRY OR WONDER NO MORE."
350 PRINT"THIS PROGRAM IS DESIGNED TO
    LET YOU"
360 PRINT"ENTER ALL THE REQUIRED DATA
    YOU'LL"
370 PRINT"NEED TO REMEMBER ABOUT YOUR
    VEHICLE."
380 PRINT"YOU CAN THEN STORE THE ENTIR
    E FILE"
390 PRINT"ON TAPE, RECALL IT AT ANY TI
    ME AND"
400 PRINT"ADD MORE DATA TO IT IF YOU W
    ISH."
420 PRINT"ENTER";
430 INPUT X
440 CLS
450 PRINT
460 PRINT"THE PROGRAM WILL BEGIN WITH
    A"
470 PRINT"MAINTENANCE RECORD FOR YOUR
    VEHICLE."
480 PRINT"THIS PART IS FOR MAINTENANCE
    & REPAIR"
490 PRINT"THAT <HAS NOT> BEEN PERFORME
    D, THAT IS,"
500 PRINT"IT IS A MAINTENANCE & REPAIR
    SERVICE"
510 PRINT"INTERVAL LOG, WHEN EACH ARE
    SUPPOSED"
520 PRINT"TO BE PERFORMED - MONTH(S) O
    R MILES."
530 PRINT
540 PRINT"OWNERS NAME";
```

```
550 INPUT N$
560 PRINT"VEHICLE I.D. NUMBER";
570 INPUT I$
580 PRINT"WARRANTY START DATE (M/D/Y)"
    ;
590 INPUT D$
595 INPUT"LENGTH OF WARRANTY (MONTHS)"
    ;D
596 INPUT"LENGTH OF WARRANTY (MILES)";
    DD
600 PRINT"MAKE & MODEL OF VEHICLE";
610 INPUT M$
620 PRINT"YEAR VEHICLE WAS MANUFACTURE
    D";
630 INPUT Y$
640 PRINT"ENGINE DISPLACEMENT (SIZE)";
650 INPUT E$
660 PRINT
670 PRINT"** MAINTENANCE & REPAIR SERV
    ICE INTERVAL **"
680 PRINT
690 PRINT"ANSWER EACH OF THE FOLLOWING
    "
700 PRINT"WITH <MONTHS OR MILES> THAT
    EACH"
710 PRINT"ARE SUPPOSED TO BE PERFORME
    D."
720 PRINT"IF THERE ARE OTHER ITEMS THA
    T ARE"
730 PRINT"NOT COVERED HERE YOU CAN ENT
    ER"
740 PRINT"THEM LATER."
745 PRINT"(ENTER ONLY NUMERICAL CONTEN
    T, THAT"
746 PRINT"IS, 12 MONTHS, ENTER <12> ON
    LY)"
750 PRINT
760 I=1
770 PRINTA$(I);
780 INPUT M(I):I=I+1
790 PRINTA$(I);
800 INPUT M(I):I=I+1
```

```
810 PRINTA$(I);
820 INPUT M(I):I=I+1
830 PRINTA$(I);
840 INPUT M(I):I=I+1
850 PRINTA$(I);
860 INPUT M(I):I=I+1
880 PRINT
890 PRINT"** ";A$(I);" **"
900 PRINT:I=I+1
910 PRINTA$(I);
920 INPUT M(I):I=I+1
930 PRINTA$(I);
940 INPUT M(I):I=I+1
950 PRINTA$(I);
960 INPUT M(I)
970 PRINT
980 PRINT"THAT IS THE PARTIAL LIST OF
    ITEMS."
990 PRINT"DO YOU NEED TO ENTER MORE (Y
    /N)";
1000 INPUT A$
1010 IF A$="N" THEN 1100
1020 I=I+1
1030 PRINT"TO EXIT...JUST PRESS ENTER."
1040 PRINT
1050 INPUT"ENTER ITEM";A$(I)
1060 IF A$(I)="" THEN 1100
1070 INPUT"MONTHS OR MILES TO BE PERFOR
     MED";M(I)
1080 I=I+1
1090 GOTO1040
1100 REM SERVICE & REPAIR COMPLETED
1110 CLS:W1=I
1120 PRINT
1130 PRINT"** SERVICE & REPAIR RECORD *
     *"
1140 PRINT
1150 PRINT"THIS PART OF THE PROGRAM WIL
     L"
1160 PRINT"LET YOU ENTER ALL SERVICE &"
1170 PRINT"REPAIRS THAT HAVE BEEN PERFO
     RMED"
```

159

```
1180 PRINT"ON YOUR ";Y$;" ";M$
1190 PRINT
1192 PRINT"DO YOU HAVE SERVICE OR REPAI
     RS"
1195 INPUT"THAT NEED TO BE ENTERED NOW
     (Y/N)";A$
1198 IF A$="N" THEN 1360
1200 PRINT"TO EXIT ENTRYS...JUST PRESS
     ENTER."
1205 J=1
1210 PRINT
1220 PRINT"SERVICE / REPAIRS COMPLETED"
     ;
1230 INPUT R$(J)
1235 IF R$(J)="" THEN J=J-1:W2=J:GOTO13
     60
1240 PRINT"DATE OF SERVICE";
1250 INPUT R1$(J)
1260 PRINT"MILEAGE AT SERVICE";
1270 INPUT R2(J)
1280 PRINT"SERVICE SHOP (NAME & ADDRESS
     )";
1290 INPUT R3$(J)
1300 PRINT"TOTAL COST OF SERVICE"
1310 PRINT"(IF COVERED BY WARRANTY, ENT
     ER 0 (ZERO))";
1330 INPUT R4(J)
1340 J=J+1
1350 GOTO1210
1360 REM DATA TO CASSETTE
1370 CLS
1380 PRINT
1382 PRINT"SEE DATA BEFORE SAVING ON TA
     PE (Y/N)";
1385 INPUT A$:IF A$="Y" THEN P=1:GOTO18
     00
1390 PRINT"ALL COMPLETED DATA WILL NOW
     BE"
1400 PRINT"LOADED ON CASSETTE TAPE."
1410 PRINT"READY TAPE PLAYER, THEN PRES
     S ENTER";
1420 INPUT A$
```

```
1430 PRINT#-1,W1,W2
1440 PRINT"SAVING VEHICLE DATA....."
1450 PRINT#-1,N$,I$,D$,D,DD,M$,Y$,E$
1460 FOR I=1TOW1:PRINT#-1,A$(I),M(I):NE
     XT
1470 FOR I=1TOW2
1480 PRINT#-1,R$(I),R1$(I),R2(I),R3$(I)
     ,R4(I)
1490 NEXT
1500 PRINT
1510 PRINT"DATA NOW ON TAPE....."
1520 PRINT"PRESS ENTER TO EXIT";
1530 CLS
1540 PRINT:GOTO1870
1600 REM DATA FROM CASSETTE
1610 CLS
1620 PRINT
1630 PRINT"READY PLAYER (PLACE IN PLAY
     MODE)."
1640 PRINT"PRESS ENTER";
1650 INPUT A$
1660 INPUT#-1,W1,W2
1670 PRINT"LOADING VEHICLE DATA."
1680 INPUT#-1,N$,I$,D$,D,DD,M$,Y$,E$
1690 FOR I=1TOW1:INPUT#-1,A$(I),M(I):NE
     XT
1700 FOR I=1TOW2
1710 INPUT#-1,R$(I),R1$(I),R2(I),R3$(I)
     ,R4(I)
1720 NEXT
1730 PRINT
1740 PRINT"LOADING OF DATA COMPLETED...
     .."
1750 PRINT"PRESS ENTER";
1760 INPUT A$
1800 REM PRINT DATA
1810 CLS
1820 PRINT
1825 IF P=1 THEN 1880
1830 PRINT"ENTER TODAYS DATE (M/D/Y)";
1840 INPUT D1$
1850 PRINT"ENTER ODOMETER READING (MILE
     AGE)";
```

```
1860 INPUT M1
1870 PRINT
1880 PRINT"1) LIST MAINTENANCE INTERVAL
     S"
1890 PRINT"2) LIST MAINTENANCE THAT IS
     DUE"
1895 PRINT TAB(3);"(PLUS WARRANTY INFOR
     MATION)"
1900 PRINT"3) LIST SERVICE / REPAIRS CO
     MPLETED"
1910 PRINT"4) ADD MORE DATA TO PRESENT
     LIST"
1920 PRINT"5) END PROGRAM"
1930 PRINT
1940 PRINT"ENTER CHOICE";
1950 INPUT X
1960 ON X GOTO 1970,2300,2600,3300,3500
1970 CLS
1980 PRINT
1990 I=1
1995 IF W1>12 THEN T=12 ELSE T=W1
2000 PRINT"REQUIRED MAINTENANCE / SERVI
     CE";
2010 PRINT TAB(35);"INTERVAL (MONTHS /
     MILES)"
2020 FOR Y=0TO120:SET(Y,6):NEXT
2030 PRINT
2040 PRINTA$(I);:GOSUB3000
2050 IF I<=T THEN 2040
2140 PRINT
2150 PRINT"PRESS ENTER TO EXIT";
2160 INPUT A$
2170 CLS
2180 PRINT
2190 IF I<>W1 THEN 2210
2200 CLS:PRINT:GOSUB3100
2205 IF P=1 P=0:GOTO1390
2206 GOTO1870
2210 CLS:PRINT
2220 T=W1:I=I+1
2230 GOTO2000
2300 REM MAINTENANCE / SERVICE DUE
```

```
2310 CLS
2320 PRINT
2330 PRINT"***** MAINTENANCE / SERVICE
     DUE *****"
2335 PRINT
2340 I=1:TT=0:T1=0
2345 GOSUB2350:GOTO2372
2350 D1=VAL(LEFT$(D$,2))
2360 D2=VAL(LEFT$(D1$,2))
2370 D3=ABS(D1-D2)+1:RETURN
2372 GOSUB2900
2375 PRINT"VEHICLE IN OPERATION";D3;"MO
     NTHS.":PRINT
2380 IF M(I)=D3 THEN PRINTA$(I):T1=1:T2
     =1
2382 IF TT=0 AND M(I)<D3 AND A$(I)<>""
     THEN PRINT"PAST DUE: ";A$(I):T1=1:
     T2=1
2385 IF TT=1 AND T1=0 AND ABS(M1-M(I))<
     =100 PRINTA$(I):T2=1
2390 I=I+1:IF I=6 THEN I=7
2394 T1=0:IF I<=W1 THEN 2380
2395 IF TT=1 THEN 2440
2400 I=1
2410 D3=M1
2420 TT=1
2430 GOTO2380
2440 PRINT
2442 IF T2=0 PRINT"NO MAINTENANCE IS DU
     E NOW."
2445 IF ABS(DD-M1)=0 THEN 2455
2450 IF ABS(DD-M1)<=500 THEN 2490
2452 GOTO2460
2455 PRINT"YOUR WARRANTY HAS EXPIRED...
     ":GOTO2530
2460 GOSUB2350:GOSUB2900
2465 IF D3>D THEN 2455
2470 IF ABS(D-D3)<=0 THEN 2505
2475 IF ABS(D-D3)<=3 THEN 2510
2480 GOTO2530
2490 PRINT"YOUR WARRANTY EXPIRES WITHIN
     ";
```

```
2500 PRINT ABS(DD-M1);"MILES.....";GOTO
     2530
2505 PRINT"YOUR WARRANTY EXPIRES THIS M
     ONTH...";GOTO2530
2510 PRINT"THEIR ARE";ABS(D-D3);
2520 PRINT"MONTH(S) LEFT ON YOUR WARRAN
     TY."
2530 PRINT
2540 PRINT"PRESS ENTER TO EXIT";
2550 INPUT A$
2560 GOTO2200
2600 REM SERVICE / REPAIRS COMPLETED
2610 CLS:J=1
2620 PRINT
2630 PRINT"xxx SERVICE / REPAIRS COMPLE
     TED xxx"
2640 FOR Y=0TO70:SET(Y,6):NEXT
2650 PRINT
2655 IF W2=0 PRINT"NO SERVICE OR REPAIR
      ITEMS IN FILE...";GOTO2780
2660 PRINT"SERVICE / REPAIRS:";
2670 PRINT TAB(25);R$(J)
2680 PRINT"DATE OF SERVICE:";
2690 PRINT TAB(25);R1$(J)
2700 PRINT"MILEAGE AT SERVICE:";
2710 PRINT TAB(25);R2(J)
2720 PRINT"SERVICE SHOP:";
2730 PRINT TAB(25);R3$(J)
2740 PRINT"COST OF SERVICE";
2750 IF R4(J)=0 PRINT TAB(25);"WARRANTY
     ";GOTO2770
2760 PRINT TAB(25);USING G$;R4(J)
2770 IF J<>W2 THEN 2790
2780 PRINT:INPUT"PRESS ENTER";A$
2782 CLS:IF P=1 P=0:GOTO1390
2785 GOTO1870
2790 PRINT
2800 PRINT"PRESS ENTER TO CONTINUE LIST
     ";
2810 INPUT A$
2820 J=J+1
2830 CLS
```

```
2840 GOTO2620
2900 D4=VAL(RIGHT$(D$,2))
2905 D5=VAL(RIGHT$(D1$,2))
2910 D6=ABS(D4-D5)
2915 IF D6=1 THEN 2925
2920 RETURN
2925 D7=D1:D8=1
2930 D7=D7+1:D8=D8+1
2935 IF D7=13 THEN D7=1:D6=0
2940 IF D7<>D2 OR D6<>0 THEN 2930
2950 D3=D8
2960 GOTO2920
3000 PRINTTAB(40);M(I);
3010 IF M(I)<100 PRINT TAB(50);"MONTHS"
     :GOTO3030
3020 PRINT TAB(50);"MILES"
3030 I=I+1
3040 IF I=6 I=7
3050 RETURN
3100 REM WARRANTY INFORMATION (CONT)
3110 PRINT"WARRANTY INFORMATION (CONTIN
     UED)"
3120 PRINT
3130 PRINT"OWNER: ";N$
3140 PRINT"VEHICLE I.D. NUMBER: ";I$
3150 PRINT"WARRANTY START DATE: ";D$
3160 PRINT"LENGTH OF WARRANTY (MONTHS):
     ";D
3170 PRINT"LENGTH OF WARRANTY (MILES):
     ";DD
3180 PRINT"MAKE & MODEL: ";M$
3190 PRINT"YEAR OF MANUFACTURE: ";Y$
3200 PRINT"ENGINE SIZE: ";E$
3210 PRINT
3220 PRINT"PRESS ENTER TO EXIT";
3230 INPUT A$
3240 CLS
3250 PRINT
3260 RETURN
3300 REM MORE DATA
3310 CLS
3320 PRINT
```

```
3330 PRINT"1) MAINTENANCE TO BE PERFORM
     ED"
3340 PRINT"2) SERVICE & REPAIRS COMPLET
     ED"
3350 PRINT
3360 PRINT"SELECT";
3370 INPUT A
3380 ON A GOTO 1020,3400
3400 IF W2=0 THEN 1205
3410 J=J+1
3420 CLS
3430 GOTO1210
3500 REM END
3510 CLS
3520 PRINT
3530 PRINT"END OF VEHICLE MAINTENANCE P
     ROGRAM..."
3540 END
10000 REM DATA
10010 DATA CHANGE ENGINE OIL
10020 DATA REPLACE ENGINE OIL FILTER
10030 DATA REPLACE SPARK PLUGS
10040 DATA REPLACE ENGINE COOLANT
10050 DATA LUBRICATION (GENERAL)
10060 DATA EMISSION CONTROL DEVICES
10070 DATA CHECK DRIVE BELT CONDITION &
      TENSION
10080 DATA CHECK & ADJUST IDLE SPEEDS
10090 DATA CHECK & ADJUST CHOKE SYSTEM
```

HOME INVENTORY

Can you recall every item in your home, valuable or otherwise? Do each of your valuable items have your Social Security number inscribed on them? If you can't remember, this programs for you. You can input every item in your home, from one end to the other. Where the item is located and whether or not it has your Social Security number inscribed on it. Then the entire data file can be transferred to cassette tape, you can add to it anytime you acquire new items. Then, if your home is burglarized, you'll know exactly what items are missing by recalling the stored data file.

The data file should be kept in a fire-proof container (along with this program) in the event of a fire, so you'll have it ready for insurance purposes.

SAMPLE RUN

HOME INVENTORY

1) BEGIN A INVENTORY FILE
2) ADD TO EXISTING FILE
3) LIST ALL INVENTORY ITEMS
4) SAVE INVENTORY ON TAPE
5) LOAD INVENTORY FROM TAPE
6) MAKE CHANGES IN INVENTORY LIST
7) ITEMS CONTAINING S.S. NUMBER
8) END INVENTORY PROGRAM

SELECT? 1

MAKING AN INVENTORY FILE WILL BE
QUITE SIMPLE. AFTERWARDS YOU WILL
HAVE A COMPLETE FILE ON EVERYTHING
YOU OWN (OR INCLUDED IN THE FILE).
YOU CAN THEN SAVE THE ENTIRE FILE
ON CASSETTE TAPE FOR FUTURE REF-
ERENCE, (BE SURE TO STORE IT IN A
FIRE-PROOF CONTAINER) IN CASE YOUR
HOME IS BURGLARLIZED OR ALL OF YOUR
PROPERTY IS LOST IN A FIRE.
BE SURE TO CHECK WITH YOUR INSURANCE
AGENT, TO BE SURE HE HAS EVERY ITEM
YOU ENTER IN THIS LOG, IN HIS FILE.

PRESS ENTER TO BEGIN? <ENTER>

DATE OF INVENTORY? 01/01/80
ITEMS INSURED WITH (NAME)? BLUE BELL
STREET ADDRESS? 1234 SOUTH SECOND ST.
CITY & STATE? YOUR CITY U.S.A.
ZIP CODE? 00001
PHONE NUMBER? 900-555-5555
POLICY NUMBER? 1234567
TYPE OF INSURANCE? FIRE/THEFT

ITEM # 1 ? MICROWAVE OVEN
SERIAL NUMBER OF ITEM? 12345

WHERE LOCATED IN HOUSE? <u>KITCHEN</u>
DECLARED VALUE OF MICROWAVE OVEN? <u>500</u>
IS YOUR SOCIAL SECURITY NUMBER
ENGRAVED ON THIS ITEM (Y/N)? <u>Y</u>

CONTINUE ITEMS INTO FILE (Y/N)? <u>Y</u>

ITEM # 2 ? <u>COLOR T.V.</u>
SERIAL NUMBER OF ITEM? <u>343455</u>
WHERE LOCATED IN HOUSE? <u>LIVINGROOM</u>
DECLARED VALUE OF COLOR T.V.? <u>1200</u>
IS YOUR SOCIAL SECURITY NUMBER
ENGRAVED ON THIS ITEM (Y/N)? <u>Y</u>

CONTINUE ITEMS INTO FILE (Y/N)? Y

ITEM # 3 ? <u>COMPUTER</u>
SERIAL NUMBER OF ITEM? <u>WE34111</u>
WHERE LOCATED IN HOUSE? <u>DEN</u>
DECLARED VALUE OF COMPUTER? <u>2000</u>
IS YOUR SOCIAL SECURITY NUMBER
ENGRAVED ON THIS ITEM (Y/N)? <u>Y</u>

CONTINUE ITEMS INTO FILE (Y/N)? <u>Y</u>

ITEM # 4 ? <u>DINING ROOM SET</u>
SERIAL NUMBER OF ITEM? <u>RT5555</u>
WHERE LOCATED IN HOUSE? <u>DININGROOM</u>
DECLARED VALUE OF DINING ROOM SET? <u>300</u>
IS YOUR SOCIAL SECURITY NUMBER
ENGRAVED ON THIS ITEM (Y/N)? <u>N</u>

CONTINUE ITEMS INTO FILE (Y/N)? Y

ITEM # 5 ? <u>WATER BED</u>
SERIAL NUMBER OF ITEM? <u>DFG444Q</u>
WHERE LOCATED IN HOUSE? <u>BEDROOM</u>
DECLARED VALUE OF WATER BED? <u>1000</u>
IS YOUR SOCIAL SECURITY NUMBER
ENGRAVED ON THIS ITEM (Y/N)? <u>N</u>

CONTINUE ITEMS INTO FILE (Y/N)? <u>Y</u>

ITEM # 6 ? <u>WASHER</u>
SERIAL NUMBER OF ITEM? <u>99000Q</u>
WHERE LOCATED IN HOUSE? <u>WASHROOM</u>
DECLARED VALUE OF WASHER? <u>300</u>
IS YOUR SOCIAL SECURITY NUMBER
ENGRAVED ON THIS ITEM (Y/N)? <u>N</u>

CONTINUE ITEMS INTO FILE (Y/N)? <u>Y</u>

ITEM # 7 ? <u>DRYER</u>
SERIAL NUMBER OF ITEM? <u>ERWW45</u>
WHERE LOCATED IN HOUSE? <u>WASHROOM</u>
DECLARED VALUE OF DRYER? <u>300</u>
IS YOUR SOCIAL SECURITY NUMBER
ENGRAVED ON THIS ITEM (Y/N)? <u>N</u>

CONTINUE ITEMS INTO FILE (Y/N)? <u>Y</u>

ITEM # 8 ? <u>RECLINER</u>
SERIAL NUMBER OF ITEM <u>122311</u>
WHERE LOCATED IN HOUSE? <u>LIVINGROOM</u>
DECLARED VALUE OF RECLINER? <u>300</u>
IS YOUR SOCIAL SECURITY NUMBER
ENGRAVED ON THIS ITEM (Y/N)? <u>N</u>

CONTINUE ITEMS INTO FILE (Y/N)? <u>N</u>

PRESS ENTER? <ENTER>

H O M E   I N V E N T O R Y

1) BEGIN A INVENTORY FILE
2) ADD TO EXISTING FILE
3) LIST ALL INVENTORY ITEMS
4) SAVE INVENTORY ON TAPE
5) LOAD INVENTORY FROM TAPE
6) MAKE CHANGES IN INVENTORY LIST
7) ITEMS CONTAINING S.S. NUMBER
8) END INVENTORY PROGRAM

SELECT? <u>7</u>

THE FOLLOWING ITEMS HAVE
YOUR SOCIAL SECURITY NUMBER
ENGRAVED ON THEM
ITEM #1 MICROWAVE OVEN
ITEM #2 COLOR TV
ITEM #3 COMPUTER

PRESS ENTER? <ENTER>

HOME INVENTORY

1) BEGIN A INVENTORY FILE
2) ADD TO EXISTING FILE
3) LIST ALL INVENTORY ITEMS
4) SAVE INVENTORY ON TAPE
5) LOAD INVENTORY FROM TAPE
6) MAKE CHANGES IN INVENTORY LIST
7) ITEMS CONTAINING S.S. NUMBER
8) END INVENTORY PROGRAM

SELECT? 8

END OF INVENTORY PROGRAM . . . .

Just a short list of inventory items in this sample run. In your actual
sample run you should also input who the item is manufactured by
along with the name of the item. Each piece of jewelry should be
listed separately, so they can be identified quickly. If you have more
than 100 items be sure to change the DIM statements in lines 30 &
40.

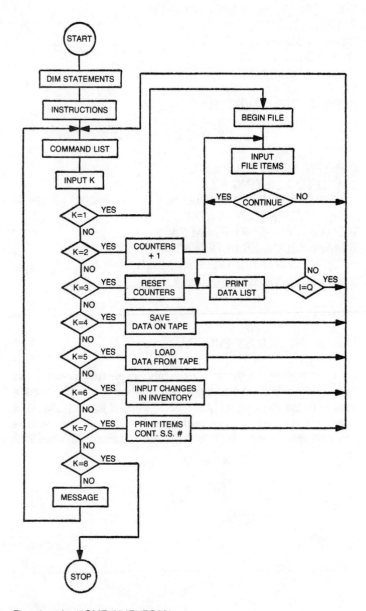

Flowchart for HOME INVENTORY

172

Program Listing

```
10 REM PROGRAM TITLE: HOME INVENTORY
20 CLEAR 1000
30 DIM I$(100),N$(100),L$(100),V(100)
40 DIM A$(100)
50 W$="$$#####.##"
80 CLS
90 PRINTTAB(15);"H O M E    I N V E N
   T O R Y"
100 PRINT
110 PRINT"1) BEGIN A INVENTORY FILE"
120 PRINT"2) ADD TO EXISTING FILE"
130 PRINT"3) LIST ALL INVENTORY ITEMS"
140 PRINT"4) SAVE INVENTORY ON TAPE"
150 PRINT"5) LOAD INVENTORY FROM TAPE"
160 PRINT"6) MAKE CHANGES IN INVENTORY
    LIST"
165 PRINT"7) ITEMS CONTAINING S.S. NUM
    BER"
170 PRINT"8) END INVENTORY PROGRAM"
180 PRINT
190 PRINT"SELECT";
200 INPUT K
210 ON K GOTO 250,700,800,1300,1500,17
    00,1930,2000
220 PRINT"THE NUMBER YOU HAVE SELECTED"
230 PRINT"IS NOT IN THIS PROGRAM...TRY
    AGAIN."
240 FOR X=1TO1500:NEXT:CLS:PRINT:GOTO8
    0
250 CLS:PRINT
260 PRINT"MAKING AN INVENTORY FILE WIL
    L BE"
270 PRINT"QUITE SIMPLE. AFTERWARDS YOU
    WILL"
280 PRINT"HAVE A COMPLETE FILE ON EVER
    YTHING"
290 PRINT"YOU OWN (OR INCLUDED IN THE
    FILE)."
300 PRINT"YOU CAN THEN SAVE THE ENTIRE
    FILE"
```

173

```
310 PRINT"ON CASSETTE TAPE FOR FUTURE
    REF-"
320 PRINT"ERENCE, (BE SURE TO STORE IT
    IN A"
330 PRINT"FIRE-PROOF CONTAINER) IN CAS
    E YOUR"
340 PRINT"HOME IS BURGLARIZED OR ALL O
    F YOUR"
350 PRINT"PROPERTY IS LOST IN A FIRE."
360 PRINT"BE SURE TO CHECK WITH YOUR I
    NSURANCE"
370 PRINT"AGENT, TO BE SURE HE HAS EVE
    RY ITEM"
380 PRINT"YOU ENTER IN THIS LOG, IN HI
    S FILE."
385 PRINT
390 PRINT"PRESS ENTER TO BEGIN";
400 INPUT X
410 CLS
420 PRINT
430 INPUT"DATE OF INVENTORY";D$
440 INPUT"ITEMS INSURED WITH (NAME)";N
    $
450 INPUT"STREET ADDRESS";N1$
460 INPUT"CITY & STATE";N2$
470 INPUT"ZIP CODE";N3$
480 INPUT"PHONE NUMBER";N4$
490 INPUT"POLICY NUMBER";P$
500 INPUT"TYPE OF INSURANCE";T$
505 I=1
510 PRINT
520 PRINT"ITEM #";I;
530 INPUT I$(I)
540 PRINT"SERIAL NUMBER OF ITEM";
550 INPUT N$(I)
560 PRINT"WHERE LOCATED IN HOUSE";
570 INPUT L$(I)
580 PRINT"DECLARED VALUE OF ";I$(I);
590 INPUT V(I)
600 PRINT"IS YOUR SOCIAL SECURITY NUMB
    ER"
610 PRINT" ENGRAVED ON THIS ITEM (Y/N)"
    ;
```

```
620 INPUT A$(I)
630 IF A$(I)="N" THEN 660
635 IF H=1 THEN 660
640 PRINT"ENTER YOUR SOCIAL SECURITY N
    UMBER";
650 INPUT S$
655 H=1
660 PRINT
665 IF I>=99 THEN 725
670 PRINT"CONTINUE ITEMS INTO FILE (Y/
    N)";
680 INPUT U$
690 IF U$="N" THEN 730
700 I=I+1
710 CLS
720 PRINT:GOTO520
725 PRINT"THAT IS";I;"ITEMS, ALL YOU C
    AN ENTER"
726 PRINT"WITH PROGRAM AS IT IS,,,,,"
730 Q=I
740 PRINT
750 PRINT"PRESS ENTER";
760 INPUT X
770 GOTO80
800 CLS
830 I=1:L=1
835 PRINTTAB(18);"** INVENTORY LIST **"
840 PRINT"ITEM" TAB(20);"SERIAL #";
850 PRINTTAB(35);"LOCATION" TAB(53);"V
    ALUE"
860 PRINT
870 PRINTI$(I) TAB(20);N$(I);
880 PRINT TAB(35);L$(I) TAB(50);USING
    W$;V(I)
890 IF L>=10 THEN 920
900 IF I<>Q THEN 910
905 GOTO1000
910 I=I+1:L=L+1:GOTO870
920 PRINT
930 PRINT"PRESS ANY KEY TO CONTINUE LI
    ST"
940 X$=INKEY$:IF X$="" THEN 940
```

175

```
950 I=I+1:L=1
960 CLS
970 GOTO840
1000 REM INSURANCE DATA PRINT-OUT
1005 IF JJ=1 JJ=0:GOTO1900
1010 FOR X=0TO127:SET(X,41):NEXT
1020 GOTO1060
1025 FOR X=1TO2500:NEXT
1030 PRINT@896,"
                        ";
1040 PRINT@896,;
1050 RETURN
1060 GOSUB1030
1070 PRINT"REMAINING DATA WILL BE PRINT
    ED"
1080 GOSUB1025
1090 PRINT"IN THIS AREA....."
1100 GOSUB1025
1110 PRINT"DATE OF INVENTORY: ";D$
1120 GOSUB1025
1130 PRINT"NAME OF INSURANCE AGENT: ";N
    $
1140 GOSUB1025
1150 PRINT"STREET ADDRESS: ";N1$
1160 GOSUB1025
1170 PRINT"CITY & STATE: ";N2$
1180 GOSUB1025
1190 PRINT"ZIP CODE: ";N3$
1200 GOSUB1025
1210 PRINT"PHONE NUMBER: ";N4$
1220 GOSUB1025
1230 PRINT"POLICY NUMBER: ";P$
1240 GOSUB1025
1250 PRINT"TYPE OF INSURANCE: ";T$
1260 GOSUB1025
1270 GOTO1900
1300 REM DATA TO RECORDER
1310 CLS
1320 PRINT
1330 PRINT"READY TAPE PLAYER (PLACE"
1340 PRINT"IN RECORD MODE) THEN"
1350 PRINT"PRESS ENTER";
```

```
1360 INPUT X
1370 PRINT#-1,Q
1380 PRINT"SAVING DATA....."
1390 FOR I=1TOQ
1400 PRINT#-1,I$(I),N$(I),L$(I),V(I),A$
     (I):NEXT
1410 PRINT#-1,D$,N$,N1$,N2$,N3$,N4$,P$,
     T$
1420 PRINT"DATA NOW ON TAPE....."
1430 PRINT
1440 PRINT"PRESS ENTER TO RETURN"
1450 PRINT"TO COMMAND LIST";
1460 INPUT X
1470 GOTO80
1500 REM DATA FROM TAPE
1510 CLS
1520 PRINT
1530 PRINT"PLACE CASSETTE IN PLAY MODE"
1540 PRINT"PRESS ENTER";
1550 INPUT X
1560 INPUT#-1,Q
1570 PRINT"LOADING DATA....."
1575 FOR I=1TOQ
1580 INPUT#-1,I$(I),N$(I),L$(I),V(I),A$
     (I):NEXT
1590 INPUT#-1,D$,N$,N1$,N2$,N3$,N4$,P$,
     T$
1600 PRINT"DATA IN MEMORY....."
1610 PRINT
1620 PRINT"PRESS ENTER";
1630 INPUT X
1640 GOTO80
1700 REM CHANGES IN LIST
1710 CLS
1720 PRINT
1730 PRINT"ENTER NUMBER OF ITEM";
1740 INPUT N
1745 JJ=1
1750 PRINT"ITEM #";N;": ";I$(N)
1755 PRINT"CHANGE TO";
1760 INPUT I$(N)
1770 PRINT"SERIAL NUMBER: ";N$(N)
```

```
1775 PRINT"CHANGE TO";
1780 INPUT N$(N)
1790 PRINT"LOCATION: ";L$(N)
1795 PRINT"CHANGE TO";
1800 INPUT L$(N)
1810 PRINT"DECLARED VALUE: ";V(N)
1815 PRINT"CHANGE TO";
1820 INPUT V(N)
1830 PRINT
1840 PRINT"MAKE MORE CHANGES IN"
1850 PRINT"INVENTORY ITEMS (Y/N)";
1860 INPUT A$
1870 IF A$="Y" THEN 1700
1880 FOR X=1TO1200:NEXT
1890 GOTO80
1900 PRINT@896,"PRESS ANY KEY"
1910 X$=INKEY$:IF X$="" THEN 1910
1920 GOTO80
1930 REM ITEMS CONTAINING S.S. NUMBER
1935 CLS:PRINT
1940 PRINT"THE FOLLOWING ITEMS HAVE"
1950 PRINT"YOUR SOCIAL SECURITY NUMBER"
1960 PRINT"ENGRAVED ON THEM."
1970 FOR I=1TOQ
1980 IF A$(I)="Y" THEN PRINT@256,"ITEM
     #";I;" ";I$(I) ELSE 1996
1990 FOR X=1TO1900:NEXT X
1995 PRINT@256,"
                 "
1996 NEXT
1997 PRINT"PRESS ENTER";
1998 INPUT X
1999 GOTO80
2000 REM END OF PROGRAM
2010 CLS
2020 PRINT
2030 PRINT"END OF INVENTORY PROGRAM....."
2040 END
2100 REM THE DIM STATEMENTS LINES
2110 REM 30 & 40 WILL LET YOU
2120 REM ENTER UP TO 100 ITEMS
2130 REM IF YOU HAVE MORE THAN
2140 REM 100 ITEMS JUST CHANGE
2150 REM THE DIM STATEMENTS AT
2160 REM THE ABOVE LINES TO SUITE
2170 REM YOUR NEEDS
```

MEDICINE LOG

Whether you keep a file of medicine purchased for income tax records, or just to keep up with all the medicines that come into your home, you will find this program quite useful.

Perhaps you need a prescription refilled, you can recall the list of medicines from your log and have an instant printout of the prescription number, type of medicine, doctor's name, etc. All the data you need to recall will be as close as your computer.

SAMPLE RUN

>>>MEDICINE LOG<<<

PROCESS DATA FROM TAPE? <u>NO</u>

REQUIRE INSTRUCTIONS? <u>YES</u>

DO YOU USE ENOUGH MEDICINE EACH
YEAR TO USE IT AS A DEDUCTION
ON YOUR INCOME TAX?
IF YOU HAVE A PRESCRIPTION REFILLED
DO YOU KNOW EXACTLY WHERE TO LOOK
FOR THE RX NUMBER?
IF YOU ANSWERED YES TO EITHER ONE OF
THE ABOVE QUESTIONS OR YOU JUST
WANT TO KEEP A LOG OF PRESCRIPTIONS
THIS PROGRAM WILL DO THAT FOR YOU.

PRESS ENTER? <ENTER>

NOTICE: THE DATA YOU INPUT INTO THIS
LOG WILL NOT TAKE THE PLACE OF YOUR
ORIGINAL RX RECEIPTS . . . . .

A LIST OF INFORMATION YOU'LL NEED
TO INPUT IS:

(1) PRESCRIPTION FOR (NAME OF PERSON)
(2) DATE OF PRESCRIPTION
(3) PRESCRIPTION NUMBER
(4) DOCTORS NAME
(5) CONTENTS OF PRESCRIPTION
(6) AMOUNT OF PRESCRIPTION

PRESS ENTER TO BEGIN? <ENTER>

TO CANCEL INPUTS INTO LOG, PRESS
<ENTER> ONLY FOR <PRESCRIPTION FOR>

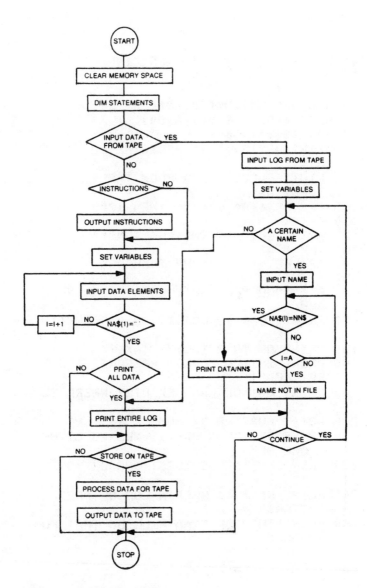

Flowchart for MEDICINE LOG

Program Listing

```
10 REM PROGRAM TITLE: MEDICINE LOG
20 CLS
30 CLEAR 1000
40 DIM NA$(50),D$(50),N$(50)
50 DIM E$(50),C$(50),A(50)
60 D$="$$#####.##"
70 PRINTTAB(10);">>> MEDICINE LOG <<<"
80 PRINT
90 PRINT"PROCESS DATA FROM TAPE";
100 INPUT A$
105 IF LEFT$(A$,1)="Y" THEN 1220
110 PRINT
120 PRINT"REQUIRE INSTRUCTIONS";
130 INPUT A$
140 IF LEFT$(A$,1)="N" THEN 430
150 PRINT
160 PRINT"DO YOU USE ENOUGH MEDICINE E
    ACH"
170 PRINT"YEAR TO USE IT AS A DEDUCTIO
    N"
180 PRINT"ON YOUR INCOME TAX ?"
190 PRINT"IF YOU HAVE A PRESCRIPTION R
    EFILLED"
200 PRINT"DO YOU KNOW EXACTLY WHERE TO
     LOOK"
210 PRINT"FOR THE RX NUMBER ?"
220 PRINT"IF YOU ANSWERED YES TO EITHE
    R ONE OF"
230 PRINT"THE ABOVE QUESTIONS OR YOU J
    UST"
240 PRINT"WANT TO KEEP A LOG OF PRESCR
    IPTIONS"
250 PRINT"THIS PROGRAM WILL DO THAT FO
    R YOU."
255 PRINT
260 INPUT"PRESS ENTER";X
270 CLS
280 PRINT
290 PRINT"NOTICE: THE DATA YOU INPUT I
    NTO THIS"
```

```
300 PRINT"LOG WILL NOT TAKE THE PLACE
    OF YOUR"
310 PRINT"ORIGINAL RX RECEIPTS....."
320 PRINT
330 PRINT"A LIST OF INFORMATION YOU'LL
    NEED"
340 PRINT"TO INPUT IS:"
350 PRINT
355 PRINT"(1) PRESCRIPTION FOR (NAME O
    F PERSON)"
360 PRINT"(2) DATE OF PRESCRIPTION"
370 PRINT"(3) PRESCRIPTION NUMBER"
380 PRINT"(4) DOCTORS NAME"
390 PRINT"(5) CONTENTS OF PRESCRIPTION"
400 PRINT"(6) AMOUNT OF PRESCRIPTION"
410 PRINT
420 INPUT"PRESS ENTER TO BEGIN LOG";X
430 CLS
440 PRINT
450 PRINT"TO CANCEL INPUTS INTO LOG, P
    RESS"
460 PRINT"<ENTER> ONLY FOR <PRESCRIPTI
    ON FOR>"
470 PRINT
480 I=0
485 INPUT"PRESCRIPTION FOR";NA$(I)
486 GOTO610
490 PRINT"DATE OF PRESCRIPTION";
500 INPUT D$(I)
510 PRINT"PRESCRIPTION NUMBER";
520 INPUT N$(I)
530 REM LINE 520 USES A STRING BECAUSE
     SOME
540 REM RX NUMBERS ARE ALPHANUMERIC
550 PRINT"DOCTORS NAME";
560 INPUT E$(I)
570 PRINT"CONTENTS";
580 INPUT C$(I)
590 PRINT"PRESCRIPTION AMOUNT";
600 INPUT A(I)
605 GOTO640
610 IF NA$(I)<>"" THEN 490
```

```
620 A=I
630 GOTO700
640 I=I+1
650 PRINT
660 GOTO485
700 CLS
710 PRINT
720 PRINT"DO YOU WANT THE LIST PRINTED
    ";
730 INPUT I$
740 IF LEFT$(I$,1)="N" THEN 1060
750 CLS:I=0:J=0:K=1:PRINT
760 IF I=A THEN 890
762 PRINT"PRESCRIPTION FOR:";
765 PRINTTAB(30);NA$(I)
770 PRINT"DATE OF PRESCRIPTION:";
780 PRINTTAB(30);D$(I)
790 PRINT"PRESCRIPTION NUMBER:";
800 PRINTTAB(30);N$(I)
810 PRINT"EXPIRATION DATE:";
820 PRINTTAB(30);E$(I)
830 PRINT"PRESCRIPTION CONTENTS:";
840 PRINTTAB(30);C$(I)
850 PRINT"PRESCRIPTION AMOUNT:";
860 PRINTTAB(28);USING D$;A(I)
870 PRINT
875 J=J+1:IF J<>2 THEN I=K:GOTO760
880 IF I<>A THEN 900
890 GOTO1000
900 J=0:I=I+1:K=K+2
910 GOSUB5000
930 GOTO760
1000 X=0
1010 PRINT
1020 X=X+1
1030 IF X<=4 THEN 1010
1040 GOSUB5000
1050 IF M=1 THEN 1400
1055 IF M=3 THEN 1695
1060 CLS
1070 PRINT
1080 PRINT"STORE LOG ON TAPE (Y/N)";
```

```
1090 INPUT I$
1100 IF I$="N" THEN 1700:REM TO END
1105 PRINT
1110 PRINT"READY PLAYER....."
1120 INPUT"THEN PRESS <ENTER>";X
1130 PRINT#-1,A
1140 PRINT
1150 PRINT"PROCESSING DATA....."
1160 FOR I=0TOA
1170 PRINT#-1,NA$(I),D$(I),N$(I),E$(I),
     C$(I),A(I)
1180 NEXT
1190 PRINT
1200 PRINT"PROCESSING OF DATA FINISHED."
1210 GOTO1400
1220 CLS
1230 PRINT
1240 PRINT"PLACE CASSETTE IN PLAYER, PR
     ESS"
1250 PRINT"THE <PLAY> BUTTON, THEN <ENT
     ER>";
1260 INPUT X
1270 INPUT#-1,A
1280 PRINT"PROCESSING INTO MEMORY....."
1290 FOR I=0TOA
1300 INPUT#-1,NA$(I),D$(I),N$(I),E$(I),
     C$(I),A(I)
1310 NEXT
1320 PRINT
1330 PRINT"DATA IN MEMORY."
1340 PRINT
1350 PRINT"(1) SEE ENTIRE FILE"
1355 PRINT"(2) SPECIFIC NAME IN LOG"
1356 PRINT"(3) CANCEL PROGRAM"
1360 PRINT
1365 INPUT"SELECT";X
1370 ON X GOTO 1375,1600,1700
1375 M=1
1380 GOTO750
1400 REM ADD TO PRESENT LIST
1410 PRINT
1420 PRINT"(1) ADD TO PRESENT LIST"
```

```
1430 PRINT"(2) START ANOTHER FILE"
1440 PRINT"(3) CANCEL PROGRAM"
1450 PRINT
1460 INPUT"SELECTION (1,2 OR 3)";X
1470 ON X GOTO 1500,430,1700
1500 I=I+1
1510 CLS
1520 PRINT
1530 GOTO485
1600 REM SPECIFIC NAME IN LOG
1610 PRINT
1620 PRINT"ENTER NAME";
1630 INPUT NN$
1640 I=0
1650 IF NA$(I)<>NN$ THEN 1680
1660 M=3:J=0:K=1
1670 GOTO760
1680 IF I<>A THEN I=I+1:GOTO1650
1690 PRINT"NAME NOT IN FILE.....":GOTO1
     696
1695 PRINT"END OF LISTING UNDER: ";NN$
1696 FOR XX=1TO2500:NEXT
1697 GOTO1340
1700 REM END
1710 CLS
1720 PRINT
1730 PRINT"END OF ** MEDICINE LOG **"
1740 END
5000 PRINT"PRESS ANY KEY TO CONTINUE...
     .."
5010 Q$=INKEY$
5020 IF Q$="" THEN 5010
5030 RETURN
```

SETTING UP A YARD SALE

So now your house is full of useless items that you want to pass on to someone else in a yard sale. Have no fear, you can input all those items into this program, plus amounts you want to sell them for. You can, during the actual yard sale, place the program on "SCAN/ SOLD". The computer will show you the list of items from the yard sale, you can scan each item, indicating if that item has been sold or not. If sold, it will be deleted from the yard sale list and be placed on a separate list, including amount received for the item.

SAMPLE RUN

SETTING UP A YARD SALE (ITEMS)

INPUT PREVIOUS DATA FROM TAPE? <u>NO</u>

SEE INSTRUCTIONS? <u>YES</u>

SO YOU HAVE NUMEROUS ITEMS TO GET
RID OF AND YOU DON'T KNOW WHERE
TO START? YOU HAVE A COMPUTER, WHY
NOT START THERE? THIS PROGRAM IS
DESIGNED TO HELP YOU SET UP AND
COMPLETE A YARD SALE. YOU WILL BE
ABLE TO ENTER EACH ITEM, IT'S PRICE
AND WHETHER IT HAS BEEN SOLD (DURING
THE ACTUAL YARD SALE).

PRESS ENTER? <ENTER>

IF SOMEONE HAS ASKED FOR A CERTAIN
ITEM, YOU CAN LIST THE ITEMS TO SEE
IF YOU HAVE THAT ITEM FOR SALE (FOR
LARGE YARD SALES). DURING THE ACTUAL
YARD SALE YOU CAN PUT THE ITEMS ON
"SCAN/SOLD", THE COMPUTER WILL 'SCAN'
EACH ITEM OF YOUR COMPLETED LIST, A
(BLOCK) WILL BE PLACED NEXT
TO EACH ITEM, IF YOU HAVE SOLD IT
THAT ITEM WILL GO TO A SEPARATE 'SOLD'
LIST WITH IT'S PRICE. THEN IT WILL BE
DELETED FROM THE ACTUAL YARD SALE LIST.
ALL OF THIS WILL BECOME MORE CLEARER
AS YOU PROGRESS THROUGH THE PROGRAM.

PRESS ENTER? <ENTER>

TO EXIT ALL ENTRYS IN ITEM FILE
JUST PRESS 'ENTER', FOR 'ITEM'.

DATE OF YARD SALE? <u>01/01/81</u>
NAME OF ITEM? <u>CHAIR</u>

188

SELLING PRICE OF ITEM? <u>20</u>

NAME OF ITEM? <u>COUCH</u>
SELLING PRICE OF ITEM? <u>25</u>

NAME OF ITEM? <u>CLOTHES (ASSORTED)</u>
SELLING PRICE OF ITEM? <u>20</u>

NAME OF ITEM? <u>BOOKS (ASSORTED)</u>
SELLING PRICE OF ITEM? <u>10</u>

NAME OF ITEM? <u>LAWN CHAIRS</u>
SELLING PRICE OF ITEM? <u>4</u>

NAME OF ITEM? <u>MAGAZINES (ASSORTED)</u>
SELLING PRICE OF ITEM? <u>3</u>

NAME OF ITEM? <u>CURTAINS (3 SETS)</u>
SELLING PRICE OF ITEM? <u>5</u>

NAME OF ITEM? <u>CHAIRS (4)</u>
SELLING PRICE OF ITEM? <u>20</u>

DO YOU WANT TO PROCEED TO
"SCAN/SOLD" NOW (Y/N)? <u>N</u>

THE LIST WILL BE PRINTED BEFORE
WE CONTINUE . . .

NAME OF ITEM	SELLING PRICE
CHAIR	$20.00
COUCH	$25.00
CLOTHES (ASSORTED)	$20.00
BOOKS (ASSORTED)	$10.00
LAWN CHAIRS	$4.00
MAGAZINES (ASSORTED)	$3.00
CURTAINS (3 SETS)	$5.00
CHAIRS (4)	$20.00

PRESS ENTER? <ENTER>

DO YOU WANT TO STORE THE

COMPLETED ITEM LIST ON TAPE (Y/N)? Y

The most unique area of this program would be the SCAN/SOLD, here each item is scanned while you input if the item is sold or not. Items that are sold are placed on a separate list. You can make up your yard sale items well in advance of the actual yard sale so you'll know exactly what you want to get rid of.

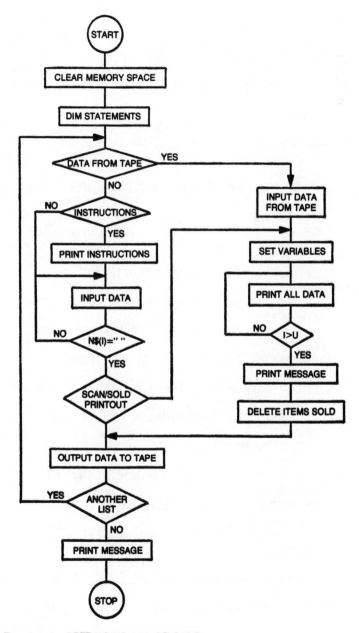

Flowchart for SETTING UP A YARD SALE

Program Listing

```
10 REM PROGRAM TITLE: SETTING UP
20 REM A YARD SALE (ITEMS)
30 CLEAR1000
40 DIM N$(50),P(50),A$(50),T(50)
45 DIM Q$(50),R(50)
50 X$=CHR$(34):Y$=CHR$(143)
60 Q$="$$####.##"
70 CLS
80 PRINT
90 PRINTTAB(10);"SETTING UP A YARD SA
   LE (ITEMS)"
100 PRINT
110 PRINT"INPUT PREVIOUS DATA FROM TAP
    E";
120 INPUT A$
130 IF A$="Y" OR A$="YES" THEN 820
140 PRINT"SEE INSTRUCTIONS";
150 INPUT A$
160 IF A$="NO" OR A$="N" THEN 455
170 PRINT
180 PRINT "SO YOU HAVE  NUMEROUS ITEMS
     TO GET"
190 PRINT"RID OF AND YOU DON'T KNOW WH
    ERE"
200 PRINT"TO START? YOU HAVE A COMPUTE
    R, WHY"
210 PRINT"NOT START THERE? THIS PROGRA
    M IS"
220 PRINT"DESIGNED TO HELP YOU SET UP
    AND"
230 PRINT"COMPLETE A YARD SALE. YOU WI
    LL BE"
240 PRINT"ABLE TO ENTER EACH ITEM, IT'
    S PRICE"
250 PRINT"AND WHETHER IT HAS BEEN SOLD
     (DURING"
260 PRINT"THE ACTUAL YARD SALE)."
270 PRINT
280 INPUT"PRESS ENTER";X:CLS
300 PRINT"IF SOMEONE HAS ASKED FOR A C
    ERTAIN"
310 PRINT"ITEM, YOU CAN LIST THE ITEMS
     TO SEE"
320 PRINT"IF YOU HAVE THAT ITEM FOR SA
    LE (FOR"
```

```
330 PRINT"LARGE YARD SALES). DURING TH
    E ACTUAL"
340 PRINT"YARD SALE YOU CAN PUT THE IT
    EMS ON"
350 PRINT X$;"SCAN/SOLD";X$;", ";
360 PRINT"THE COMPUTER WILL 'SCAN'"
370 PRINT"EACH ITEM OF YOUR COMPLETED
    LIST, A"
380 PRINT Y$;" (BLOCK) WILL BE PLACED
    NEXT"
390 PRINT"TO EACH ITEM, IF YOU HAVE SO
    LD IT"
400 PRINT"THAT ITEM WILL GO TO A SEPAR
    ATE 'SOLD'"
410 PRINT"LIST WITH IT'S PRICE. THEN I
    T WILL BE"
420 PRINT"DELETED FROM THE ACTUAL YARD
    SALE LIST."
430 PRINT"ALL OF THIS WILL BECOME MORE
    CLEARER"
440 PRINT"AS YOU PROGRESS THROUGH THE
    PROGRAM."
445 PRINT
450 INPUT"PRESS ENTER";X
455 CLS
460 PRINT
470 PRINT"TO EXIT ALL ENTRYS IN ITEM F
    ILE"
480 PRINT"JUST PRESS 'ENTER', FOR 'ITE
    M'."
490 PRINT
495 INPUT"DATE OF YARD SALE";D$
500 I=1
510 INPUT"NAME OF ITEM";N$(I)
520 IF N$(I)="" THEN I=I-1:U=I:GOTO570
530 INPUT"SELLING PRICE OF ITEM";P(I)
540 PRINT
550 I=I+1
560 GOTO510
570 CLS
580 PRINT
590 PRINT"DO YOU WANT TO PROCEED TO"
600 PRINTX$;"SCAN/SOLD";X$;" NOW (Y/N)";
610 INPUT A$
620 IF A$="Y" THEN 1000 ELSE 900
630 PRINT
```

```
640 PRINT"DO YOU WANT TO STORE THE"
650 PRINT"COMPLETED ITEM LIST ON TAPE
    (Y/N)";
660 INPUT A$
670 IF A$="N" THEN RR=1:GOTO2300
680 REM LIST TO TAPE
690 PRINT
700 PRINT"PLACE UNIT IN <RECORD MODE>"
710 PRINT"AND PRESS <ENTER>";
720 INPUT A$
730 PRINT#-1,D,Q,U
735 IF D=0 THEN 745
740 FOR I=1TOD:PRINT#-1,N$(I),P(I):NEXT
745 IF Q=0 THEN JJ=1:GOTO760
750 FOR I=1TOQ:PRINT#-1,A$(I),T(I):NEXT
760 PRINT#-1,D$
765 IF JJ=1 THEN FOR I=1TOU:PRINT#-1,N
    $(I),P(I):NEXT
766 FOR I=1TOU:PRINT#-1,Q$(I),R(I):NEXT
770 PRINT
780 PRINT"YARD SALE LIST NOW ON TAPE..."
790 PRINT"PRESS ENTER";
800 INPUT A$
810 GOTO2310
820 REM LIST FROM TAPE
830 PRINT
840 PRINT"PLACE UNIT IN <PLAY> MODE"
850 PRINT"AND PRESS <ENTER>";
860 INPUT A$
865 INPUT#-1,D,Q,U
866 IF D=0 THEN 877
870 PRINT"LOADING DATA LIST..."
875 FOR I=1TOD:INPUT#-1,N$(I),P(I):NEXT
877 IF Q=0 THEN JJ=1:GOTO885
880 FOR I=1TOQ:INPUT#-1,A$(I),T(I):NEXT
885 INPUT#-1,D$
888 IF JJ=1 THEN FOR I=1TOU:INPUT#-1,N
    $(I),P(I):NEXT
889 FOR I=1TOU:INPUT#-1,Q$(I),R(I):NEXT
890 PRINT
895 PRINT"DATA LIST IN MEMORY..."
896 PRINT
897 INPUT"PRESS ENTER FOR LIST";A$
898 CLS
899 PRINT:GOTO1800
900 PRINT
```

```
910 PRINT"THE LIST WILL BE PRINTED BEF
    ORE"
920 PRINT"WE CONTINUE..."
930 FOR X=1TO1200:NEXT
940 W=1:CLS
950 GOTO1120
1000 REM "SCAN/SOLD" ITEMS
1010 CLS
1020 PRINT
1030 PRINT"ALL THE ITEMS YOU HAVE ENTER
     ED"
1040 PRINT"WILL NOW BE 'SCANNED'. A   ";
1045 PRINTY$;"   WILL
1050 PRINT"BE PLACED NEXT TO EACH ITEM,
     IF"
1060 PRINT"IT HAS BEEN SOLD, PRESS THE
     <SPACE"
1070 PRINT"BAR>. IF NOT PRESS <ENTER>."
1075 PRINT"THE BLOCK WILL CONTINUE TO"
1080 PRINT"EACH ITEM UNTIL ALL ITEMS HA
     VE"
1090 PRINT"BEEN ";X$;"SCANNED";X$;".
1095 PRINT:Q=1
1100 INPUT"PRESS ENTER TO BEGIN";X
1110 CLS
1120 I=1:J=192:E=1:GOSUB1125:GOTO1130
1125 IF U<=12 THEN T=U ELSE T=10
1128 RETURN
1130 PRINT
1140 PRINT TAB(5);"NAME OF ITEM";
1150 PRINT TAB(40);"SELLING PRICE"
1160 PRINT
1170 PRINT TAB(7);N$(I);
1180 PRINT TAB(40);USING Q$;P(I)
1190 Q$(I)=N$(I):R(I)=P(I)
1260 I=I+1
1270 IF I<=T THEN 1170
1285 T=T+10
1290 IF T>U THEN T=U
1295 IF W=1 THEN 1310
1300 GOSUB1370
1310 IF I>U THEN Q=Q-1:GOTO1600
1315 GOSUB1325
1320 J=192:GOTO1130
1325 IF W=1 THEN PRINT:PRINT:GOTO1340
1330 PRINT@J+64,;
```

195

```
1340 INPUT"PRESS ENTER TO CONTINUE";X
1350 CLS
1360 RETURN
1370 PRINT@J,Y$;
1380 A$=INKEY$:IF A$="" THEN 1380
1390 IF A$=" " THEN 1490
1400 PRINT@J," ";
1410 E=E+1:J=J+64
1420 IF E=I THEN RETURN
1430 GOTO1370
1490 A$(Q)=N$(E)
1500 T(Q)=P(E)
1510 N$(E)="":P(E)=0
1520 Q=Q+1
1530 PRINT@J+2,"SOLD";
1540 GOTO1400
1600 REM PRINT LIST AGAIN
1605 IF W=1 THEN PRINT:GOTO1620
1610 PRINT@J+64,;
1620 INPUT"PRESS ENTER";X
1630 CLS
1640 PRINT
1645 IF RR=1 RETURN
1650 IF W=1 W=0:GOTO630
1660 REM ITEMS DELETED FROM LIST
1670 I=1:D=1
1680 IF N$(I)="" THEN 1700
1690 N$(D)=N$(I):P(D)=P(I)
1695 D=D+1
1700 IF I<>U THEN 1720
1710 D=D-1:GOTO1740
1720 I=I+1
1730 GOTO1680
1740 GOTO630
1800 IF JJ=1 THEN 1910
1810 IF D<>0 THEN 1910
1850 REM ALL ITEMS SOLD
1855 PRINT"DATE OF YARD SALE: ";D$
1860 PRINT
1870 PRINT"ALL ITEMS HAVE BEEN SOLD"
1880 PRINT"THAT WERE CONTAINED IN YOUR"
1890 PRINT"YARD SALE LIST....."
1900 FOR K=1TO1200:NEXT:V=1
1910 I=1:RR=1
1915 IF D=0 AND Q=0 THEN T=U:GOTO1950
1920 IF D<=10 THEN T=D ELSE T=10
```

196

```
1930 IF Q<=10 THEN W=Q ELSE W=10
1950 PRINT"DATE OF YARD SALE: ";D$
1955 I=1
1960 PRINT
1965 IF V=1 THEN 2170
1970 PRINT TAB(10);"YARD SALE ITEM";
1980 PRINT TAB(40);"SELLING PRICE"
1990 PRINT
2000 PRINT TAB(12);N$(I);
2010 PRINT TAB(40);USING Q$;P(I)
2030 IF N$(I+1)="" THEN 2060
2032 IF I<=T THEN 2050
2035 T=T+10:IF T>D THEN T=D
2040 IF I>D THEN 2060
2045 GOSUB1620:CLS:GOTO1960
2050 I=I+1:GOTO2000
2060 PRINT
2065 FOR K=1TO1500:NEXT
2070 PRINT"ALL THE ABOVE ITEMS HAVE"
2080 PRINT"<NOT> BEEN SOLD FROM YOUR"
2090 PRINT"YARD SALE..."
210C PRINT
2110 GOSUB1620
2112 IF JJ=1 THEN 2310
2115 IF Q=0 THEN 2310
2120 I=1
2130 PRINT
2140 PRINT TAB(10);"YARD SALE ITEM";
2150 PRINT TAB(40);"SELLING PRICE"
2160 PRINT
2170 PRINT TAB(12);A$(I);
2180 PRINT TAB(40);USING Q$;T(I)
2190 S=T(I)+S
2200 IF I<=W THEN 2240
2210 W=W+10
2220 IF W>Q THEN W=Q
2225 IF I>Q THEN 2245
2230 GOSUB1620:CLS:GOTO2140
2240 I=I+1
2242 IF A$(I)<>"" THEN 2170
2245 FOR K=1TO1500:NEXT:PRINT
2250 PRINT"ALL THE ABOVE ITEMS <HAVE>"
2260 PRINT"BEEN SOLD FROM YOUR YARD"
2270 PRINT"SALE...TOTAL AMOUNT RECEIVED:";
2280 PRINT USING Q$;S
2290 FOR K=1TO1200
```

```
2300 GOSUB1620
2310 REM MORE DATA
2320 IF RR=0 RR=1
2325 PRINT
2340 PRINT"1) 'SCAN' LIST"
2350 PRINT"2) MAKE ANOTHER LIST"
2360 PRINT"3) END PROGRAM"
2370 PRINT
2380 PRINT"SELECT";
2390 INPUT X
2400 ON X GOTO 2530,2450,2600
2450 FOR I=1TOU
2460 N$(I)="":P(I)=0
2470 A$(I)="":T(I)=0
2480 NEXT
2490 S=0
2500 PRINT"MEMORY CLEARED....."
2510 PRINT:GOSUB1620
2520 GOTO490
2530 FOR I=1TOU
2540 A$(I)="":T(I)=0
2550 N$(I)=Q$(I):P(I)=R(I)
2560 NEXT:S=0:RR=0
2570 GOTO1000
2580 N$(I)=A$(I):P(I)=T(I)
2590 GOTO2560
2600 REM END OF PROGRAM
2610 PRINT
2620 PRINT"END OF YARD SALE PROGRAM."
2630 END
2700 REM THE DIM STATEMENTS LINES
2710 REM 40 & 45 WILL LET YOU INPUT
2720 REM UP TO 50 YARD SALE ITEMS
2730 REM YOU CAN INCREASE OR DECREASE
2740 REM THIS AMOUNT TO SUIT YOUR NEEDS
```

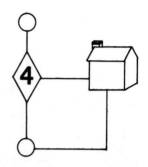

Programs for the Dinette or Den

Occasions To Remember. Forget nothing with this program.

Morning Organizer. Input and organize your morning, from 6:00 a.m. until 11:59 a.m.

Evening Organizer. Having a party? You can even enter the guests' names with this program.

Household Chores. Your computer will make all of the decisions on who is supposed to do what.

Magazine Topics to Remember. Want a magazine article, but can't remember where it's at? You'll always know with this program.

Weather Conditions. You won't be left out in the rain using this mass storage weather program.

OCCASIONS TO REMEMBER

So you forgot your nephew's birthday because last years calendar expired and was thrown away, and that's where you had the date marked? This program is designed to let you enter each and every item you'll ever need to remember, from birthdays to doctor's appointments to luncheon engagements.

You can (and should) store the entire file on tape, so it will be there and ready when you need it. Also, the completed file can be updated at your convenience. Make a file for day to day, or make it for items months from now.

SAMPLE RUN

OCCASIONS TO REMEMBER

INPUT DATA FROM RECORDER? <u>NO</u>

PRINT INSTRUCTIONS? <u>YES</u>

MISSED YOUR FRIENDS BIRTHDAY, 'CAUSE
YOU COULDN'T REMEMBER THE EXACT DATE?
THIS PROGRAM WON'T LET YOU FORGET!!
WHETHER IT BE A BIRTHDAY, ANNIVERSARY
APPOINTMENT OR JUST A SPECIAL OCCASION
AFTER YOU ENTER THE DATA AND STORE IT
ON TAPE, YOU'LL NEVER FORGET IT AGAIN.

PRESS A KEY? < SPACE BAR>

DATA WILL BE ENTERED AS FOLLOWS:

A) THE ITEM ITSELF
B) TIME OF ITEM (WITHOUT THE COLON)
C) DATE OF ITEM (M/D/Y)

A POSSIBLE LIST OF ITEMS WILL
BE PRINTED, IF YES - ENTER 'Y'
IF NO - ENTER 'N'. YOU CAN ADD
YOUR OWN ITEMS LATER ON IN THE
PROGRAM.

PRESS A KEY TO BEGIN? <SPACE BAR>

ITEMS (Y/N):

BIRTHDAY? <u>N</u>
ANNIVERSARY? <u>N</u>
APPOINTMENT? <u>Y</u>
ENTER TIME FOR THE APPOINTMENT? 10.A.M.
ENTER DATE FOR APPOINTMENT (M/D/Y)? <u>01/20/81</u>
LOCATION FOR APPOINTMENT? <u>DOCTORS OFFICE</u>

ARE THERE OTHER ITEMS YOU WANT
TO REMEMBER? <u>NO</u>

The list could go on and on. With the program as it stands, you can
input up to 25 items. To increase this, increase the numbers in the
dimension statements.

202

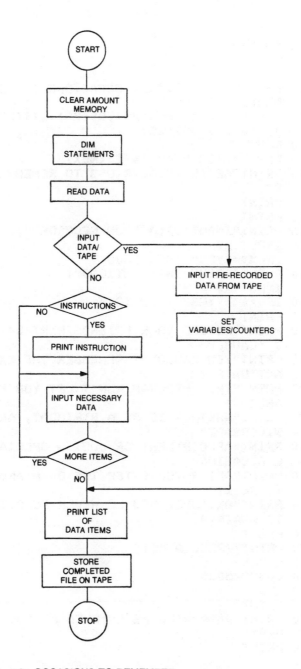

Flowchart for OCCASIONS TO REMEMBER

Program Listing

```
1000 REM PROGRAM TITLE: OCCASIONS TO RE
     MEMBER
1010 CLEAR 1000:DIM G(25),G$(25),IT$(25
     ),TT$(25),DD$(25)
1020 CLS
1030 FOR I=1TO3:READ I$(I):NEXT
1040 PRINTTAB(15);"OCCASIONS TO REMEMBE
     R"
1050 PRINT
1052 PRINT
1055 PRINT"INPUT DATA FROM RECORDER";
1056 INPUT X$
1058 IF X$="YES" THEN 3600
1060 PRINT"PRINT INSTRUCTIONS";
1070 INPUT X$
1080 IF X$<>"YES" THEN 1375
1090 PRINT
1100 PRINT"MISSED YOUR FRIENDS BIRTHDAY
     , 'CAUSE"
1110 PRINT"YOU COULDN'T REMEMBER THE EX
     ACT DATE ?"
1120 PRINT"THIS PROGRAM WON'T LET YOU F
     ORGET !!"
1130 PRINT"WHETHER IT BE A BIRTHDAY, AN
     NIVERSARY"
1140 PRINT"APPOINTMENT OR JUST A SPECIA
     L OCCASION"
1150 PRINT"AFTER YOU ENTER THE DATA AND
     STORE IT"
1160 PRINT"ON TAPE, YOU'LL NEVER FORGET
     IT AGAIN."
1170 PRINT
1180 PRINT"PRESS A KEY"
1190 A=780
1200 GOSUB25000
1210 CLS
1220 PRINT
1230 PRINT"DATA WILL BE ENTERED AS FOLL
     OWS:"
1240 PRINT
```

```
1250 PRINT"A) THE ITEM ITSELF"
1260 PRINT"B) TIME OF ITEM (WITHOUT THE
     COLON)"
1270 PRINT"C) DATE OF ITEM (M/D/Y)"
1280 PRINT
1290 PRINT"A POSSIBLE LIST OF ITEMS WIL
     L"
1300 PRINT"BE PRINTED, IF YES - ENTER '
     Y'"
1310 PRINT"IF NO - ENTER 'N'. YOU CAN A
     DD"
1320 PRINT"YOUR OWN ITEMS LATER ON IN T
     HE"
1330 PRINT"PROGRAM."
1340 PRINT
1350 PRINT"PRESS A KEY TO BEGIN"
1360 A=853
1370 GOSUB25000
1375 CLS
1380 PRINT:I=1:SD=1
1390 PRINT"ITEMS (Y/N):":PRINT
1400 PRINT I$(I);
1410 INPUT Q$(I)
1415 IF Q$(I)="Y" THEN R(I)=I
1420 I=I+1
1430 IF I<>4 THEN1400 ELSE I=1
1435 IF R(I)=0 THEN I=I+1
1440 REM ALL NO ANSWERS ?
1450 IF R(1)+R(2)+R(3)=0 THEN JH=1:GOTO
     2500
1460 IF R(I)=0 THEN I=I+1
1500 CLS:PRINT
1505 IF I$(I)="" THEN2500
1510 PRINT"ENTER TIME FOR THE ";I$(I);
1520 INPUT T$(I)
1530 IF RIGHT$(T$(I),4)<>"A.M." AND RIG
     HT$(T$(I),4)<>"P.M." THEN PRINT"TR
     Y AGAIN, ALSO ENTER A.M. OR P.M.";
     PRINT:GOTO1510
1540 PRINT"ENTER DATE FOR ";I$(I);" (M/
     D/Y)";
1550 INPUT D$(I)
```

```
1560 IF LEN(D$(I))<>6 AND LEN(D$(I))<>7
     AND LEN(D$(I))<>8 THEN PRINT"ENTE
     R DATE AGAIN, AS: 10/10/81 (EXAMPL
   E):PRINT:GOTO1540
1562 IF RR=1 THEN2670
1565 ON R(I) GOTO1570,1800,1900
1570 PRINT"WOULD YOU LIKE TO ENTER NAME
     S"
1580 PRINT"OF GUESTS THAT WILL ATTEND T
     HE ";I$(I);
1590 INPUT I$
1600 IF LEFT$(I$,1)="Y" THEN1630
1610 REM GOTO ANOTHER QUESTION
1620 GOTO1690
1630 PRINT"HOW MANY DO YOU EXPECT";
1640 INPUT G
1650 PRINT"ENTER THESE";G;"GUESTS NOW."
1660 FOR J=1TOG
1670 INPUT G$(J)
1680 NEXT
1685 G2=G
1690 PRINT"WHERE WILL THE ";I$(I);" TAK
     E PLACE";
1700 INPUT P$(I)
1705 GOTO1800
1710 I=I+1
1720 IF I<>4 AND R(I)=0 THEN1710
1730 GOTO1500
1800 PRINT"WHOM IS THE ";I$(I);" FOR";
1810 INPUT N$(I)
1820 GOTO1710
1900 PRINT"LOCATION FOR ";I$(I);
1910 INPUT L$(I)
1920 GOTO1710
2500 REM ANY OTHER ITEMS ?
2510 PRINT
2520 PRINT"ARE THEIR OTHER ITEMS YOU WA
     NT"
2530 PRINT"TO REMEMBER";
2540 INPUT X$
2550 IF X$<>"YES" THEN2700
2555 RR=1
```

```
2560 PRINT"HOW MANY ITEMS";
2570 INPUT G1
2580 PRINT"ENTER TITLE, TIME & DATE FOR
     THE"
2585 PRINT G1;"ITEMS."
2590 FOR J=1TOG1
2600 INPUT"TITLE OF ITEM"; IT$(J)
2610 PRINT"TIME";
2620 INPUT TT$(J)
2630 PRINT"DATE";
2640 INPUT DD$(J)
2650 NEXT
2700 REM PRINTOUT LIST BEFORE STORING
2710 REM ON TAPE
2720 CLS
2730 PRINTTAB(15);"** OCCASIONS TO REME
     MBER **"
2740 PRINT
2750 PRINTTAB(0);"OCCASION" TAB(25);"TI
     ME";
2760 PRINTTAB(45);"DATE OF OCCASION"
2770 FOR X=0TO122:SET(X,9):NEXT
2780 PRINT:I=1
2790 IF R(I)=0 THEN 2850
2840 PRINTTAB(0);I$(I) TAB(25);T$(I) TA
     B(48);D$(I)
2850 I=I+1
2860 IF I<>4 THEN2790
2870 IF RR=1 THEN 2890
2880 GOTO2960
2890 REM PRINTOUT REST OF ITEMS
2900 J=1
2910 PRINTTAB(0);IT$(J) TAB(25);TT$(J);
2920 PRINTTAB(48);DD$(J)
2930 J=J+1
2940 IF J<>G1+1 THEN2910
2950 REM MORE ITEMS ?
2960 FOR X=0TO122:SET(X,43):NEXT
2970 I=1:K=1:V=1000
2980 GOTO3020
2990 PRINT@965,"
                                      ";
```

```
2995 REM 48 SPACES AT LINE 2990
3000 PRINT@965,;
3005 FOR XX=1TOV:NEXT
3010 RETURN
3020 GOSUB2990:IF JH=1 THEN 3340
3030 PRINT"OTHER DATA ITEMS WILL BE PRI
     NTED HERE";
3040 GOSUB3005:GOSUB2990
3050 PRINT"AFTER YOU HAVE VIEWED EACH I
     TEM OF THE";
3060 GOSUB3005:GOSUB2990
3070 PRINT"REMAINING DATA -- PRESS THE
     <SPACE BAR>";
3080 GOSUB3005:GOSUB2990
3085 V=V-500
3090 IF R(I)=0 AND I<=4 THEN I=I+1:GOTO
     3090
3095 IF I=2 THEN 3120 ELSE IF I=3 THEN
     3310
3098 IF I>=4 THEN 3320
3100 PRINT I$(I);" WILL TAKE PLACE AT "
     ;P$(I);
3110 GOSUB4000:GOSUB2990
3120 PRINT"THE ";I$(I);" IS FOR ";N$(I)
     ;
3130 GOSUB4000:GOSUB2990
3135 IF I=2 THEN3290
3140 IF G<>0 OR G2<>0 THEN 3210
3150 GOTO3290
3200 GOSUB4000:GOSUB2990
3210 PRINT"THEIR WILL BE";G;"GUESTS AT
     THE ";I$(I);
3220 GOSUB4000:GOSUB2990
3230 PRINT"THE GUESTS NAMES ARE: ";
3240 PRINT G$(K);
3250 GOSUB4000:GOSUB2990
3260 K=K+1
3265 IF R1=1 AND K<>G+1 THEN3240 ELSE I
     F K=G+1 THEN R1=0:GOTO3290
3270 IF K<>G2+1 THEN3240
3280 G2=0
3290 IF I=3 THEN 3310 ELSE I=I+1
```

```
3300 GOTO3090
3310 IF R(3)<>0 THEN 3330
3320 V=V+1000:GOSUB2990:GOTO3350
3330 PRINT"LOCATION FOR ";I$(3);" IS TH
     E ";L$(3);
3340 GOSUB4000:GOSUB2990
3350 PRINT"PRESS <SPACE BAR> WHEN FINIS
     HED VIEWING";
3360 GOSUB4000
3370 IF SD=1 THEN 3390
3380 REM GOTO END
3385 CLS:PRINT:GOTO3560
3390 CLS
3400 PRINT
3410 PRINT"DATA WILL NOW BE STORED ON"
3420 PRINT"CASSETTE TAPE, WHEN READY,"
3430 PRINT"PRESS ENTER";
3440 INPUT XX$
3450 PRINT
3460 PRINT"STORING DATA ON TAPE....."
3465 PRINT#-1,JH,RR
3470 IF JH=1 THEN 3520
3480 FOR I=1TO4:PRINT#-1,T$(I),D$(I):NE
     XT
3485 PRINT#-1,R(1),R(2),R(3)
3490 PRINT#-1,G
3500 FOR I=1TOG:PRINT#-1,G$(I):NEXT
3510 PRINT#-1,P$(1),N$(1),N$(2),L$(3)
3515 IF RR<>1 THEN 3540
3520 PRINT#-1,G1
3530 FOR I=1TOG1:PRINT#-1,IT$(I),TT$(I)
     ,DD$(I):NEXT
3540 PRINT
3550 PRINT"TRANSFER COMPLETE....."
3560 PRINT
3570 PRINT"END OF PROGRAM....."
3580 END
3600 PRINT
3610 PRINT"PLACE CASSETTE IN PLAYER....
     ."
3620 PRINT"PLACE IN PLAY MODE, AND PRES
     S"
```

```
3630 PRINT"ENTER";
3640 INPUT X$
3650 PRINT
3655 PRINT"INPUTTING DATA....."
3660 INPUT#-1,JH,RR
3665 IF JH=1 THEN3710
3670 FOR I=1TO4:INPUT#-1,T$(I),D$(I):NE
     XT
3675 INPUT#-1,R(1),R(2),R(3)
3680 INPUT#-1,G
3690 FOR I=1TOG:INPUT#-1,G$(I):NEXT:R1=
     1
3700 INPUT#-1,P$(1),N$(1),N$(2),L$(3)
3705 IF RR<>1 THEN3730
3710 INPUT#-1,G1
3720 FOR I=1TOG1:INPUT#-1,IT$(I),TT$(I)
     ,DD$(I):NEXT
3730 PRINT
3740 PRINT"DATA IN MEMORY...."
3750 PRINT
3760 PRINT"PRESS ANY KEY FOR PRINTOUT"
3770 A=859
3780 GOSUB25000
3790 GOTO2720
4000 REM KEY CLOSURE
4010 X$=INKEY$
4020 IF X$<>" " THEN 4010
4030 RETURN
10000 DATA BIRTHDAY,ANNIVERSARY,APPOINTM
      ENT
25000 REM KEY CLOSURE
25005 A$=INKEY$
25010 PRINT@A,CHR$(143)
25020 FOR J=1TO100:NEXT
25030 PRINT@A," "
25040 FOR J=1TO50:NEXT
25050 IF A$="" THEN 25005
25060 RETURN
```

MORNING ORGANIZER

If you have problems getting yourself organized in the morning, stay up too late, or just had a few too many at the party the night before, this program should help you through the morning. It's best to input all the items you want to remember the day or night before, that way when you arise the next morning all you need do is load the data file containing your organizing items. The computer will print the items you entered, plus the time for each so you can get yourself organized easier.

SAMPLE RUN
MORNING ORGANIZER
(ROUTINE)

RETRIEVE DATA FROM TAPE (Y/N)? <u>N</u>

INSTRUCTIONS? N

ENTER THE MONTH? <u>JANUARY</u>
ENTER THE DAY YOU WISH TO
BEGIN (MONDAY, TUESDAY, ETC.)? <u>MONDAY</u>
ENTER THE DATE FOR MONDAY? <u>10</u>
ENTER THE YEAR? <u>1981</u>

NOW YOU WILL ENTER ALL THE
NECESSARY DATA TO MAKE THE
ORGANIZER EFFECTIVE. YOU WILL
BEGIN BY ENTERING THE TIME FOR
THE 1 ST THING YOU WANT TO
REMEMBER, AND SO ON.
THE FORMAT FOR ENTERING TIME
WILL BE 700, 915, ETC.
ENTER WITHOUT THE COLON, THE
COMPUTER WILL DO THAT.

ENTER TIME FOR ITEM 1 ? <u>930</u>
NUMBER 1 ITEM TO REMEMBER:
ENTER THIS ITEM NOW, APPOINTMENT,
VISIT, OTHER THINGS TO DO, FOR
THE TIME YOU HAVE ENTERED?
<u>CALL DENTIST FOR APPOINTMENT</u>

ITEM NUMBER: 1
TIME: 09:30 A.M.
TO REMEMBER:
CALL DENTIST FOR APPOINTMENT
FOR THE DATE: JANUARY 10, 1981 (MONDAY)

ARE THEIR ANY OTHER ITEMS YOU
WANT TO LIST FOR MONDAY JANUARY 10 ?
<u>YES</u>

ITEMS WILL NOW BE STORED ON
CASSETTE TAPE, PLACE RECORDER
IN RECORD MODE & PRESS ENTER?

DO YOU WISH TO ENTER AND
SAVE MORE MEMO'S? <u>YES</u>

WE WILL CONTINUE....

IF MONTH AND YEAR ARE THE SAME
AS PREVIOUSLY ENTERED, JUST
PRESS ENTER FOR MONTH, YEAR.

ENTER THE MONTH? <u>JANUARY</u>
ENTER THE DAY YOU WISH TO
BEGIN (MONDAY, TUESDAY, ETC.)? <u>WEDNESDAY</u>
ENTER THE DATE FOR WEDNESDAY? <u>12</u>
ENTER THE YEAR? <u>1981</u>

ENTER TIME FOR ITEM 4 ? <u>830</u>
NUMBER 4 ITEM TO REMEMBER:
<u>CALL DOCTORS OFFICE / APPOINTMENT</u>

ITEM NUMBER: 4

TIME: 08:30 A.M.
TO REMEMBER:
CALL DOCTORS OFFICE / APPOINTMENT
FOR THE DATE: JANUARY 12 1981 (WEDNESDAY)

ARE THERE ANY OTHER ITEMS YOU
WANT TO LIST FOR WEDNESDAY JANUARY 12 ?
NO

ITEMS WILL NOW BE STORED ON
CASSETTE TAPE, PLACE RECORDER
IN RECORD MODE & PRESS ENTER?

DO YOU WISH TO ENTER AND
SAVE MORE MEMO'S? <u>NO</u>

SO-LONG....

RUN COMPLETE

When inputing items for one morning try not to exceed 10, unless
you insert, dimension statements at the beginning of the program.

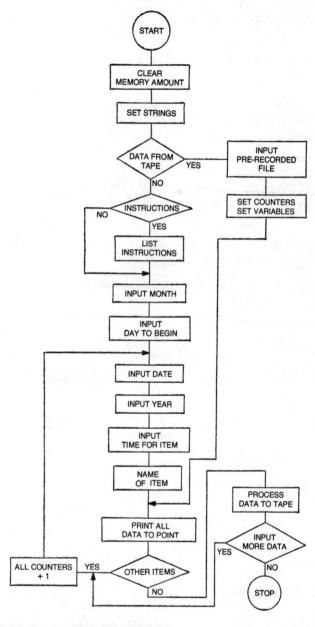

Flowchart for MORNING ORGANIZER

214

PROGRAM Listing

```
900 REM PROGRAM TITLE: MORNING ORGANIZER
1000 CLS
1010 CLEAR1000:Z$="A.M."
1020 PRINTTAB(15);"MORNING ORGANIZER"
1025 PRINTTAB(19);"(ROUTINE)"
1030 PRINT
1040 PRINT"RETRIEVE DATA FROM TAPE (Y/N)";
1050 INPUT II$
1055 IF II$="Y" THEN2600
1060 PRINT
1070 PRINT"INSTRUCTIONS";
1080 INPUT I$
1090 IF I$="NO" THEN1440
1100 IF I$="YES" THEN1150
1110 PRINT I$;"?  DOES THIS ANSWER IMPLY T
     HAT"
1120 PRINT"YOUR NOT SURE ??"
1130 FOR X=1TO2000:NEXT
1140 GOTO1060
1150 REM INSTRUCTIONS
1160 PRINT"SO YOU HAD A PARTY LAST NIGHT A
     ND YOU CAN'T"
1170 PRINT"REMEMBER WHAT YOU WERE"
1180 PRINT"SUPPOSED TO DO THIS MORNING ?"
1190 PRINT"OR, YOUR MEMORY ISN'T THE BEST
1195 PRINT"IN THE WORLD AND YOU DON'T WANT"
1200 PRINT"EVERYONE ELSE TO KNOW THAT,"
1210 PRINT"BECAUSE YOU HAVE MEMO'S TACKED"
1220 PRINT"ALL AROUND THE HOUSE ?"
1230 PRINT:INPUT"PRESS ENTER";X
1235 CLS:PRINT
1240 PRINT"WELL, YOUR THE OWNER OF A"
1250 PRINT"COMPUTER. AND BEING SO YOU DON'
     T"
1260 PRINT"NEED A MEMO PAD OR PEN TO JOT D
     OWN"
1270 PRINT"WHAT YOU WERE SUPPOSTED TO"
1275 PRINT"REMEMBER. YOU CAN TYPE IT INTO"
1280 PRINT"THE COMPUTER AND LET <IT>"
1290 PRINT"REMEMBER FOR YOU."
```

```
1300 PRINT:PRINT"PRESS ENTER";
1310 INPUT I$
1320 CLS:PRINT
1330 PRINT"THIS PROGRAM IS CALLED MORNING"
1340 PRINT"ORGANIZER. IT WILL HELP YOU REM
     -"
1350 PRINT"EMBER ALL THAT YOU ARE SUPPOSE
     D"
1360 PRINT"TO, FROM 6:00 A.M. TIL' 11:59 A
     .M."
1370 PRINT"THE ENTIRE FILE WILL BE PROCESS
     ED"
1375 PRINT"TO THE CASSETTE PLAYER FOR YOUR'
1380 PRINT"REFERENCE. THIS WILL DETER ANYO
     NE"
1385 PRINT"ELSE FROM SEEING YOUR MEMO'S."
1390 PRINT
1440 PRINT
1450 PRINT"SO PRESS ENTER TO GET STARTED";
1460 INPUT I$
1470 CLS:PRINT:I=1:II=1
1472 PRINT"ENTER THE MONTH";
1475 INPUT M$(I)
1480 PRINT"ENTER THE DAY YOU WISH TO"
1490 PRINT"BEGIN (MONDAY, TUESDAY, ETC.)";
1510 INPUT D$(I)
1520 PRINT"ENTER THE DATE FOR ";D$(I);
1530 INPUT D(I)
1540 PRINT"ENTER THE YEAR";
1550 INPUT Y$(I)
1555 IF RR=1 GOSUB2500
1560 PRINT:IF RR=1 THEN1680
1570 PRINT"NOW YOU WILL ENTER ALL THE"
1580 PRINT"NECESSARY DATA TO MAKE THE"
1590 PRINT"ORGANIZER EFFECTIVE. YOU WILL"
1600 PRINT"BEGIN BY ENTERING THE TIME FOR"
1610 PRINT"THE ";I;"ST THING YOU WANT TO"
1620 PRINT"REMEMBER, AND SO ON."
1630 PRINT"THE FORMAT FOR ENTERING TIME"
1640 PRINT"WILL BE 700, 915, ETC."
1650 PRINT"ENTER WITHOUT THE COLON, THE"
1660 PRINT"COMPUTER WILL DO THAT."
```

```
1670 PRINT
1680 PRINT"ENTER TIME FOR ITEM #";II;
1690 INPUT T$
1700 T=LEN(T$)
1710 IF T<=3 THEN1730
1720 Q$=MID$(T$,1,2):GOTO3000
1730 Q$="0"+MID$(T$,1,1)
1735 GOTO3000
1740 W$=RIGHT$(T$,2)
1745 H$(I)=Q$+W$+CHR$(32)+Z$
1750 FOR TI=1TO1000:NEXT
1760 CLS:PRINT
1770 PRINT"NUMBER ";II;" ITEM TO REMEMBER:"
1780 IF RR=1 THEN1820
1790 PRINT"ENTER THIS ITEM NOW, APPOINTMEN
     T,"
1800 PRINT"VISIT, OTHER THINGS TO DO, FOR"
1810 PRINT"THE TIME YOU HAVE ENTERED."
1820 INPUT IT$(I)
1830 PRINT
1840 PRINT"ITEM NUMBER: ";II
1850 PRINT"TIME: ";LEFT$(H$(I),2)+":"+RIGH
     T$(H$(I),7)
1860 PRINT"TO REMEMBER:"
1870 PRINTIT$(I)
1880 PRINT"FOR THE DATE: ";
1890 PRINT M$(I);" ";D(I);" ";
1900 PRINTY$(I);"  (";D$(I);")"
1910 PRINT:IF RR=2 THEN2200
1915 RR=1
1920 PRINT"ARE THEIR ANY OTHER ITEMS YOU"
1930 PRINT"WANT TO LIST FOR ";
1940 PRINTD$(I);"  ";M$(I);" ";D(I);
1950 INPUT II$
1960 IF II$="YES" THEN1980
1970 GOTO2000
1980 I=I+1:II=II+1
1990 M$(I)=M$(I-1):D$(I)=D$(I-1)
1995 D(I)=D(I-1):Y$(I)=Y$(I-1)
1998 GOTO1670
2000 PRINT
2010 PRINT"ITEMS WILL NOW BE STORED ON"
```

```
2020 PRINT"CASSETTE TAPE, PLACE RECORDER"
2030 PRINT"IN RECORD MODE & PRESS ENTER";
2040 INPUT X$
2060 GOSUB2800:GOTO2400
2070 PRINT
2080 PRINT"WE WILL CONTINUE....."
2090 PRINT
2100 PRINT"IF MONTH AND YEAR ARE THE SAME"
2110 PRINT"AS PREVIOUSLY ENTERED, JUST"
2120 PRINT"PRESS ENTER FOR MONTH, YEAR."
2130 FOR TI=1TO2500:NEXT
2140 CLS:PRINT
2150 I=1:II=II+1
2160 GOTO1472
2200 REM CONTINUE OUTPUT
2210 REM IF NOT COMPLETE FOR TIME
2220 IF I<>N THEN2240
2230 GOTO2300:REM COMPLETE
2240 I=I+1
2250 PRINT
2260 PRINT"PRESS ENTER TO CONTINUE";
2270 INPUT XX
2280 CLS
2290 GOTO1830
2300 PRINT
2310 PRINT"THIS CONCLUDES MEMO'S FOR"
2320 PRINT"THE DAY AND TIME YOU REQUESTED."
2330 PRINT
2340 PRINT"SO-LONG....."
2350 PRINT
2360 PRINT
2370 END
2400 REM CONTINUE MEMO'S ?
2405 PRINT
2410 PRINT"DO YOU WISH TO ENTER AND"
2420 PRINT"SAVE MORE MEMO'S";
2430 INPUT II$
2440 IF LEFT$(II$,1)<>"Y" THEN2330
2450 GOTO2070
2500 REM MONTH, YEAR THE SAME AS
2510 REM WAS ALREADY INPUT
2520 IF M$(I)="" THEN M$(I)=M$(I-1)
```

```
2530 IF Y$(I)="" THEN Y$(I)=Y$(I-1)
2540 RETURN
2600 REM INPUT DATA FROM TAPE
2610 PRINT
2620 PRINT"PLACE CASSETTE PLAYER IN PLAY"
2630 PRINT"MODE AND ENTER THE"
2635 PRINT"DAY YOU WISH TO RECEIVE";
2640 INPUT DA$
2645 N=1:PRINT
2650 PRINT"RECEIVING DATA....."
2660 INPUT#-1,I
2670 INPUT#-1,M$(N),D$(N),D(N),Y$(N),IT$(N)
2680 INPUT#-1,H$(N)
2690 IF N<>I THEN2720
2700 RR=2:CLS
2705 IF D$(1)<>DA$ THEN2645
2710 I=1:GOTO1830
2720 N=N+1
2730 GOTO2670
2800 REM DATA TO BE TRANSFERRED TO
2810 REM CASSETTE TAPE
2820 N=1:PRINT
2830 PRINT"SAVING DATA ON TAPE....."
2840 PRINT#-1,I
2850 PRINT#-1,M$(N),D$(N),D(N),Y$(N),IT$(N)
2860 PRINT#-1,H$(N)
2870 IF N<>I THEN 2890
2880 RETURN
2890 N=N+1
2900 GOTO2850
3000 REM CHECK TIME FOR CORRECT
3010 REM ENTRY NOT GREATER THAN
3020 REM 11:59 A.M.
3030 TT=VAL(Q$(I))
3040 IF TT>11 THEN3060
3050 GOTO1740
3060 PRINT
3070 PRINT"THE TIME YOU HAVE ENTERED IS"
3080 PRINT"GREATER THAN 11:59 A.M. ENTER"
3090 PRINT"AGAIN....."
3100 GOTO1670
3200 REM IF YOU REALLY WANT TO
```

```
3210 REM KEEP ANYONE ELSE FROM
3220 REM SEEING YOUR MEMO'S YOU
3230 REM CAN ADD SOME SORT OF CODE
3240 REM NUMBER AT THE OUTPUT
3250 REM TO THE CASSETTE TAPE
3260 REM THIS WAY THE CODE WILL
3270 REM HAVE TO BE RECALLED
3280 REM BEFORE ANY DATA CAN BE
3290 REM READ FROM THE CASSETTE
3300 REM TAPE PLAYER
3310 REM BUT BE SURE TO ADD A
3320 REM MATCHING INPUT# (SAME
3330 REM AS PRINT#) OR YOU'LL
3340 REM END UP WILL LOSS OF DATA
3350 REM YOUR CODE COULD BE
3360 REM INSERTED BEFORE THE
3370 REM VARIABLE I, LINE 2840
3380 REM FOR THE PRINT# AND YOUR
3390 REM INPUT# (CODE) COULD BE
3400 REM INSERTED BEFORE THE
3410 REM VARIABLE I, LINE 2660
```

EVENING ORGANIZER

This program takes over where the previous one left off. You can organize your evenings more efficiently. If you are having a party enter the word 'party.' The program will ask you if you want to enter the names of guests that are to attend.

SAMPLE RUN
** EVENING ORGANIZER **
(ROUTINE)

INPUT DATA FROM CASSETTE? <u>NO</u>

LIST INSTRUCTIONS? <u>YES</u>

THIS PROGRAM IS CALLED EVENING
ORGANIZER, TO HELP YOU REMEMBER
AND SORT-OUT ALL THE THINGS THAT
OCCUR AFTER 12:00 P.M.

YOU CAN LIST APPOINTMENTS, VISITS,
PARTIES YOU'LL HAVE, AND EVEN THE
LIST OF GUESTS THAT ARE TO
ATTEND YOUR PARTIES.
OF COURSE YOU CAN STORE OTHER
THINGS YOU WANT TO REMEMBER,
THE ABOVE IS JUST AN EXAMPLE.

PRESS A KEY <SPACE BAR>

YOU WILL ENTER ALL DATA YOU
WISH, FOR A CERTAIN TIME AND
DAY, THEN THE DATA WILL BE
PROCESSED TO CASSETTE TAPE.

ENTER DATE (MONTH / DAY / YEAR)
(EXAMPLE: 01/01/81)? <u>3/17/81</u>

ENTER COMPLETE DATE AGAIN...ADD
LEADING ZERO'S WHERE NECESSARY.

ENTER DATE (MONTH / DAY / YEAR)
EXAMPLE: 01/01/81? <u>03/17/81</u>
NOW ENTER THE DAY, FOR ABOVE
DATE (SATURDAY, SUNDAY, ETC.)? <u>TUESDAY</u>
NOW ENTER THE TIME OF THE ITEM
YOU WANT TO REMEMBER.
EXAMPLE: 7:00 P.M. - ENTER TIME
700, WITHOUT THE COLON & WITHOUT

P.M. ? 500
ENTER THE ITEM YOU WANT TO
REMEMBER FOR: 5 00 P.M.
GET EVERYTHING READY FOR PARTY

WOULD YOU LIKE TO ENTER
THE NAMES OF THE GUESTS
THAT WILL ATTEND YOUR PARTY? NO

COMPLETE DATE FOR ITEM: TUESDAY MARCH 17 1981
TIME FOR ITEM: 5 00 P.M.
ITEM TO REMEMBER:
GET EVERYTHING READY FOR PARTY
ARE THERE OTHER ITEMS NEEDED TO
BE STORED FOR TUESDAY MARCH 17 1981? YES

NOW ENTER THE TIME OF THE ITEM
YOU WANT TO REMEMBER.
P.M.? 530 ENTER THE ITEM YOU WANT TO
REMEMBER FOR: 5 30 P.M.
CALL TO SEE IF AUTO IS FINISHED

COMPLETE DATE FOR ITEM: TUESDAY MARCH 17 1981
TIME FOR ITEM: 5 30 P.M.
ITEM TO REMEMBER:
CALL TO SEE IF AUTO IS FINISHED
ARE THERE OTHER ITEMS NEEDED TO
BE STORED FOR TUESDAY MARCH 17 1981? YES

NOW ENTER THE TIME OF THE ITEM
YOU WANT TO REMEMBER.
P.M. ? 700

ENTER THE ITEM YOU WANT TO
REMEMBER FOR: 7 00 P.M.
CALL GUESTS IF HAVEN'T ARRIVED

COMPLETE DATE FOR ITEM: TUESDAY MARCH 17 1981
TIME FOR ITEM: 7 00 P.M.
ITEM TO REMEMBER:
CALL GUESTS IF HAVEN'T ARRIVED
ARE THEIR OTHER ITEMS NEEDED TO
BE STORED FOR TUESDAY MARCH 17 1981? YES

NOW ENTER THE TIME OF THE ITEM
YOU WANT TO REMEMBER.
P.M. ? <u>800</u>

ENTER THE ITEM YOU WANT TO
REMEMBER FOR: 8 00 P.M.
<u>CANCEL IF GUESTS HAVEN'T ARRIVED!!</u>

COMPLETE DATE FOR ITEM: TUESDAY MARCH 17 1981
TIME FOR ITEM: 8 00 P.M.
ITEM TO REMEMBER:
CANCEL IF GUESTS HAVEN'T ARRIVED!!
ARE THERE OTHER ITEMS NEEDED TO
BE STORED FOR TUESDAY MARCH 17 1981? <u>NO</u>

IF YOU HAVEN'T DONE SO YET, PLACE
A FRESH CASSETTE TAPE IN PLAYER.
PLACE IN RECORD MODE, THEN PRESS
ENTER? <ENTER>

DATA LOADED ON CASSETTE TAPE.
DO YOU HAVE OTHER DATES AND
ITEMS TO INPUT? <u>NO</u>

END OF EVENING ORGANIZER.....
FILES CLOSED.....

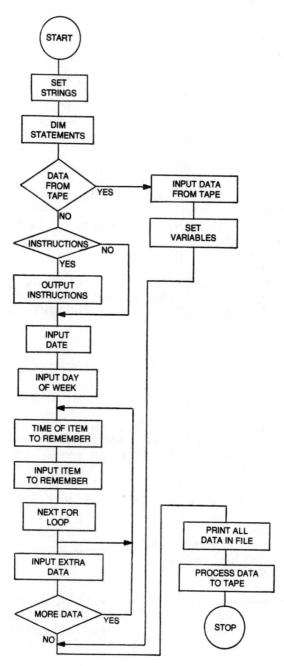

Flowchart for EVENING ORGANIZER

225

Program Listing

```
10 REM PROGRAM TITLE: EVENING ORGANIZER
20 CLEAR1500:DIM M$(12),N$(50)
30 CLS:U$=" ":Q$="P.M.":E=1
40 FOR I=1TO12:READ M$(I):NEXT
50 PRINTTAB(15);"** EVENING ORGANIZER **"
60 PRINTTAB(22);"(ROUTINE)"
65 PRINT
70 PRINT"INPUT DATA FROM CASSETTE";
80 INPUT A$
90 IF A$="YES" THEN GG=1:GOTO1500
100 PRINT
110 PRINT"LIST INSTRUCTIONS";
120 INPUT A$
130 IF A$="NO" THEN360
140 PRINT
150 PRINT"THIS PROGRAM IS CALLED EVENING"
160 PRINT"ORGANIZER, TO HELP YOU REMEMBER"
170 PRINT"AND SORT-OUT ALL THE THINGS THA
    T"
180 PRINT"OCCUR AFTER 12:00 P.M."
190 PRINT
200 PRINT"YOU CAN LIST APPOINTMENTS, VISI
    TS,"
210 PRINT"PARTIES YOU'LL HAVE, AND EVEN T
    HE"
220 PRINT"LIST OF GUESTS THAT ARE TO"
230 PRINT"ATTEND YOUR PARTIES."
240 PRINT"OF COURSE YOU CAN STORE OTHER"
250 PRINT"THINGS YOU WANT TO REMEMBER,"
260 PRINT"THE ABOVE IS JUST AN EXAMPLE."
265 REM SEE REM STATEMENTS LINES 2400-258
    0
270 PRINT.
280 PRINT"PRESS A KEY"
290 P=908:GOSUB5000
300 CLS
310 PRINT
320 PRINT"YOU WILL ENTER ALL DATA YOU"
330 PRINT"WISH, FOR A CERTAIN TIME AND"
340 PRINT"DAY, THEN THE DATA WILL BE"
350 PRINT"PROCESSED TO CASSETTE TAPE."
360 PRINT
```

```
370 PRINT"ENTER DATE (MONTH / DAY / YEAR)"
380 PRINT"(EXAMPLE: 01/01/81)";
390 INPUT D$
395 GOTO6100
400 PRINT"NOW ENTER THE DAY, FOR ABOVE"
410 PRINT"DATE (SATURDAY, SUNDAY, ETC.)";
420 INPUT DT$
430 PRINT"NOW ENTER THE TIME OF THE ITEM"
440 PRINT"YOU WANT TO REMEMBER."
445 IF E>=2 THEN490
460 PRINT"EXAMPLE: 7:00 P.M. - ENTER TIME"
470 PRINT"700, WITHOUT THE COLON & WITHOU
    T"
480 PRINT"P.M.";
490 INPUT T$(E)
495 GOSUB900
500 PRINT
510 PRINT"ENTER THE ITEM YOU WANT TO"
520 PRINT"REMEMBER FOR:    ";
530 PRINT TM$(E)
540 INPUT Y$(E)
550 FOR I=1TO LEN(Y$(E))
560 IF MID$(Y$(E),I,5)="PARTY" THEN580
570 NEXT:GOTO600
580 REM ENTER NAMES FOR PARTY ?
590 GOTO1000
600 M=VAL(LEFT$(D$,2))
605 W$=DT$+CHR$(32)+M$(M)+CHR$(32)+MID$(D
    $,4,2)+" "+CHR$(32)+"19"+RIGHT$(D$,2)
610 REM PRINTOUT ENTIRE DATA
620 CLS:LL=0:J=384:JK=448
630 PRINT
640 PRINT"COMPLETE DATE FOR ITEM: ";
650 PRINT W$
655 PRINT
660 PRINT"TIME FOR ITEM: ";
670 PRINT TM$(E)
675 PRINT
680 PRINT"ITEM TO REMEMBER:"
690 FOR I=1TOLEN(Y$(E))
700 PRINT@J,MID$(Y$(E),I,1)
710 LL=LL+1:J=J+1
```

```
720 IF LL>=50 AND MID$(Y$(E),I,1)=CHR$(32
    ) THEN J=JK:LL=0
730 REM LINE 720 WILL KEEP WORDS IN A 'NE
    AT' FORMAT
740 NEXT
750 PRINT:IF GG=1 THEN FOR U=1TOLEN(Y$(E)
    ):IF MID$(Y$(E),U,5)="PARTY" THEN1900
    ELSE NEXT:GOTO1970
755 IF G$="YES" AND AT<>0 GOSUB2200
760 PRINT"ARE THEIR OTHER ITEMS NEEDED TO"
770 PRINT"BE STORED FOR ";W$;
780 INPUT II$
790 IF II$="YES" THEN810
800 GOTO1200:REM STORE TO CASSETTE
810 E=E+1
820 GOTO430
900 L=LEN(T$(E))
910 IF L>=4 THEN940
920 TT$=LEFT$(T$(E),1)+U$+RIGHT$(T$(E),2)
930 GOTO950
940 TT$=LEFT$(T$(E),2)+U$+RIGHT$(T$(E),2)
950 TM$(E)=TT$+CHR$(32)+Q$
960 RETURN
1000 PRINT
1010 PRINT"WOULD YOU LIKE TO ENTER"
1020 PRINT"THE NAMES OF THE GUESTS"
1030 PRINT"THAT WILL ATTEND YOUR PARTY";
1040 INPUT G$
1050 IF G$="NO" THEN600
1060 PRINT"HOW MANY DO YOU EXPECT TO ATTEN
     D";
1070 INPUT AT
1080 Z=1
1090 PRINT"ENTER THEIR FIRST NAMES ONLY"
1094 FOR H=1TO1000:NEXT:PRINT@896,"
1095 PRINT@896,"GUEST #";Z;
1100 INPUT N$(Z)
1110 IF Z=1 PRINT`832,"TO CLOSE LIST, JUST
     PRESS ENTER FOR A NAME.":FOR H=1TO12
     00:NEXT
1120 IF N$(Z)="" THEN600
```

```
1130 Z=Z+1
1140 GOTO1095
1200 REM ITEMS TO BE STORED ON CASSETTE
1210 CLS
1220 PRINT
1230 PRINT"IF YOU HAVEN'T DONE SO YET, PLA
     CE"
1240 PRINT"A FRESH CASSETTE TAPE IN PLAYER
     ."
1250 PRINT"PLACE IN RECORD MODE, THEN PRES
     S"
1260 PRINT"ENTER"
1270 P=262:GOSUB 5000
1280 V=1
1290 PRINT#-1,E,W$,G$,Z:REM DATE
1300 PRINT#-1,TM$(V):REM TIME
1310 PRINT#-1,Y$(V):REM ITEM
1320 IF G$="YES" AND MM<>1 PRINT:PRINT:GOS
     UB2000
1325 IF V<>E THEN1340
1330 GOTO1350
1340 V=V+1:IF MM=1 THEN1290 ELSE 1300
1350 E=1:PRINT:PRINT
1360 PRINT"DATA LOADED ON CASSETTE TAPE."
1370 PRINT"DO YOU HAVE OTHER DATES AND"
1380 PRINT"ITEMS TO INPUT";
1390 INPUT A$
1400 IF RIGHT$(A$,1)="O" THEN2360
1410 FOR JK=1TO1500:NEXT
1420 CLS
1430 GOTO360
1500 REM INPUT FROM CASSETTE
1510 PRINT
1520 PRINT"READY CASSETTE PLAYER, THEN"
1530 PRINT"PRESS ENTER"
1540 P=396:GOSUB5000
1550 V=1
1560 INPUT#-1,E,W$,G$,Z
1570 INPUT#-1,TM$(V)
1580 INPUT#-1,Y$(V)
1590 IF G$="YES" AND H=0 THEN 1650
1600 IF V<>E THEN 1630
```

```
1610 V=E:E=1:GOTO610:REM PRINTOUT
1630 V=V+1
1640 IF H>0 THEN1560 ELSE 1570
1650 REM INPUT NAMES
1660 H=1
1670 INPUT#-1,N$(H)
1680 IF H<>Z THEN1700
1690 GOTO1600
1700 H=H+1
1710 GOTO1670
1900 REM CHECK FOR PARTY NAMES
1910 IF G$="YES" THEN1930
1920 GOTO1970
1930 PRINT"NAMES OF GUESTS TO ATTEND:"
1940 FOR I=1TOZ
1950 PRINTN$(I)
1960 NEXT
1970 IF E<>V THEN 1990
1980 GOTO2300
1990 E=E+1:FOR JK=1TO1500:NEXT:PRINT:PRINT
     :GOTO610
2000 REM STORE NAMES TO CASSETTE
2010 VV=1
2020 PRINT"NAMES OF YOUR GUESTS WILL"
2030 PRINT"NOW BE PROCESSED TO TAPE."
2040 PRINT"PRESS ENTER"
2050 P=524:GOSUB5000
2060 PRINT#-1,N$(VV)
2070 IF VV<>Z THEN2090
2080 MM=1:RETURN
2090 VV=VV+1
2100 GOTO2060
2200 REM PRINT GUESTS NAMES FOR PARTY
2210 AA=1:AB=2
2220 H=1
2230 PRINTTAB(0);N$(AA) TAB(10);N$(AB)
2240 IF H<>Z THEN2260
2250 PRINT:AT=0:RETURN
2260 AA=AA+2:AB=AB+2
2270 H=H+1
2280 GOTO2230
2300 REM END -- CONT
```

```
2310 PRINT
2320 PRINT"WOULD YOU LIKE TO LOAD"
2330 PRINT"MORE DATA FROM TAPE PLAYER";
2340 INPUT A$
2350 IF A$="YES" THEN1500
2360 PRINT
2370 PRINT"END OF EVENING ORGANIZER....."
2380 PRINT"FILES CLOSED....."
2390 END
2400 REM IF YOU INTEND ON STORING
2410 REM MORE THAN 10 ITEMS PER
2420 REM TIME SLOT YOU'LL NEED TO
2430 REM ADD APPROPRIATE DIM STATEMENTS
2440 REM FOR THE FOLLOWING STRING$ -
2450 REM AND VARIABLES:
2460 REM T$,TM$ AND Y$
2470 REM YOU'LL HAVE ENOUGH SPACE
2480 REM OPEN FOR 50 NAMES PER
2490 REM PARTY, DINNER EVENT OR
2500 REM GATHERING YOU CAN CHANGE
2510 REM THIS AMOUNT AT LINE 20
2520 REM N$ FOR NAMES
2530 REM IF YOU ARE PLANNING ON
2540 REM ENTERING GUESTS NAMES FOR
2550 REM PARTIES YOU MUST INCLUDE
2560 REM THE WORD 'PARTY' WHEN YOU
2570 REM ENTER THE ITEM (LINES 510
2580 REM THROUGH 540
5000 PRINT@P,CHR$(140);
5010 FOR HH=1TO100:NEXT
5020 PRINT@P," ";
5030 FOR HH=1TO50:NEXT
5040 Z$=INKEY$
5050 IF Z$="" THEN5000
5060 RETURN
6000 DATA JANUARY,FEBRUARY,MARCH,APRIL
6010 DATA MAY,JUNE,JULY,AUGUST
6020 DATA SEPTEMBER,OCTOBER,NOVEMBER
6030 DATA DECEMBER
6100 REM CHECK D$ FOR LEADING ZERO'S
6110 IF MID$(D$,5,1)=CHR$(47) THEN6130
6120 GOTO400
```

```
6130 PRINT
6140 PRINT"ENTER COMPLETE DATE AGAIN...ADD"
6150 PRINT"LEADING ZERO'S WHERE NECESSARY."
6160 GOTO360
```

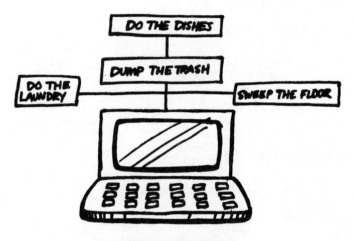

HOUSEHOLD CHORES

Have children? Old enough to do chores around the house but put up an argument everytime? After you input all necessary data information, the computer will sort out the chores and assign each of your children an equal amount of work. At the end of the day you input whether the chore was completed or not, and decide whether you want to input a deduction in allowance for chores not completed. This file can be kept for 1 week, 2 weeks or 1 month, depending on how often you pay the allowance. At the end of that period the computer will print a total allowance for each child.

SAMPLE RUN

**** HOUSEHOLD CHORES ****

INPUT CHORE FILE FROM TAPE? <u>NO</u>

NEED INSTRUCTIONS? <u>NO</u>

HOW MANY CHILDREN IN YOUR HOME
DO CHORES? <u>4</u>
DO YOU WANT TO LOG THIS FILE
TO BASE ALLOWANCE FOR:
1) * ONCE A WEEK *
2) * EVERY TWO WEEKS *
3) * ONCE A MONTH *

SELECT (1,2 OR 3)? <u>1</u>

INPUT THE 4 CHILDRENS NAMES:

<u>ANNAJEAN</u>
<u>DONNA</u>
<u>BRIAN</u>
<u>CLIFFORD</u>

HOW MANY CHORES WILL EACH CHILD DO? <u>2</u>

YOU MUST INPUT 8 CHORES
BE SPECIFIC.
<u>CLEAN BEDROOM(S)</u>
<u>SWEEP FLOORS</u>
<u>MOP FLOORS</u>
<u>WAX FLOORS</u>
<u>VACUUM CARPET</u>
<u>CLEAN BATHROOM</u>
<u>DO ALL LAUNDRY</u>
<u>WASH WINDOWS</u>

HOW MUCH ALLOWANCE WILL YOU
PAY EACH CHILD, FOR EACH
CHORE COMPLETED? <u>.75</u>

CHILDS NAME	CHORE TO COMPLETE	COMPLETED ?
ANNAJEAN	VACUUM CARPET	YES / NO ? Y
ANNAJEAN	CLEAN BEDROOM(S)	YES / NO ? Y
BRIAN	MOP FLOORS	YES / NO ? Y
BRIAN	DO ALL LAUNDRY	YES / NO ? Y
CLIFFORD	WAX FLOORS	YES / NO ? Y
CLIFFORD	WASH WINDOWS	YES / NO ? Y
DONNA	CLEAN BATHROOM	YES / NO ? Y
DONNA	SWEEP FLOORS	YES / NO ? Y

DO YOU WANT THE COMPUTER TO
MAKE DEDUCTIONS ON ALLOWANCE
FOR CHORES NOT COMPLETED? YES
DEDUCTIONS HAVE BEEN MADE.

ALL NECESSARY DATA IN MEMORY.

YOU SELECTED THIS FILE TO
BE COMPLETED IN A WEEK
THERE ARE 6 DAYS LEFT.

On each of the next 6 days, you would answer the opening question
with a YES. At the end of the last day, the allowances are computed
automatically.

FILE COMPLETE....
TOTAL ALLOWANCES TO BE PAID FOR 7 DAYS
ANNAJEAN $10.50
BRIAN $10.50
CLIFFORD $10.50
DONNA $10.50

If you have more than 6 people doing chores, you will have to add
more K variables to the PRINT#-1 and INPUT#-1 statements. The
present 6 are K1-K6. If the number of total chores is greater than
20, you will have to put larger numbers in the DIM statements. If
the number of people doing chores exceeds 11, dimension variable
I.

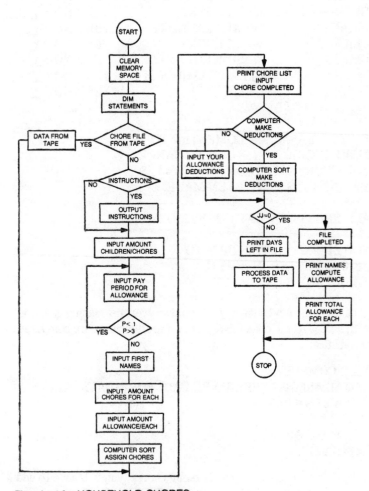

Flowchart for HOUSEHOLD CHORES

236

Program Listing

```
10 REM PROGRAM TITLE: HOUSEHOLD CHORES
20 RANDOM
30 CLS:J=1
40 CLEAR 1000
50 DIM N$(20),C$(25),C(20),H$(25),Q$(
   25)
55 DIM A$(25),A(25)
60 IF RR<>1 THEN T=1
70 DL$="$$###.##"
100 PRINTTAB(10);"**** HOUSEHOLD CHORE
    S ****"
110 PRINT
112 INPUT"INPUT CHORE FILE FROM TAPE";
    A$
115 IF A$="YES" THEN RR=1:GOTO 2080
116 PRINT
120 INPUT"NEED INSTRUCTIONS";A$
130 IF A$="NO" THEN 400
140 PRINT
150 PRINT"DO YOU HAVE CHILDREN THAT AR
    E OLD"
160 PRINT"ENOUGH TO KNOW BETTER BUT ST
    ILL"
170 PRINT"ARGUE WHEN IT COMES TO DOING
     CHORES ?"
180 PRINT"AFTER YOU INPUT THE NECESSAR
    Y DATA"
190 PRINT"THE COMPUTER WILL CHOOSE WHO
     WILL DO"
200 PRINT"WHICH CHORE."
210 PRINT"THEIR ALLOWANCE WILL BE BASE
    D ON"
220 PRINT"CHORES COMPLETED. YOU (OR TH
    E"
230 PRINT"COMPUTER) CAN SUBTRACT AN AM
    OUNT"
240 PRINT"FOR A CHORE THAT WASN'T FINI
    SHED."
250 PRINT
260 INPUT"PRESS <ENTER>";A$
```

```
270 CLS
280 PRINT
290 PRINT"IF THEY (YOUR CHILDREN) DO N
    OT"
300 PRINT"COMPLETE THE REQUIRED CHORE,
     THAT"
310 PRINT"THE COMPUTER HAS SELECTED (R
    ANDOMLY)"
320 PRINT"YOU CAN LET THE COMPUTER MAK
    E DEDUCTIONS"
330 PRINT"FROM THEIR ALLOWANCE (50% OF
     WHAT"
340 PRINT"YOU ENTER FOR THE CHORE), RE
    MIND"
350 PRINT"THEM THAT ONCE THE DATA HAS
    BEEN ENTERED"
360 PRINT"INTO THE COMPUTER (FOR A CHO
    RE THEY"
370 PRINT"DIDN'T DO) IT CAN'T BE REVER
    SED !!"
380 PRINT
390 INPUT"PRESS <ENTER> TO BEGIN FILE"
    ;A$
400 CLS
410 PRINT
420 REM INPUT NECESSARY DATA
440 PRINT"HOW MANY CHILDREN IN YOUR HO
    ME"
450 INPUT"DO CHORES";C
460 PRINT"DO YOU WANT TO LOG THIS FILE"
465 PRINT"TO BASE ALLOWANCE FOR:"
470 PRINT"1) * ONCE A WEEK *"
480 PRINT"2) * EVERY TWO WEEKS *"
490 PRINT"3) * ONCE A MONTH *"
500 PRINT
510 INPUT"SELECT (1,2 OR 3)";P
520 IF P=1 P=7:D$="A WEEK":GOTO570
530 IF P=2 P=15:D$="TWO WEEKS":GOTO570
540 IF P=3 P=30:D$="A MONTH":GOTO570
550 PRINT"INVALID RESPONCE...TRY AGAIN
    ."
560 GOTO500
```

```
570 PRINT
580 PRINT"INPUT THE";C;"CHILDRENS NAME
    S:"
590 FOR I=1TOC
600 INPUT N$(I):NEXT
610 REM ONLY FIRST NAMES
620 I=1:K=1
630 IF MID$(N$(I),K,1)=" " THEN PRINT:
    GOTO670
640 IF K<>LEN(N$(I)) THEN K=K+1:GOTO63
    0
650 IF I<>C THEN I=I+1:K=1:GOTO630
660 GOTO690
670 PRINT"FIRST NAME ONLY...PLEASE, TR
    Y AGAIN."
680 GOTO570
690 CLS
700 PRINT
710 PRINT"HOW MANY CHORES WILL EACH CH
    ILD DO";
720 INPUT M1
725 M=C*M1
730 IF M1>=2 GOSUB1000
735 PRINT
740 PRINT"YOU MUST INPUT";M;"CHORES"
745 PRINT"BE SPECIFIC."
750 FOR I=1TOM
760 INPUT C$(I):NEXT
765 IF RR=1 THEN 810
770 PRINT
780 PRINT"HOW MUCH ALLOWANCE WILL YOU"
790 PRINT"PAY EACH CHILD, FOR EACH"
795 PRINT"CHORE COMPLETED";
800 INPUT A
810 PRINT
820 PRINT"PRESS ENTER AND COMPUTER WIL
    L"
830 PRINT"SORT-OUT LIST AND ASSIGN CHO
    RES";
840 INPUT X
850 CLS:PRINTCHR$(23):PRINT
860 PRINT"SORTING LIST....."
```

```
870 FOR I=1TOM:C(I)=I:NEXT:I=1
880 E=RND(M)
890 IF C(E)=0 THEN 880
900 H$(I)=C$(E):Q$(I)=N$(E)
910 C(E)=0
960 IF I<>M THEN I=I+1:GOTO880
970 GOTO1100
1000 REM SETS OF NAMES
1010 I=C+1:N=C+2
1020 N$(I)=N$(I-C)
1030 N$(N)=N$(N-C)
1040 IF N<=M THEN 1060
1050 RETURN
1060 I=I+2:N=N+2
1070 GOTO1020
1100 I=1:X=0
1110 IF Q$(I)<=Q$(I+1) THEN 1170
1120 A$=Q$(I+1):Q$(I+1)=Q$(I)
1130 Q$(I)=A$
1140 R$=H$(I+1):H$(I+1)=H$(I)
1150 H$(I)=R$
1160 X=1
1170 I=I+1
1180 IF I<>M THEN 1110
1190 IF X=1 THEN 1100
1200 REM CHART PRINTOUT
1205 IF RR=1 THEN T=T+1:CLS:GOTO1350
1210 CLS:PRINT
1230 PRINT"A CHART WILL NOW BE PRINTED."
1235 PRINT"THE CHILDS NAME, AND CHORE T
     O"
1240 PRINT"COMPLETE WILL BE IN THIS CHA
     RT."
1245 PRINT"TO THE RIGHT OF THE VIDEO YO
     U"
1250 PRINT"WILL SEE THE WORD, COMPLETED
     ?"
1255 PRINT"THE COMPUTER WILL GO THROUGH"
1260 PRINT"THE ENTIRE LIST OF NAMES & C
     HORES."
1265 PRINT"TO THE RIGHT OF THE CHORE IT
     WILL"
```

```
1270 PRINT"PRINT <YES/NO>, IF CHORE WAS
     COM-"
1275 PRINT"PLETED PRESS 'Y' IF NOT PRES
     S 'N'."
1280 PRINT"THE COMPUTER WILL THEN ADVAN
     CE"
1285 PRINT"TO THE NEXT CHORE."
1290 PRINT
1295 INPUT"PRESS ENTER TO BEGIN";X:CLS
1350 REM CHART
1370 PRINT"CHILDS NAME";
1380 PRINTTAB(25);"CHORE TO COMPLETE";
1390 PRINTTAB(50);"COMPLETED ?"
1395 FOR X=0TO127:SET(X,3):NEXT
1400 PRINT
1410 I=1
1420 PRINTQ$(I); TAB(25);H$(I)
1430 IF I<>M THEN 1450
1440 GOTO1470
1450 I=I+1
1460 GOTO1420
1470 REM CHORE COMPLETED ?
1480 I=1:L=180
1490 PRINT@976,"PRESS Y (YES) OR N (NO)
     ";
1500 PRINT@L,"YES / NO";
1510 X$=INKEY$
1520 A$(I)=X$
1530 IF X$="" THEN 1510
1540 IF I<>M THEN 1560
1550 GOTO1590
1560 PRINT@L,"          ";
1570 L=L+64:I=I+1
1580 GOTO1500
1585 PRINT@976,"T H A N K   Y O U
     ";
1590 FOR X=1TO2500:NEXT:CLS
1595 FOR I=1TOM:IF A$(I)="N" THEN J=J:N
     EXT ELSE J=J+1:NEXT
1600 IF J=M THEN FOR I=1TOM:A(I)=A:NEXT
     :GOTO1850
1605 I=1:PRINT
```

```
1610 PRINT"DO YOU WANT THE COMPUTER TO"
1620 PRINT"MAKE DEDUCTIONS ON ALLOWANCE"
1630 PRINT"FOR CHORES NOT COMPLETED";
1640 INPUT I$
1650 IF I$="NO" THEN 1750
1660 REM DEDUCTIONS
1680 IF A$(I)="Y" THEN A(I)=A:GOTO1700
1690 A(I)=A-.50
1700 IF I<>M THEN I=I+1:GOTO1680
1720 PRINT"DEDUCTIONS HAVE BEEN MADE."
1730 REM GOTO DATA ON TAPE
1740 GOTO1870
1750 PRINT
1760 IF A$(I)="Y" THEN A(I)=A:GOTO1810
1770 PRINT"CHILDS NAME: ";Q$(I)
1780 PRINT"CHORE NOT COMPLETED: ";H$(I)
1790 INPUT"INPUT YOUR DEDUCTION ";DE
1800 A(I)=A-DE
1810 IF I<>M THEN I=I+1:GOTO1760
1820 PRINT
1830 PRINT"THAT COMPLETES DEDUCTIONS."
1840 GOTO1870
1850 PRINT
1860 PRINT"ALL CHORES COMPLETED, NO DED
     UCTIONS."
1870 PRINT
1880 PRINT"ALL NECESSARY DATA IN MEMORY
     ."
1890 JJ=ABS(P-T):GOSUB3000
1900 IF JJ=0 THEN PRINT"FILE COMPLETED.
     ....":GOTO3300
1910 PRINT"YOU SELECTED THIS FILE TO"
1920 PRINT"BE COMPLETED IN ";D$
1930 PRINT"THERE ARE";JJ;"DAYS LEFT."
1940 PRINT
1950 PRINT"DATA WILL NOW BE PROCESSED T
     O"
1960 PRINT"TAPE, PLACE IN RECORD MODE,"
1970 INPUT"AND PRESS <ENTER>";X
1980 PRINT#-1,M,A,T,C,P
1990 FOR I=1TOM
2000 PRINT#-1,N$(I)
```

```
2010 NEXT
2015 PRINT#-1,K1,K2,K3,K4,K5,K6
2020 PRINT
2030 PRINT"PROCESSING COMPLETED....."
2040 PRINT"THAT COMPLETES THE FILE FOR"
2050 PRINT"THIS DAY....."
2060 GOTO3420:REM END
2070 CLS
2080 PRINT
2090 PRINT"PLACE PLAYER IN PLAY MODE,"
2100 INPUT"AND PRESS <ENTER>";X
2110 INPUT#-1,M,A,T,C,P
2120 FOR I=1TOM
2130 INPUT#-1,N$(I)
2140 NEXT
2145 INPUT#-1,K1,K2,K3,K4,K5,K6
2150 PRINT
2160 PRINT"DATA IN MEMORY....."
2170 INPUT"PRESS <ENTER> TO ADD TO FILE
     ";X
2180 CLS
2190 GOTO690
3000 REM ALLOWANCE TOTAL
3010 I=1:U=M1:B=1
3020 A1=A(I)+A1
3030 IF I<>U THEN I=I+1:GOTO3020
3040 A(B)=A1:A1=0:GOTO3100
3050 I=I+1:U=U+M1:B=B+1
3060 IF U<=M THEN 3020
3070 RETURN
3100 ON B GOTO 3110,3120,3130,3140,3150
     ,3160
3110 K1=A(B)+K1:GOTO3050
3120 K2=A(B)+K2:GOTO3050
3130 K3=A(B)+K3:GOTO3050
3140 K4=A(B)+K4:GOTO3050
3150 K5=A(B)+K5:GOTO3050
3160 K6=A(B)+K6:GOTO3050
3170 REM IF YOU INPUT MORE THAN
3180 REM 6 CHILDREN FOR THE FILE
3190 REM INCREASE <K> AND
3200 REM ADD THE LINES TO <LINE>
```

243

```
3210 REM 3100
3300 REM PRINT TOTAL ALLOWANCE
3305 FOR X=1TO3000:NEXT
3310 CLS
3320 PRINT
3325 PRINT"TOTAL ALLOWANCES TO BE PAID
     FOR";P;"DAYS"
3330 I=1:G=220
3335 PRINT
3340 PRINT N$(I)
3350 IF I<>C THEN I=I+1:GOTO3340
3360 PRINT@G,USING DL$;K1;:GOSUB3500
3370 PRINT@G,USING DL$;K2;:GOSUB3500
3380 IF K3<>0 PRINT@G,USING DL$;K3;:GOS
     UB3500
3390 IF K4<>0 PRINT@G,USING DL$;K4;:GOS
     UB3500
3400 IF K5<>0 PRINT@G,USING DL$;K5;:GOS
     UB3500
3410 IF K6<>0 PRINT@G,USING DL$;K6;
3420 PRINT:PRINT
3430 PRINT"END OF FILE PROGRAM....."
3440 END
3500 G=G+64
3510 RETURN
```

MAGAZINE TOPICS TO REMEMBER

This program will let you input all the necessary data to keep up with and locate articles easily. Title of article, magazine date, and a brief description of the article can be entered. Recalling the data will be easier than what you went through to get the magazine itself!

SAMPLE RUN

INPUT DATA FROM RECORDER? <u>NO</u>

SEE INSTRUCTIONS ? <u>YES</u>

HAVE A MAGAZINE WITH AN INTER-
ESTING ARTICLE IN IT YOU WANT
TO REMEMBER ?
WELL, THIS IS THE PROGRAM YOU'VE
BEEN LOOKING FOR...YOU CAN ENTER
EVERYTHING, FROM THE TITLE OF THE
MAGAZINE TO A SHORT SUMMARY OF THE
ARTICLE.

THEN AT ANY TIME YOU DESIRE YOU CAN
RECALL THE LIST (FROM TAPE), GET A
COMPLETE LISTING OF MAGAZINE TITLES,
PAGE OF ARTICLES, THEN PULL OUT THE
RIGHT MAGAZINE FROM YOUR COLLECTION
WITHOUT HAVING TO THUMB THROUGH EACH
AND EVERY ONE.

PRESS ENTER? <ENTER>

WHEN FINISHED INPUTTING THE
INFORMATION, PRESS ENTER FOR
DATE OF MAGAZINE.....

ENTER DATE OF MAGAZINE (M/D/Y) ? <u>9/28/81</u>
TITLE OF MAGAZINE ? <u>INFO WORLD</u>
TITLE OF ARTICLE ? <u>STATE OF MICROCOMPUTING: SOFT
WARES BRING HARD CASH</u>
PAGE NUMBER ? <u>14</u>

ENTER A BRIEF SUMMARY OF ARTICLE (Y/N) ? <u>Y</u>
ENTER A BRIEF SUMMARY WITH 200
CHARACTERS OR LESS ? <u>ARTICLE RANKS THE TOP SEL-
LING SOFTWARE IN THE COUNTRY, BY NUMBERS SOLD
AND DOLLARS.</u>

ENTER DATE OF MAGAZINE (M/D/Y) ? <u>9/28/81</u>
TITLE OF MAGAZINE ? <u>COMPUTERWORLD</u>
TITLE OF ARTICLE ? <u>UNOS SIMILAR TO (BUT DIFFERENT</u>
<u>FROM) UNIX</u>
PAGE NUMBER ? <u>4</u>

ENTER A BRIEF SUMMARY OF ARTICLE (Y/N) ? <u>Y</u>
ENTER A BRIEF SUMMARY WITH 200
CHARACTERS OR LESS ? <u>THE CRDS UNIVERSE COMPUTER</u>
<u>HAS AN OPERATING SYSTEM CALLED UNOS THAT IS</u>
<u>MORE INTERACTIVE THAN UNIX (BELL"S MULTIUSER</u>
<u>OPERATING SYSTEM FOR THE PDP-11) YET HAS MANY OF</u>
<u>THE SAME FEATURES. THE AMAZING THING IS THAT IT</u>
<u>WAS WRITTEN IN C LANGUAGE ON A PDP-11 AND TOOK</u>
<u>ONLY TWO WEEKS TO TRANSFER TO A 68000 SYSTEM.</u>

SORRY....YOU"VE EXCEEDED THE CHAR-
ACTER AMOUNT, TRY AGAIN...

ENTER A BRIEF SUMMARY WITH 200
CHARACTERS OR LESS ? <u>CRDS UNIVERSE (M68000) USES</u>
<u>UNOS WHICH IS SIMILAR TO UNIX BUT MORE INTERAC-</u>
<u>TIVE. WRITTEN IN C ON PDP-11 AND TRANSFERRED IN 2</u>
<u>WEEKS.</u>

ENTER DATE OF MAGAZINE ? <ENTER>

***MAGAZINE ARTICLES ***

<DATE>   <MAGAZINE>
9/28/81   INFOWORLD

<ARTICLE>   <PAGE NUMBER>
STATE OF MICROCOMPUTING: SOFT WARES BRING HARD
CASH 14

<SUMMARY>
ARTICLE RANKS THE TOP SELLING SOFTWARE IN THE
COUNTRY, BY NUMBERS SOLD AND DOLLARS.

PRESS ENTER TO CONTINUE LIST ? <ENTER>

*** MAGAZINE ARTICLES ***

<DATE>   <MAGAZINE>
9/28/81   COMPUTERWORLD

<ARTICLE>   < PAGE NUMBER >
UNOS SIMILAR TO (BUT DIFFERENT FROM) UNIX   4

<SUMMARY>
CRDS UNIVERSE (M68000) USES UNOS WHICH IS SIMILAR
TO UNIX BUT MORE INTERACTIVE. WRITTEN IN C ON
DPD-11 AND TRANSFERRED IN 2 WEEKS.

(1) PRINT LIST
(2) SAVE ON TAPE
(3) LOAD FROM TAPE
(4) MAKE A FILE
(5) CANCEL PROGRAM

2
PLACE IN RECORD MODE.....
AND PRESS ENTER ? <ENTER>

(1) PRINT LIST
(2) SAVE ON TAPE
(3) LOAD FROM TAPE
(4) MAKE A FILE
(5) CANCEL PROGRAM
5
END OF MAGAZINE PROGRAM.....

Be sure to read the remarks at the end of the program listing.

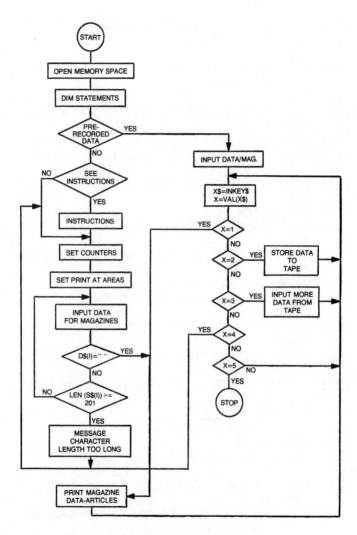

Flowchart for MAGAZINE TOPICS TO REMEMBER

Program Listing

```
1000 REM PROGRAM TITLE: MAGAZINE TOPICS
1010 REM TO REMEMBER
1020 CLEAR1000
1030 DIM D$(15),T$(15),A$(15),P(15),I$(
     15),S$(15)
1040 CLS
1080 PRINT"INPUT DATA FROM RECORDER";
1090 INPUT A$
1100 IF A$="YES" THEN 2220
1110 PRINT"SEE INSTRUCTIONS";
1120 INPUT A$
1130 IF A$="NO" THEN 2000
1140 CLS
1150 GOSUB1460
1160 PRINT"HAVE A MAGAZINE WITH AN INTE
     R-"
1170 PRINT"ESTING ARTICLE IN IT YOU WAN
     T"
1180 PRINT"TO REMEMBER ?"
1190 PRINT"WELL, THIS IS THE PROGRAM YO
     U'VE"
1200 PRINT"BEEN LOOKING FOR...YOU CAN E
     NTER"
1210 PRINT"EVERYTHING, FROM THE TITLE O
     F THE"
1220 PRINT"MAGAZINE TO A SHORT SUMMARY
     OF THE"
1230 PRINT"ARTICLE."
1235 FOR X=1TO4000:NEXT:CLS
1238 GOSUB1460
1240 PRINT"THEN AT ANY TIME YOU DESIRE
     YOU CAN"
1250 PRINT"RECALL THE LIST (FROM TAPE),
     GET A"
1260 PRINT"COMPLETE LISTING OF MAGAZINE
     TITLES,"
1270 PRINT"PAGE OF ARTICLES, THEN PULL
     OUT THE"
1280 PRINT"RIGHT MAGAZINE FROM YOUR COL
     LECTION"
```

```
1290 PRINT"WITHOUT HAVING TO THUMB THRO
     UGH EACH"
1300 PRINT"AND EVERY ONE."
1310 PRINT
1320 PRINT"PRESS ENTER";
1330 INPUT A$
1340 CLS
1350 PRINT
1360 PRINT"WHEN FINISHED INPUTTING THE"
1370 PRINT"INFORMATION, PRESS ENTER FOR"
1380 PRINT"DATE OF MAGAZINE....."
1390 FOR X=1TO2500:NEXT
1400 CLS
1410 PRINT
1420 I=1:C=0
1430 GOTO1520
1440 PRINT@0,;
1450 RETURN
1460 PRINT@64,;
1470 RETURN
1480 PRINT@128,;
1490 RETURN
1500 PRINT@192,;
1510 RETURN
1520 GOSUB1440
1530 INPUT"ENTER DATE OF MAGAZINE (M/D/
     Y)";D$(I)
1535 IF D$(I)="" THEN 1800
1540 GOSUB1460
1550 INPUT"TITLE OF MAGAZINE";T$(I)
1560 GOSUB1480
1570 INPUT"TITLE OF ARTICLE";A$(I)
1580 GOSUB1500
1590 INPUT"PAGE NUMBER";P(I)
1600 CLS
1610 GOSUB1440
1620 INPUT"ENTER A BRIEF SUMMARY OF ART
     ICLE (Y/N)";I$(I)
1630 IF I$(I)="N" THEN 1760
1640 GOSUB1460
1650 PRINT"ENTER A BRIEF SUMMARY WITH 2
     00"
```

251

```
1660 PRINT"CHARACTERS OR LESS";
1670 INPUT S$(I)
1680 IF LEN(S$(I))>=201 THEN 1700
1690 GOTO1760
1700 GOSUB1500
1710 PRINT"SORRY...YOU'VE EXCEEDED THE
     CHAR-"
1720 PRINT"ACTER AMOUNT, TRY AGAIN..."
1730 FOR X=1TO2500:NEXT
1740 CLS
1750 GOTO1640
1760 I=I+1
1770 CLS
1780 GOTO1520
1800 REM PRINT ENTIRE LIST
1810 C=(I-1)
1815 IF I=0 THEN 1970
1820 CLS:PRINT:I=1
1830 PRINTTAB(10);"*** MAGAZINE ARTICLE
     S ***"
1840 PRINT
1850 PRINTTAB(0);"<DATE>" TAB(30);"<MAG
     AZINE>"
1855 PRINTTAB(0);D$(I);:IF LEN(T$(I))>=
     8 PRINTTAB(25);T$(I) ELSE PRINTTAB
     (31);T$(I)
1858 PRINT
1860 PRINTTAB(0);"<ARTICLE>" TAB(30);"<
     PAGE NUMBER>"
1870 PRINTTAB(0);A$(I) TAB(34);P(I):PRI
     NT
1880 IF I$(I)="Y" THEN PRINTTAB(17);"<S
     UMMARY>":PRINTTAB(0);S$(I)
1890 IF I<>C THEN 1910
1900 GOTO2000
1910 PRINT
1920 PRINT"PRESS ENTER TO CONTINUE LIST
     ";
1930 INPUT X$
1940 CLS
1950 I=I+1
1960 GOTO1830
```

```
1970 REM NO LIST
1980 PRINT@192,"NO LIST IN MEMORY....."
2000 FOR X=0TO127:SET(X,41):NEXT:X=0
2010 PRINT@896,"(1) PRINT LIST";
2020 PRINT@914,"(2) SAVE ON TAPE";
2030 PRINT@934,"(3) LOAD FROM TAPE";
2040 PRINT@968,"(4) MAKE A FILE";
2045 PRINT@990,"(5) CANCEL PROGRAM";
2050 X$=INKEY$
2060 IF X$="" THEN 2050
2070 X=VAL(X$)
2080 ON X GOTO 1800,2090,2220,1340,2340
2090 REM LIST TO TAPE
2100 CLS
2110 PRINT
2120 PRINT"PLACE IN RECORD MODE....."
2130 PRINT"AND PRESS ENTER";
2140 INPUT Q$
2150 PRINT#-1,C
2160 FOR I=1TOC
2170 PRINT#-1,D$(I),T$(I),A$(I),P(I),I$
     (I)
2180 IF I$(I)<>"N" THEN PRINT#-1,S$(I)
2190 NEXT
2200 CLS
2210 GOTO2000
2220 REM LIST FROM TAPE
2230 CLS
2240 PRINT
2250 PRINT"PLACE IN PLAY MODE....."
2260 PRINT"AND PRESS ENTER";
2265 INPUT Q$
2270 INPUT#-1,C
2280 FOR I=1TOC
2290 INPUT#-1,D$(I),T$(I),A$(I),P(I),I$
     (I)
2300 IF I$(I)<>"N" THEN INPUT#-1,S$(I)
2310 NEXT
2320 GOTO2200
2330 REM TERMINATE PROGRAM
2340 CLS
2350 PRINT
```

```
2360 PRINT"END OF MAGAZINE PROGRAM....."
2370 END
2400 REM THE DIM STATEMENT LINE 1030
2410 REM WILL LET YOU ENTER UP TO 15
2420 REM MAGAZINE TITLES AND INFORMATION
2430 REM YOU CAN ADD MORE TO THIS
2440 REM BY INCREASING THAT DIM
2450 REM STATEMENT -- BUT BE SURE TO
2460 REM HAVE ALL THE STRINGS AND
2470 REM VARIABLES THE SAME AMOUNT
2480 REM THESE ARE D$,T$,A$,P,I$ & S$
```

WEATHER CONDITIONS

Temperatures, rainfall, and general forecasts can be stored with this program. It is handy for anyone who wants to keep a log of the many changing weather conditions. After about a year's worth of keeping the weather data you should begin to make your own forecasts.

SAMPLE RUN

                    ...WEATHER CONDITIONS...
                        ....LOG.........

INPUT RECORDED DATA? <u>NO</u>

PRINT INSTRUCTIONS? <u>NO</u>

INPUT CURRENT MONTH? <u>MARCH</u>
INPUT DAY OF MONTH? <u>1</u>

INPUT GENERAL FORECASTS FOR
MARCH 1 ? <u>CLOUDY - WARMER</u>
LOW TEMPERATURE? <u>40</u>
HIGH TEMPERATURE? <u>66</u>
RAINFALL (IF NONE - INPUT 0)? <u>0</u>
THE ABOVE DATA WILL HELP YOU
FORECAST FUTURE WEATHER BY
KEEPING A FILE FOR AT LEAST
1 (ONE) YEAR.

PRESS ENTER FOR COMMAND LIST? <ENTER>

1) TEMPERATURES
2) TOTAL RAINFALL
30 GENERAL FORECAST(S)
4) SAVE DATA ON TAPE
5) LOAD DATA FROM TAPE
6) ADD DATA TO CURRENT FILE
7) TERMINATE PROGRAM

INPUT CHOICE? <u>6</u>

STARTING DATE OF WEATHER LOG MARCH 1
TOTAL DAYS IN FILE = 1

INPUT GENERAL FORECASTS FOR
MARCH 2 ? <u>CLOUDY - RAIN - COOLER</u>
LOW TEMPERATURE? <u>30</u>
HIGH TEMPERATURE? <u>58</u>
RAINFALL (IF NONE - INPUT 0)? <u>.4</u>

PRESS ENTER FOR COMMAND LIST? <ENTER>

1) TEMPERATURES
2) TOTAL RAINFALL
3) GENERAL FORECAST(S)
4) SAVE DATA ON TAPE
5) LOAD DATA FROM TAPE
6) ADD DATA TO CURRENT FILE
7) TERMINATE PROGRAM

INPUT CHOICE? 1

STARTING DATE OF WEATHER LOG MARCH 1
TOTAL DAYS IN FILE = 2

ENTER MONTH FOR TEMPERATURES ?<u>MARCH</u>

SORTING TEMPERATURES.....
MARCH. . . . . . .
LOWEST TEMPERATURE TO DATE: 30 DEGREES.
HIGHEST TEMPERATURE TO DATE: 66 DEGREES.

DAY	LOW TEMPERATURES	HIGH TEMPERATURES
1	40	66
2	30	58

AVERAGE LOW TEMPERATURE: 35
AVERAGE HIGH TEMPERATURE: 62

PRESS ENTER FOR COMMAND LIST? <ENTER>

1) TEMPERATURES
2) TOTAL RAINFALL
3) GENERAL FORECAST(S)
4) SAVE DATA ON TAPE
5) LOAD DATA FROM TAPE
6) ADD DATA TO CURRENT FILE
7) TERMINATE PROGRAM

INPUT CHOICE? <u>7</u>

STARTING DATE OF WEATHER LOG MARCH 1
TOTAL DAYS IN FILE = 3
END OF WEATHER CONDITIONS (LOG)

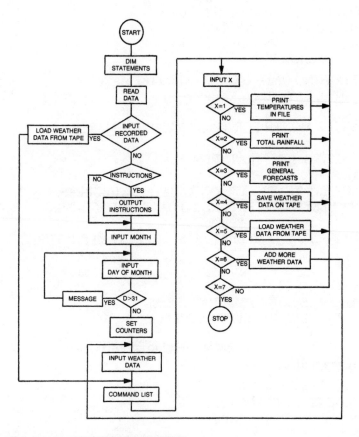

Flowchart for WEATHER CONDITIONS

258

```
Program Listing
10 REM PROGRAM TITLE: WEATHER CONDITI
   ONS (LOG)
20 CLS
30 CLEAR1000
35 DIM L(65),H(65),J(65),P(31),PP(12)
40 DIM Q(12),D(12),M$(12),A(12)
42 DIM F$(31),R(31),RR(31)
45 FOR I=1TO12:Q(I)=I:PP(I)=I:NEXT
50 FOR I=1TO12:READ D(I):NEXT
60 FOR I=1TO12:READ M$(I):NEXT
62 FOR I=1TO31:P(I)=I:NEXT
65 I=1:D$="DEGREES":T$="TEMPERATURE"
70 PRINT TAB(15);"...WEATHER CONDITIO
   NS..."
75 PRINT TAB(15);"..........LOG......
   ....."
80 PRINT
90 PRINT"INPUT RECORDED DATA";
100 INPUT I$
110 IF I$="YES" THEN 2300
120 PRINT"PRINT INSTRUCTIONS";
130 INPUT I$
140 IF I$="NO" THEN 500
150 CLS
160 PRINT
190 PRINT"THIS PROGRAMS IS DESIGNED TO
    LET"
200 PRINT"YOU ENTER WEATHER DATA, FROM
    GENERAL"
210 PRINT"FORCAST TO RAIN AMOUNTS. THI
    S DATA CAN"
220 PRINT"BE STORED ON A DAY TO DAY BA
    SIS."
230 PRINT"THEREFORE, IF YOU NEED THE F
    ORECAST BUT"
240 PRINT"DON'T HAVE TIME TO CATCH IT
    FROM OTHER"
250 PRINT"SOURCES YOU CAN LOAD THAT DA
    TA FROM"
260 PRINT"TAPE."
270 PRINT
280 INPUT"<ENTER>";I$
290 CLS
```

```
300 PRINT
310 PRINT"AFTER STORING ABOUT 1 YEAR O
    F"
320 PRINT"WEATHER INFORMATION, YOU CAN
    USE THAT"
330 PRINT"STORED DATA TO FORECAST YOUR
    OWN WEATHER!!"
340 PRINT"(KEEP IN MIND, THIS PROGRAM
    IS NOT"
350 PRINT"DESIGNED TO 'TEACH' YOU HOW
    TO FORECAST"
360 PRINT"THE WEATHER, TO DO THAT WOUL
    D TAKE MORE"
370 PRINT"THAN ONE COMPUTER PROGRAM.)"
380 PRINT"AFTER YOU ENTER A STARTING D
    ATE FOR THE"
385 PRINT"WEATHER LOG, THE COMPUTER WI
    LL ADVANCE"
390 PRINT"EACH DAY BY 1. ENTRYS CAN BE
    ON A DAY TO"
395 PRINT"DAY BASIS, OR YOU CAN INPUT
    DATA UP TO"
400 PRINT"1 MONTH BEFORE SAVING THE DA
    TA ON TAPE."
405 PRINT
410 INPUT"<ENTER>";I$
415 CLS:PRINT
420 PRINT"GENERAL FORCASTS, TEMPERATUR
    ES AND RAIN-"
425 PRINT"FALL AMOUNTS CAN BE RECALLED
    AT ANYTIME."
430 PRINT"THE COMPUTER WILL ALSO PRINT
    LOW & HIGH"
435 PRINT"TEMPERATURES, AND AVERAGE TE
    MPERATURES"
440 PRINT"UP TO THE DAY(S) IN FILE."
500 REM DATA
510 PRINT
520 INPUT"INPUT CURRENT MONTH";M$
522 Z$=M$
525 FOR I=1TO12:IF M$=M$(I) THEN J=D(I
    ):A=I:PP(A)=0:NEXT:ELSE NEXT
530 INPUT"INPUT DAY OF MONTH";D
540 IF D>31 PRINT"INVALID ENTRY, INPUT
    AGAIN.":GOTO530
560 D1=D:F1=D:I=1:W=1:P(A)=D
```

260

```
565 PRINT
570 PRINT"INPUT GENERAL FORECAST FOR"
580 PRINT M$;" ";D1;
590 INPUT F$(I)
600 PRINT"LOW ";T$;
605 INPUT L(I)
610 PRINT"HIGH ";T$;
615 INPUT H(I)
620 INPUT"RAINFALL (IF NONE - INPUT 0)
    ";R(I)
630 RR(W)=D1
660 T=I:PRINT
662 IF D1=J THEN P=1:GOTO2000
670 W=W+1:IF W>=3 THEN 710
675 PRINT"THE ABOVE DATA WILL HELP YOU"
680 PRINT"FORECAST FUTURE WEATHER BY"
690 PRINT"KEEPING A FILE FOR AT LEAST"
700 PRINT"1 (ONE) YEAR."
710 PRINT
720 INPUT"PRESS ENTER FOR COMMAND LIST
    ";I$
730 LW(A)=0
735 CLS
740 PRINT
750 PRINT"1) ";T$;"S"
760 PRINT"2) TOTAL RAINFALL"
770 PRINT"3) GENERAL FORECAST(S)"
780 PRINT"4) SAVE DATA ON TAPE"
790 PRINT"5) LOAD DATA FROM TAPE"
800 PRINT"6) ADD DATA TO CURRENT FILE"
810 PRINT"7) TERMINATE PROGRAM"
820 PRINT
830 INPUT"INPUT CHOICE";X
840 CLS:PRINT
850 PRINT"STARTING DATE OF WEATHER ";
855 PRINT"LOG ";Z$;P(1)
870 PRINT"TOTAL DAYS IN FILE =";I
875 PRINT
880 ON X GOTO 900,970,1435,2175,2300,1
    200,1600
885 PRINT"MAKE CHOICE AGAIN, SELECTION
    NOT IN FILE.":GOTO740
900 REM AVERAGE TEMPERATURES
910 PRINT"ENTER MONTH FOR ";T$;"S";
915 INPUT C$:GOTO1150
920 FOR Y=1TO12:IF C$=M$(Y) THEN 940
```

```
930 NEXT
940 IF PP(Y)=0 THEN 1430
950 PRINT"MONTH REQUESTED, NOT IN FILE
    .":GOTO960
955 PRINT"NO DATA IN FILE FOR ";C$;"
960 GO=1:GOTO710
970 GOSUB1270:IF RE=1 RE=0:GOTO710
972 GOSUB2800:GOSUB3100
975 PRINT"RAIN AMOUNTS FOR ";C$;"."
980 G=LT:GOTO1300
985 R=(R+R(G))
990 IF G<=HT THEN G=G+1:GOTO985
995 IF R=0 THEN 1035
1010 IF R>=1 THEN W$="INCHES" ELSE W$="
    OF AN INCH"
1020 PRINT"TOTAL RAINFALL FOR ";
1025 IF FF<>0 PRINTW-FF-1 ELSE PRINT HT
1030 PRINT"DAYS =";R;" ";W$:GOTO1040
1035 PRINT"NO RAINFALL IN LOG....."
1040 R=0:FF=0:GOTO710
1050 REM FORECAST(S) FOR MONTH IN FILE
1052 GOSUB1270:IF RE=1 RE=0:GOTO710
1055 GOSUB2800:GOSUB3100
1060 G=LT:X1=1:XX=3
1065 IF F$(G)="" PRINT"NO FORECAST(S) IN
    FILE.":GOTO710
1066 PRINT"GENERAL FORECAST(S) FROM FILE:"
1070 PRINT"DAY"; F1;".....";F$(G)
1080 PRINT"LOW OF ";L(G);" ";D$
1090 PRINT"HIGH OF ";H(G);" ";D$
1092 IF X1=XX THEN 1110
1095 IF G<>HT THEN F1=F1+1:G=G+1:X1=X1+
    1:GOTO1070
1100 F1=D:GOTO710
1110 PRINT
1120 INPUT"PRESS ENTER TO CONTINUE";I$
1130 PRINT:PRINT
1140 XX=XX+3:GOTO1095
1150 REM SPELLING OF MONTH
1155 FOR Y=1TO12
1160 IF C$=M$(Y) THEN 920
1165 NEXT
1170 PRINT"CORRECT SPELLING, INPUT AGAI
    N."
1180 PRINT:GOTO900
1200 REM MORE DATA
```

```
1230 I=I+1
1240 D1=D1+1
1245 IF D1>=32 THEN A=A+1:I=I-1:GOTO2035
1260 GOTO565
1270 IF C$="" THEN 1290
1275 IF GO=1 THEN 1290
1280 RETURN
1290 PRINT"YOU MUST START WITH ";T$;"S."
1295 PRINT"SO THE COMPUTER WILL HAVE A"
1296 PRINT"MONTH TO INTERPRET DATA."
1297 RE=1:RETURN
1300 REM DAYS THAT RAIN OCCURRED
1310 IF R(G)<>0 THEN 1340
1320 IF G<>HT THEN G=G+1:GOTO1310
1330 G=LT:PRINT:GOTO985
1340 PRINT"RAIN OCCURRED ON: ";C$;RR(G)
1350 PRINT"AMOUNT: ";R(G);" ";
1360 IF R(G)<1 PRINT"OF AN INCH" ELSE P
     RINT"INCHES"
1370 GOTO1320
1430 CLS:PRINT:A=Y:TW=10
1435 IF Q(A)<>0 THEN RT=1:GOTO2000
1437 IF X=3 THEN 1050
1438 GOSUB2800:GOSUB3100
1440 IF W(A)=0 THEN W(A)=ABS(LT-HT)+1
1445 PRINT C$;". . . . . . ."IF HH=1 T
     HEN 1470
1450 PRINT"LOWEST ";T$;" TO DATE: ";LW(
     A);D$;"."
1460 PRINT"HIGHEST ";T$;" TO DATE: "HW(
     A);D$;"."
1465 PRINT
1470 PRINT"DAY" TAB(10);"LOW ";T$;"S" T
     AB(40);"HIGH ";T$;"S"
1475 IF HH=1 THEN 2990
1480 GOTO2940
1500 PRINT
1505 W(A)=ABS(LT-HT)+1
1510 G=LT:K=W(A)
1520 L=(L+L(G)):H=(H+H(G))
1530 IF G<>HT THEN G=G+1:GOTO1520
1540 L=INT(L/K):H=INT(H/K)
1545 IF F1>=8 THEN FOR KK=1TO1000:NEXT
1550 PRINT"AVERAGE LOW ";T$;": ";L
1560 PRINT"AVERAGE HIGH ";T$;": ";H
1570 L=0:H=0
```

263

```
1590 GOTO3000
1600 REM TERMINATE
1610 CLS
1620 PRINT
1630 PRINT"END OF WEATHER CONDITIONS (L
     OG)"
1640 END
2000 REM MONTH ADVANCE
2005 IF RT=1 RT=0:A(A)=I:GOTO1437
2010 IF A>=12 THEN A=1:GOTO2025
2020 DD(A)=D:Q(A)=0:A=A+1:P=0:PP(A)=0:D=1
2025 PRINT"THAT CONCLUDES THE FINAL DAY"
2030 PRINT"FOR THE MONTH OF ";M$;"."
2032 PRINT:PRINT:GOTO2100
2035 M$=M$(A):J=D(A):D1=0:D=1
2040 PRINT"DATA ENTRYS WILL NOW BEGIN"
2050 PRINT"INTO THE MONTH OF ";M$(A);"."
2060 A(A-1)=I:P=0:GOTO670
2100 REM DATA TO CASSETTE
2110 PRINT"IF YOU HAVEN'T DONE SO..."
2120 PRINT M$;" DATA MUST BE PROCESSED
     TO TAPE."
2130 PRINT
2140 PRINT"INPUT 'XX' TO SAVE DATA ON T
     APE"
2150 PRINT"PRESS 'ENTER' ONLY TO START"
2160 INPUT"ANOTHER MONTH";I$
2170 IF I$<>"XX" THEN PRINT:GOTO2035
2172 A=A-1
2175 A(A)=I:GOSUB2800
2180 PRINT"PLACE PLAYER IN RECORD MODE"
2190 INPUT"AND PRESS ENTER";I$
2200 PRINT#-1,D1,Z$,D,W,A,M$,I,J
2210 FOR E=1TOI
2220 PRINT#-1,F$(E),L(E),H(E),R(E),RR(E)
2225 PRINT#-1,A(E),M$(E),Q(E),P(E),DD(E)
     ,PP(E)
2230 NEXT
2240 PRINT M$(A);" DATA ON TAPE....."
2250 IF Q(A)=0 THEN A=A+1:GOTO2035
2260 GOTO710
2300 REM DATA FROM CASSETTE
2310 PRINT
2320 PRINT"PLACE PLAYER IN PLAY MODE"
2330 INPUT"THEN PRESS ENTER";I$
2340 INPUT#-1,D1,Z$,D,W,A,M$,I,J
```

264

```
2350 PRINT"INPUTTING WEATHER DATA..."
2360 FOR E=1TOI
2370 INPUT#-1,F$(E),L(E),H(E),R(E),RR(E)
2375 INPUT#-1,A(E),M$(E),Q(E),P(E),DD(E)
     ,PP(E)
2380 NEXT
2390 PRINT
2395 GOTO710
2500 REM HIGHEST TEMP. FOR MONTH
2501 GOSUB3100
2502 IF LT=HT THEN HW(A)=H(HT):LW(A)=L(
     LT):RETURN
2503 IF HT<LT THEN QQ=1:A=A-1:RETURN
2504 PRINT"SORTING ";T$;"S....."
2505 FOR G=1TOI:J(G)=H(G):NEXT
2510 G=1:P=0
2520 IF H(G)<=H(G+1) THEN 2560
2530 U=H(G+1):H(G+1)=H(G)
2540 H(G)=U
2550 P=1
2560 G=G+1:IF G<>I THEN 2520
2580 IF P=1 THEN 2510
2590 HW(A)=H(G)
2595 FOR G=1TOI:H(G)=J(G):NEXT
2600 REM LOWEST TEMP. FOR MONTH
2610 FOR G=1TOI:J(G)=L(G):NEXT
2620 G=1:P=0
2630 IF L(G)<=L(G+1) THEN 2670
2640 U=L(G+1):L(G+1)=L(G)
2650 L(G)=U
2660 P=1
2670 G=G+1:IF G<>I THEN 2630
2680 IF P=1 THEN 2620
2690 LW(A)=L(1)
2700 FOR G=1TOI:L(G)=J(G):NEXT
2710 CLS:RETURN
2800 REM LOW / HIGH TEMPS.
2810 ON A GOTO 2820,2830,2840,2850,2860
     ,2870,2880,2890,2900,2910,2920,2930
2820 LT=1:HT=A(1):GOTO2932
2830 LT=A(1)+1:HT=A(2):GOTO2932
2840 LT=A(2)+1:HT=A(3):GOTO2932
2850 LT=A(3)+1:HT=A(4):GOTO2932
2860 LT=A(4)+1:HT=A(5):GOTO2932
2870 LT=A(5)+1:HT=A(6):GOTO2932
2880 LT=A(6)+1:HT=A(7):GOTO2932
```

```
2890 LT=A(7)+1:HT=A(8):GOTO2932
2900 LT=A(8)+1:HT=A(9):GOTO2932
2910 LT=A(9)+1:HT=A(10):GOTO2932
2920 LT=A(10)+1:HT=A(11):GOTO2932
2930 LT=A(11)+1:HT=A(12)
2932 IF X=1 AND QQ=1 THEN QQ=0:GOTO955
2935 IF X=1 GOSUB2500
2939 RETURN
2940 REM PRINT TEMPS.
2945 FOR TT=LT TO HT
2946 PRINT F1;
2950 PRINT TAB(15);L(TT);
2960 PRINT TAB(45);H(TT)
2970 F1=F1+1
2980 IF F1=TW THEN 3030
2990 NEXT
2995 GOTO1500
3000 LT=0:HT=0
3025 Y=0:HH=0:ER=0:GOTO710
3030 INPUT"PRESS ENTER TO CONTINUE";I$
3040 CLS:PRINT
3050 HH=1:TW=TW+10
3060 GOTO1445
3100 IF Q(A)=0 THEN DD(A)=P(A):FF=ABS(D
     D(A)-D(A))+1:GOTO3120
3110 DD(A)=D
3120 F1=DD(A)
3130 RETURN
5000 DATA 31,28,31,30,31,30
5010 DATA 31,31,30,31,30,31
5020 DATA JANUARY,FEBRUARY,MARCH
5030 DATA APRIL,MAY,JUNE,JULY
5040 DATA AUGUST,SEPTEMBER,OCTOBER
5050 DATA NOVEMBER,DECEMBER
```

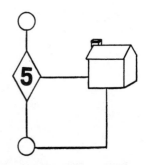

Programs for the Dinette or Kitchen

Menu Equivalents. This data program will help you in kitchen measuring.

Menu Planning. Plan all of your daily menus a week in advance and save numerous trips to the store with the use of this program.

Recipe Storage. Store all of your recipes and recall them the modern way—with your home computer!

Mixing Beverages. Store many beverage recipes from a milk shake to a Tom Collins.

Calorie Counter. You'll enjoy this one, even if you are not on a diet. The computer will select each meal for you.

Coupon Storing File. Alphabetize your coupon list and keep track of every one with this storage program.

Shopping List. Go through the coupons and the menu planner, then make out your shopping list.

MENU EQUIVALENTS

How much is this equal to? What is equivalent to what? You can get the answers fast with this program. All data elements can be changed very easily to suit your own needs.

SAMPLE RUN

MENU (MEASURING EQUIVALENTS)
PART II

AS WITH PART I, MENU (PLANNING),
THIS PROGRAM WILL SERVE AS A
GUIDE, BUT FOR MEASUREMENTS, IT WILL
ALSO HELP YOU MAKE SUBSTITUTES
FOR CERTAIN INGREDIENTS.
ONLY THE MOST POPULAR MEASUREMENTS
ARE CONTAINED IN THE DATA ELEMENTS,
BUT IF YOU LIKE YOU CAN ADD TO
OR DELETE FROM THOSE DATA LINES.

PRESS A KEY <SPACE BAR>

SELECT ONE OF THE FOLLOWING:

1) WEIGHTS & MEASURES
2) SUBSTITUTES

MAKE CHOICE BY NUMBER ONLY? 1

THE COMPUTER WILL NOT UNDERSTAND
EVERY ITEM YOU INPUT, SO WHEN YOU
INPUT SOMETHING BE PRECISE WITH
WHAT YOU WANT TO KNOW.

AN EXAMPLE MIGHT BE:
YOU WANT TO KNOW HOW MUCH 16
TABLESPOONS EQUAL, THE COMPUTER WILL ASK
<SELECT THE ITEM>?
YOU ENTER THE NUMBER FOR 'TABLESPOON'
YOU WILL THEN BE ASKED THE AMOUNT OF
TABLESPOONS YOU WANT A MEASUREMENT ON.
IF THE COMPUTER DOESN'T UNDERSTAND
WHAT YOU WANT, IT WILL PRINT

'ENTER AGAIN' OR 'CAN'T COMPLETE'.

PRESS A KEY <SPACE BAR>

SELECT ITEM? <u>1</u>

1   TEASPOON
2   TABLESPOON
3   CUP
4   OUNCES
5   OTHER MEASURES
               WEIGHTS & MEASURES

3 TEASPOONS = 1 TABLESPOON

DO YOU WISH TO SEE ANYMORE? <u>YES</u>

PRESS A KEY <SPACE BAR>

SELECT ITEM? 2

1   TEASPOON
2   TABLESPOON
3   CUP
4   OUNCES
5   OTHER MEASURES

               WEIGHTS & MEASURES

ENTER AMOUNT OF TABLESPOONS? <u>1</u>

ENTER AGAIN. . . . .PLEASE.

ENTER AMOUNT OF TABLESPOONS? <u>1</u>

CAN'T COMPLETE—INFORMATION NOT IN MEMORY.

DO YOU WISH TO SEE ANYMORE? <u>YES</u>

PRESS A KEY
SELECT ITEM? <u>2</u>

1   TEASPOON
2   TABLESPOON
3   CUP
4   OUNCES
5   OTHER MEASURES

WEIGHTS & MEASURES

ENTER AMOUNT OF TABLESPOONS? <u>4</u>

4 TABLESPOONS = 1/4 CUP

DO YOU WISH TO SEE ANYMORE? <u>YES</u>

PRESS A KEY <SPACE BAR>

SELECT ITEM? <u>3</u>

1   TEASPOON
2   TABLESPOON
3   CUP
4   OUNCES
5   OTHER MEASURES

WEIGHTS & MEASURES

ENTER AMOUNT OF CUPS? <u>8</u>

ENTER AGAIN. . . . .PLEASE.

ENTER AMOUNT OF CUPS? <u>2</u>

2 CUPS = 1 PINT

DO YOU WISH TO SEE ANYMORE? <u>NO</u>

END OF PROGRAM . . . .

As it states within the instructions, you can add to or delete any of the data items. With the SUBSTITUTE part of the program.

MENU (MEASURING EQUIVALENTS)
PART II

AS WITH PART I, MENU (PLANNING),
THIS PROGRAM WILL SERVE AS A
GUIDE, BUT FOR MEASURMENTS. IT WILL
ALSO HELP YOU MAKE SUBSTITUTES

FOR CERTAIN INGREDIENTS.
ONLY THE MOST POPULAR MEASUREMENTS
ARE CONTAINED IN THE DATA ELEMENTS,
BUT IF YOU LIKE YOU CAN ADD TO
OR DELETE FROM THOSE DATA LINES.

PRESS A KEY <SPACE BAR>

SELECT ONE OF THE FOLLOWING:

1) WEIGHTS & MEASURES
2) SUBSTITUTES

MAKE CHOICE BY NUMBER ONLY? <u>2</u>

SUBSTITUTIONS

SUBSTITUTIONS CAN COME IN VERY HANDY WHEN
YOU HAVE RUN OUT OF A CERTAIN ITEM, THEY
CAN IN FACT SAVE ANOTHER TRIP TO THE STORE-
AND WITH FUEL PRICES—WHO NEEDS THAT?

THE BIGGEST PART OF THIS SECTION OF THE PRO-
GRAM WILL BE MOSTLY PRINT STATEMENTS. YOU
CAN QUICKLY CHANGE THE DATA ELEMENTS TO
FIT YOUR NEEDS.
PRESS A KEY <SPACE BAR>

1 CUP CAKE FLOUR = 1 CUP MINUS 2 TABLESPOON ALL
PURPOSE FLOUR

1 CAKE COMPRESSED YEAST = 1 PACKAGE DRY ACTIVE
YEAST

.
.
.

Program continues printing equivalents. You may erase the ones
that are here and substitute your own, if you wish. The computer
will ask if you wish to rerun the program. A yes answer will return
you to the menu.

273

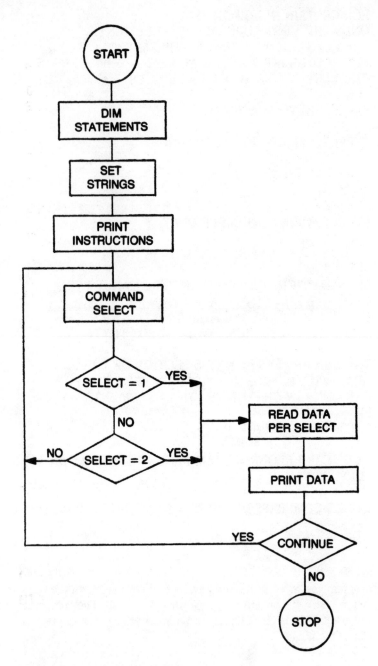

Flowchart for MENU EQUIVALENTS

274

Program Listing

```
10 REM PROGRAM TITLE: MENU (MEASURING EQ
   UIVALENTS)
20 CLS:DIM D$(70):C$=CHR$(143):GOSUB4500
30 PRINT@10,"** MENU (MEASURING EQUIVALE
   NTS) **"
40 PRINT@86,"PART II"
50 PRINT:WM$="WEIGHTS & MEASURES":SU$="S
   UBTITUTES"
60 PRINT"AS WITH PART I, MENU (PLANNING)
   , THIS PROGRAM WILL"
70 PRINT"SERVE AS A GUIDE, BUT FOR MEASU
   REMENTS. IT WILL"
80 PRINT"ALSO HELP YOU MAKE SUBSTITUTES F
   OR CERTAIN INGREDIENTS."
90 PRINT"ONLY THE MOST POPULAR MEASUREMEN
   TS ARE CONTAINED IN"
100 PRINT"THE DATA ELEMENTS, BUT IF YOU L
    IKE YOU CAN ADD TO"
110 PRINT"OR DELETE FROM THOSE DATA LINES
    ."
120 PRINT
130 PRINT"PRESS A KEY"
135 A=652
140 GOSUB5000
150 CLS:PRINT
160 PRINT"SELECT ONE OF THE FOLLOWING:"
170 PRINT
180 PRINT"1)    ";WM$
190 PRINT"2)    ";SU$
200 PRINT:PRINT"MAKE CHOICE BY NUMBER ONL
    Y"
205 A=411
210 GOSUB5000
220 ON VAL(X$) GOTO230,1200
230 CLS:PRINT
240 PRINT"THE COMPUTER WILL NOT UNDERSTAN
    D EVERY ITEM YOU"
250 PRINT"INPUT, SO WHEN YOU INPUT SOMETH
    ING BE SP-PRECISE WITH"
260 PRINT"WHAT YOU WANT TO KNOW."
270 PRINT
280 PRINT"AN EXAMPLE MIGHT BE:"
```

```
290 PRINT"YOU WANT TO KNOW HOW MUCH 16 ";
    D$(2);" EQUAL."
300 PRINT"THE COMPUTER WILL ASK <SELECT T
    HE ITEM> ?"
305 PRINT"YOU ENTER THE NUMBER FOR  '";D$
    (2);"'"
330 PRINT"YOU WILL THEN BE ASKED THE AMOU
    NT OF ";D$(2);"'s"
340 PRINT"YOU WANT A MEASUREMENT ON."
345 PRINT"IF THE COMPUTER DOESN'T UNDERST
    AND WHAT YOU WANT, IT"
350 PRINT"WILL PRINT 'ENTER AGAIN' OR 'CA
    N'T COMPLETE'."
360 PRINT
370 PRINT"PRESS A KEY"
380 IF M=1 THEN A=204:GOSUB5000:ELSE A=90
    8:GOSUB5000
390 CLS:PRINT
400 PRINT"SELECT ITEM ?":PRINT
410 FOR I=1TO4
420 PRINT I,D$(I)
430 NEXT
450 PRINTI,"OTHER MEASURES"
480 A=577:GOSUB5000
500 I=VAL(X$)
510 FOR KK=1TO500:NEXT:CLS:R=0
520 PRINT:PRINTTAB(20);WM$:PRINT
530 ON I GOTO 540,560,640,710,770
540 PRINT"3 ";D$(1);"'S = 1 ";D$(2)
550 GOTO900
560 REM TABLESPOON
570 PRINT
580 PRINT"ENTER AMOUNT OF  ";D$(2);"'S";:
    INPUT XX
590 PRINT
600 FOR U=12TO15:IF XX=VAL(D$(U)) THEN620
610 NEXT:GOSUB1000:IF R=2 THEN GOTO900 EL
    SE 560
620 PRINT XX;" ";D$(2);"'S = ";D$(U-4);"
     ";D$(3):GOTO900
630 GOTO900
640 PRINT:PRINT"ENTER AMOUNT OF ";D$(3);"
    'S";
```

```
650 INPUT CC
660 FOR U=20TO23:IF CC=VAL(D$(U)) THEN680
670 NEXT:GOSUB1000:IF R=2 GOTO900 ELSE 640
680 IF VAL(D$(U))=1 PRINT CC;" ";D$(3);"
    = ";D$(U-4);" FLUID OUNCES":PRINTCC;"
    ";D$(3);" = ";D$(17);" ";D$(5):GOTO900
685 IF VAL(D$(U))=4 THEN D$(5)="QUART" EL
    SE D$(5)="PINT"
690 PRINTCC;" ";D$(3);"'S = ";D$(U-4);" "
    ;D$(5)
700 GOTO900
710 PRINT:PRINT"ENTER THE AMOUNT OF OUNCE
    S";
720 INPUT O
730 FOR U=28TO31:IF O=VAL(D$(U)) THEN750
740 NEXT:PRINT:GOSUB1000:IF R=2 GOTO900 E
    LSE 710
750 PRINTO;" ";D$(4);" = ";D$(U-4);" ";D$
    (3);:IF VAL(D$(U-4))>=1.5 THEN PRINT"
    'S"
760 GOTO900
770 REM OTHER MEASURES
780 U=32:Q=33
790 IF U=32 THEN D$(7)="MILLILITERS" ELSE
     IF U=34 THEN D$(7)="GALLON" ELSE IF
    U=36 THEN D$(7)="PECK"
794 IF U=38 THEN D$(6)="PECK":D$(7)="BUSH
    EL"
795 IF U=40 THEN D$(6)="LITER":D$(7)="QUAR
    T"
800 PRINTD$(U);" ";D$(6);" = ";D$(Q);" ";
    D$(7)
810 U=U+2:Q=Q+2
820 IF U<>42 THEN790
830 D$(6)="QUART":D$(7)="GALLON":MM=1:GOTO
    900
840 REM OTHER MEASURES (CAN SIZES)
850 U=42:Q=43:PRINTTAB(20);"CAN SIZES":PR
    INT
855 IF U=42 PRINTD$(U);" ";D$(4)TAB(15);"
     = "TAB(18);D$(Q);" ";D$(3):GOTO865
860 PRINT "NUMBER   ";D$(U)TAB(15);" = "TA
    B(18);D$(Q);" ";D$(3);"'S
```

277

```
865 U=U+2:Q=Q+2
870 IF U<>56 THEN860
875 MM=2
900 PRINT@704,"PRESS A KEY":A=716:GOSUB50
    00
910 CLS:PRINT:IF MM=1 THEN840
920 PRINT"DO YOU WISH TO SEE ANYMORE";
930 INPUT II$
940 IF II$="YES" THEN M=1:GOTO360
950 CLS
960 GOTO1690
1000 R=R+1
1010 IF R=1 PRINT"ENTER AGAIN.....PLEASE."
     :RETURN
1020 PRINT"CAN'T COMPLETE -- INFORMATION N
     OT IN MEMORY."
1030 RETURN
1130 RETURN
1200 REM SUBTITUTIONS
1210 CLS:PRINT
1220 PRINTTAB(20);"SUBSTITUTIONS"
1230 PRINT
1240 PRINT"SUBSTITUTIONS CAN COME IN VERY H
     ANDY WHEN"
1250 PRINT"YOU HAVE RUN OUT OF A CERTAIN I
     TEM, THEY"
1260 PRINT"CAN IN FACT SAVE ANOTHER TRIP T
     O THE STORE -"
1270 PRINT"AND WITH FUEL PRICES -- WHO NEE
     DS THAT ?"
1280 PRINT
1290 PRINT"THE BIGGEST PART OF THIS SECTIO
     N OF THE PRO-"
1300 PRINT"GRAM WILL BE MOSTLY PRINT STATE
     MENTS. YOU"
1310 PRINT"CAN QUICKLY CHANGE THE DATA ELE
     MENTS TO"
1320 PRINT"FIT YOUR NEEDS."
1330 PRINT@832,"PRESS A KEY":A=844
1340 GOSUB5000
1350 REM READ DATA
1360 GOSUB4640
```

```
1370 CLS:PRINT
1380 PRINT"1 ";D$(3);" CAKE ";D$(56);" = 1
     ";D$(3);" MINUS 2 ";D$(2);" ALL PURP
     OSE ";D$(56)
1390 PRINT
1400 PRINT"1 CAKE COMPRESSED ";D$(57);" =
     1 PACKAGE ACTIVE DRY ";D$(57)
1410 PRINT
1420 PRINT"1 ";D$(3);" WHOLE ";D$(58);" =
     1/2 ";D$(3);" EVAPORATED ";D$(58);" +
     1/2 ";D$(3);" WATER + 2 1/2 ";D$(1);
     " BUTTER"
1430 PRINT
1440 PRINT"1 WHOLE ";D$(59);"  = 2 ";D$(59
     );" YOKES
1450 PRINT"8 ";D$(59);" WHITES = 1 ";D$(3)
1460 PRINT"8 ";D$(59);" YOKES  = 3/4 ";D$(
     3)
1470 PRINT
1480 PRINT"PRESS ANY KEY";A=782
1490 GOSUB5000
1500 CLS
1510 PRINT"1 SMALL FRESH ";D$(61);" = 1 ";
     D$(2);" INSTANT MINCED ";D$(61);", RE
     HYDRATED"
1515 PRINT
1520 PRINT"1 CLOVE ";D$(62);" = 1/8 ";D$(2
     );" ";D$(62);" POWDER"
1530 PRINT
1540 PRINT"1 ";D$(3);" TOMATO JUICE = 1/2
     ";D$(3);" TOMATO SAUCE + 1/2 ";D$(3);
     " WATER"
1550 PRINT
1560 PRINT"HOW MUCH OF WHAT ?"
1570 PRINT"2 ";D$(2);" BUTTER = 1 ";D$(4)
1580 PRINT"1 STICK OF BUTTER  = 1/2 ";D$(3)
1590 PRINT"1 SQUARE ";D$(60);" = 1 ";D$(4)
1600 PRINT"1 SQUARE ";D$(60);" = 3 ";D$(2)
     ;" DRY COCOA + 1 ";D$(2);" BUTTER OR
     MARGARINE"
1610 PRINT"PRESS ANY KEY";A=910
1620 GOSUB5000
```

```
1630 CLS:PRINT
1640 PRINT"END OF DATA....."
1650 PRINT
1660 PRINT"WOULD YOU LIKE TO RUN THE PROGR
     AM AGAIN";
1670 INPUT II$
1680 IF II$="YES" THEN PRINT@640,"PRESS A
     KEY":A=652:GOTO140
1690 PRINT
1700 PRINT"END OF PROGRAM.............."
1710 END
4500 REM DATA
4510 FOR I=1TO62:READ D$(I):NEXT
4520 DATA TEASPOON,TABLESPOON,CUP
4530 DATA OUNCES,PINT,QUART,GALLON
4540 DATA 1/4,1/2,3/4,1
4550 DATA 4,8,12,16
4560 DATA 8,1/2,1,1
4570 DATA 1,1,2,4
4580 DATA 2,1 1/2,1,1/2
4590 DATA 16,12,8,4
4600 DATA 1,946.4,4,1,8,1,4,1,1,1.06
4610 DATA 8,1,300,1 3/4,303,2,2,2 1/2,2 1/
     2,3 1/2
4620 DATA 3,5 3/4,10,12
4640 REM DATA FOR SUBTITUTES
4650 DATA FLOUR,YEAST,MILK,EGGS,CHOCOLATE,
     ONION,GARLIC
4660 RETURN
5000 PRINT@A,C$:FOR J=1TOK:NEXT
5010 PRINT@A,"  ":FOR J=1TOH:NEXT
5020 FOR K=1TO75:NEXT
5030 X$=INKEY$
5040 IF X$="" THEN5000
5050 RETURN
```

MENU PLANNING

Actual use of this program will help you plan all of your meals one week in advance. Planning meals this far in advance will mean you'll make fewer trips to the grocery store. The menus you store on cassette tape can be recalled by the day you wish to see.

SAMPLE RUN

MENU (PLANNING)

ANSWER YES TO THE NEXT QUESTION ONLY
IF YOU HAVE ALREADY COMPLETED THIS
PROGRAM AND HAVE MENUS ON TAPE.
STORED ON CASSETTE TAPE.

DO YOU WANT TO SEE A MENU? <u>NO</u>

PLANNING A MEAL AHEAD OF TIME WILL
SAVE ALOT OF TIME AND HEADACHES. THIS
PROGRAM WILL HELP YOU PLAN EACH MEAL
OF THE DAY, BREAKFAST, LUNCH AND SUPPER.
ALL YOU NEED DO IS INPUT THE NECESSARY
DATA AND LET THE COMPUTER DO THE REST.

EACH DAILY MEAL SHOULD BE PLANNED
SEVERAL DAYS IN ADVANCE, SO YOU'LL
BE ABLE TO TAKE ADVANTAGE OF SHOPPING
ITEMS THAT MIGHT BE ON SALE.

PRESS ENTER? <ENTER>
WHEN PUTTING TOGETHER A RECIPE,
LAY OUT ALL THE INGREDIENTS AND
UTENSILS YOU'LL NEED FOR THAT MEAL,
FOLLOW THE MEASUREMENTS EXACTLY,
YOU'LL FIND THE COOKING MUCH SIMPLER
AND PRODUCE PERFECT RESULTS.

ALWAYS REMEMBER YOUR MEALS
MUST CONTAIN SOMETHING FROM THE
4 FOOD GROUPS:
1) BREADS & CEREALS
2) FRUITS & VEGETABLES
3) MILK GROUP (INCLUDING CHEESE & ICE CREAM)
4) MEAT GROUP (INCLUDING FISH, POULTRY & EGGS)

PRESS ENTER? <ENTER>
REMEMBER THIS PROGRAM IS ONLY
A GUIDE, YOU MUST ENTER NECESSARY

DATA TO MAKE IT EFFECTIVE. THE NEXT
PART OF THE PROGRAM WILL BE STORAGE
OF MENUS FOR 7 DAYS, BE SURE YOU
ENTER ALL INFORMATION CORRECTLY AS IT
WILL BECOME A REFERENCE FOR YOUR
MEALS ONCE THE DATA IS RECORDED
ON CASSETTE TAPE.

PRESS ENTER TO BEGIN DATA STORAGE? <ENTER>

SAMPLE RUN

MENU PLANNING

ENTER CURRENT MONTH? MARCH
THE MONTH OF MARCH HAS 31 DAYS.

WHAT IS THE DAY OF THE MONTH (1,2,3 ETC.)
IF AFTER BREAKFAST, ENTER NEXT FULL DAY? 17
THERE ARE 14 DAYS LEFT IN MARCH
BUT WE'LL ONLY BE WORKING WITH 7 OF THEM FOR NOW.
ENTER THE DAY OF THE WEEK
(MONDAY, TUESDAY, WEDNESDAY, ETC.)
FOR DATA ENTERED ABOVE? TUESDAY

YOU HAVE THE FOLLOWING DAYS TO WORK WITH:

17- TUESDAY
18- WEDNESDAY
19- THURSDAY
20- FRIDAY
21- SATURDAY
22- SUNDAY
23- MONDAY

NUMBER INDICATES DATE.
PRESS ENTER? <ENTER>

WE WILL BEGIN STORAGE OF ITEMS TO BE
SERVED FOR THOSE 7 DAYS LISTED.

MEALS TO BE SERVED FOR TUESDAY.

ENTER AMOUNT OF ITEMS YOU
WILL SERVE FOR BREAKFAST? 5
ENTER THESE 5 ITEMS BY NAME:

EGGS (SCRAMBLED)
BACON (CRISP)
TOAST
JUICE
COFFEE

ITEMS FOR TUESDAY'S BREAKFAST ARE NOW IN MEM-
ORY.
WE WILL NOW ENTER DATA FOR TUESDAY'S LUNCH.

PRESS ENTER? <ENTER>

ENTER AMOUNT OF ITEMS YOU
WILL SERVE FOR LUNCH? 4
ENTER THESE 4 ITEMS BY NAME:

SLOPPY JOES
FRENCH FRIES
ICED TEA
DESSERT

ITEMS FOR TUESDAY'S LUNCH ARE NOW IN MEMORY.
WE WILL NOW ENTER DATA FOR TUESDAY'S SUPPER.

PRESS ENTER? <ENTER>

ENTER AMOUNT OF ITEMS YOU
WILL SERVE FOR SUPPER? 6
ENTER THESE 6 ITEMS BY NAME:

STEAK (TO ORDER)
BAKED POTATOES
CORN (FRESH-EARS)
GREEN BEANS
HOT ROLLS
ICED TEA

ITEMS FOR TUESDAY'S SUPPER ARE NOW IN MEMORY.
PRESS ENTER? <ENTER>

WHEN FINISHED CHECKING TUESDAY'S
MENU . . . PRESS A KEY.

BREAKFAST

EGGS (SCRAMBLED)
BACON (CRISP)
TOAST
JUICE
COFFEE

LUNCH

SLOPPY JOES
FRENCH FRIES
ICED TEA
DESSERT

SUPPER

STEAK (TO ORDER)
CORN (FRESH-EARS)
GREEN BEANS
HOT ROLLS
ICED TEA

TUESDAY MARCH 17TH
<SPACE BAR>

WE WILL NOW SAVE THIS DATA ON TAPE.
PUT CASSETTE PLAYER IN RECORD MODE,
THEN PRESS ENTER?

PRINTING DAY, MONTH, AND DATE ON TAPE.
PRINTING BREAKFAST, LUNCH, & SUPPER MENU ON TAPE
PRINTING COMPLETE

PRESS ENTER <ENTER>
.
.
.
MEALS TO BE SERVED FOR MONDAY

ENTER THE AMOUNT OF ITEMS YOU
WILL SERVE FOR BREAKFAST? <u>1</u>
ENTER THESE 1 ITEMS BY NAME:

FASTING

ITEMS FOR MONDAY'S BREAKFAST ARE NOW IN MEMORY.
WE WILL NOW ENTER DATA FOR MONDAY'S LUNCH.

PRESS ENTER? <ENTER>

ENTER THE AMOUNT OF ITEMS YOU
WILL SERVE FOR LUNCH? <u>1</u>
ENTER THESE 1 ITEMS BY NAME:

FASTING

ITEMS FOR MONDAY'S LUNCH ARE NOW IN MEMORY.
WE WILL NOW ENTER DATA FOR MONDAY'S SUPPER.

PRESS ENTER? <ENTER>

ENTER THE AMOUNT OF ITEMS YOU
WILL SERVE FOR SUPPER? <u>1</u>
ENTER THESE 1 ITEMS BY NAME:

<u>DINING OUT TONIGHT</u>

ITEMS FOR MONDAY'S SUPPER ARE NOW IN MEMORY.
PRESS ENTER? <ENTER>

WHEN FINISHED CHECKING MONDAY'S
MENU. . . PRESS A KEY

BREAKFAST

FASTING

LUNCH

FASTING

SUPPER

DINING OUT TONIGHT

MONDAY MARCH 23RD
<SPACE BAR>

WE WILL NOW SAVE THIS DATA ON TAPE.
PUT CASSETTE PLAYER IN RECORD MODE,
THEN PRESS ENTER? <ENTER>

7 DAY MENU COMPLETED . . . .
DO YOU WISH TO COMPLETE ANOTHER?

As you can see there are some limitations to the program, but with a little understanding they can be worked around.

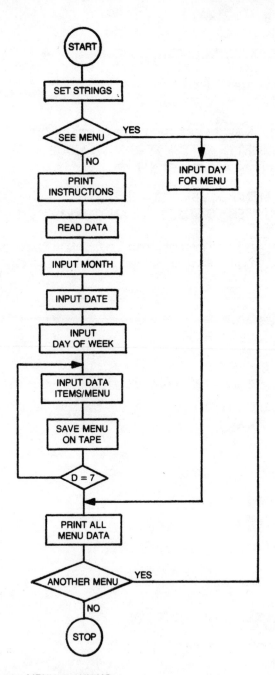

Flowchart for MENU PLANNING

Program Listing
```
10 REM PROGRAM TITLE: MENU (PLANNING)
20 CLEAR1000:DIM DT$(12),H$(30),H1$(30)
21 DIM H2$(30),D(12):CLS:GOTO30
25 B$="BREAKFAST":L$="LUNCH":S$="SUPP
   ER":RETURN
30 PRINTTAB(15);"** MENU (PLANNING) **"
40 PRINT:IF Y=1 THEN50
41 PRINT"ANSWER YES TO THE NEXT QUEST
   ION ONLY"
46 PRINT"IF YOU HAVE ALREADY COMPLETE
   D THIS"
47 PRINT"PROGRAM AND HAVE MENU'S ON T
   APE."
48 PRINT"STORED ON CASSETTE TAPE."
49 INPUT"DO YOU WANT TO SEE A MENU";I
   $:IF I$="YES"THEN 1500:ELSE Y=1:CL
   S:GOTO30
50 PRINT"PLANNING A MEAL AHEAD OF TIM
   E WILL"
51 PRINT"SAVE ALOT OF TIME AND HEADAC
   HES. THIS"
60 PRINT"PROGRAM WILL HELP YOU PLAN E
   ACH MEAL"
70 PRINT"OF THE DAY, BREAKFAST, LUNCH
   AND SUPPER."
80 PRINT"ALL YOU NEED DO IS INPUT THE
   NECESSARY"
90 PRINT"DATA AND LET THE COMPUTER DO
   THE REST."
100 PRINT
110 PRINT"EACH DAILY MEAL SHOULD BE PL
    ANNED"
120 PRINT"SEVERAL DAYS IN ADVANCE, SO
    YOU'LL"
130 PRINT"BE ABLE TO TAKE ADVANTAGE OF
    SHOPPING"
135 PRINT"ITEMS THAT MIGHT BE ON SALE."
140 PRINT:INPUT"PRESS ENTER";X:CLS:PRI
    NT
150 PRINT"WHEN PUTTING TOGETHER A RECI
    PE,"
160 PRINT"LAY OUT ALL THE INGREDIENTS
    AND"
```

```
170 PRINT"UTENSILS YOU'LL NEED FOR THA
    T MEAL,"
180 PRINT"FOLLOW THE MEASUREMENTS EXACT
    LY,"
185 PRINT"YOU'LL FIND THE COOKING MUCH
     SIMPLER"
190 PRINT"AND PRODUCE PERFECT RESULTS."
200 PRINT
210 PRINT"ALWAYS REMEMBER YOUR MEALS"
215 PRINT"MUST CONTAIN SOMETHING FROM
    THE"
220 PRINT"4 FOOD GROUPS:"
230 PRINT"1)    BREADS & CEREALS"
240 PRINT"2)    FRUITS & VEGETABLES"
250 PRINT"3)    MILK GROUP (INCLUDING C
    HEESE & ICE CREAM)"
260 PRINT"4)    MEAT GROUP (INCLUDING F
    ISH, POULTRY & EGGS)"
270 PRINT
280 INPUT"PRESS ENTER";X:CLS:PRINT
290 PRINT"REMEMBER THIS PROGRAM IS ONLY"
300 PRINT"A GUIDE, YOU MUST ENTER NECE
    SSARY"
310 PRINT"DATA TO MAKE IT EFFECTIVE. T
    HE NEXT"
320 PRINT"PART OF THE PROGRAM WILL BE
    STORAGE"
325 PRINT"OF MENU'S FOR 7 DAYS, BE SUR
    E YOU"
330 PRINT"ENTER ALL INFORMATION CORREC
    TLY AS IT"
340 PRINT"WILL BECOME A REFERENCE FOR
    YOUR"
350 PRINT"MEALS ONCE THE DATA IS RECOR
    DED"
355 PRINT"ON CASSETTE TAPE."
360 PRINT
370 INPUT"PRESS ENTER TO BEGIN DATA ST
    ORAGE";X:CLS:PRINT
375 GOSUB25:FOR I=1TO7:READ WD$(I):NEXT
380 DATA MONDAY,TUESDAY,WEDNESDAY,THUR
    SDAY
385 DATA FRIDAY,SATURDAY,SUNDAY
390 FOR I=1TO12:READ DT$(I):NEXT
400 DATA JANUARY,FEBRUARY,MARCH,APRIL,
    MAY
```

```
410 DATA JUNE,JULY,AUGUST,SEPTEMBER
415 DATA OCTOBER,NOVEMBER,DECEMBER
420 FOR I=1TO12:READ D(I):NEXT
430 DATA 31,28,31,30,31,30,31,31,30,31
    ,30,31
435 INPUT"ENTER CURRENT MONTH";D$
440 FOR I=1TO12
450 IF D$=DT$(I) THEN470
460 NEXT:PRINT"CHECK YOUR SPELLING --
    THEN TRY AGAIN.":FOR TY=1TO1500:NE
    XT:GOTO435
470 PRINT"THE MONTH OF ";D$;" HAS ";D(
    I);" DAYS."
480 PRINT:TD=D(I)
490 PRINT"WHAT IS THE DAY OF THE MONTH
    (1, 2, 3 ETC.)"
495 INPUT"IF AFTER BREAKFAST, ENTER NE
    XT FULL DAY";DA
500 L=(D(I)-DA)
510 PRINT"THERE ARE";L;"DAYS LEFT IN "
    ;D$
520 IF L>7 PRINT"BUT WE'LL ONLY BE WOR
    KING WITH 7 OF THEM FOR NOW.":PRINT
530 PRINT"ENTER THE DAY OF THE WEEK"
531 PRINT"(MONDAY, TUESDAY, WEDNESDAY,
    ETC.)"
532 PRINT"FOR DATE ENTERED ABOVE";
535 INPUT W$
540 FOR I=1TO7
550 IF W$=WD$(I) THEN565
560 NEXT:PRINT"YOU MIGHT WANT TO CORRE
    CT YOUR SPELLING, TRY AGAIN.":FOR
    TI=1TO1500:NEXT:PRINT:GOTO530
565 CLS:PRINT:JI=I
570 PRINT"YOU HAVE THE FOLLOWING DAYS
    TO WORK WITH:":PRINT
580 M=I:J=1:AD=DA
590 PRINT AD;"- "TAB(10);WD$(M)
600 U$(J)=WD$(M):M=M+1:IF M=8 THEN M=1
610 J=J+1:IF AD>=TD THEN AD=1 ELSE AD=
    AD+1
620 IF J<>8 THEN590
630 D=1:PRINT
635 PRINT"NUMBER INDICATES DATE.":PRINT
640 INPUT"PRESS ENTER";X:CLS:PRINT
```

```
650 PRINT"WE WILL BEGIN STORAGE OF ITE
    MS TO BE"
660 PRINT"SERVED FOR THOSE 7 DAYS LISTED."
670 PRINT
680 I=1:Z=1:N=1:G=1:JJ=1:Z$=B$
690 PRINT"MEALS TO BE SERVED FOR ";W$;
    ".":PRINT
700 PRINT"ENTER AMOUNT OF ITEMS YOU"
705 PRINT"WILL SERVE FOR ";Z$;
710 INPUT A
720 PRINT"ENTER THESE";A;"ITEMS BY NAME:"
740 IF I=1 THEN INPUT H$(Z):ELSE IF I=
    2 THEN INPUT H1$(N):ELSE IF I=3 TH
    EN INPUT H2$(G)
760 IF I=1 THEN Z=Z+1:ELSE IF I=2 THEN
    N=N+1:ELSE IF I=3 THEN G=G+1
765 JJ=JJ+1:IF JJ<>A+1 THEN740
840 PRINT
850 PRINT"ITEMS FOR ";W$;"'S ";Z$;" AR
    E NOW IN MEMORY."
860 IF I=1 THEN Z$=L$ ELSE IF I=2 THEN
    Z$=S$ ELSE IF I=3 THEN 880
870 PRINT"WE WILL NOW ENTER DATA FOR "
    ;W$;"'S ";Z$;"."
880 PRINT
890 INPUT"PRESS ENTER";XX
900 A(I)=A:I=I+1:JJ=1
910 CLS
920 IF I<>4 THEN PRINT:GOTO700
925 GOSUB1700
930 I=1
940 PRINT:PRINT"WHEN FINISHED CHECKING
    ";W$;"'S"
945 PRINT"MENU...PRESS A KEY.":FOR TI=
    1TO2000:NEXT:CLS
950 PRINT@64,B$:PRINT@90,L$:PRINT@114,S$
955 FOR XX=0TO123:SET(XX,6):NEXT:PRINT
    :L1=192:L2=218:L3=242
960 FOR I=1TOQ
965 PRINT@L1,H$(I);:PRINT@L2,H1$(I);:P
    RINT@L3,H2$(I)
970 L1=L1+64:L2=L2+64:L3=L3+64
980 NEXT
990 PRINT@847,W$;"    ";D$;"    ";DA ;
```

```
1000 IF DA=1 PRINT"ST" ELSE IF DA=2 PRI
     NT"ND" ELSE IF DA=3 PRINT"RD" ELSE
      IF DA>=4 PRINT"TH"
1010 ZX$=INKEY$
1020 IF ZX$="" THEN1010
1030 CLS:IF RR=2 THEN1300
1040 PRINT
1050 PRINT"WE WILL NOW SAVE THIS DATA O
     N TAPE."
1060 PRINT"PUT CASSETTE PLAYER IN RECOR
     D MODE,"
1070 PRINT"THEN PRESS ENTER";
1080 INPUT XX
1090 PRINT
1100 PRINT"PRINTING DAY, MONTH & DATE O
     N TAPE."
1105 PRINT#-1,W$
1110 PRINT#-1,D$,DA,Q
1120 GOSUB25
1130 PRINT"PRINTING ";B$;", ";L$;" & ";
     S$;" MENU ON TAPE."
1140 FOR I=1TOQ:PRINT#-1,H$(I),H1$(I),H
     2$(I):NEXT
1150 PRINT"PRINTING COMPLETE."
1160 PRINT
1170 PRINT"PRESS ENTER";
1180 INPUT XX:CLS:PRINT
1190 IF D=7 THEN 1600:ELSE D=D+1:W$=U$(
     D):DA=DA+1:FOR I=1TO3:A(I)=0:NEXT:
     FOR I=1TOQ:H$(I)="":H1$(I)="":H2$(
     I)="":NEXT:CLS:GOTO670
1200 PRINT
1210 INPUT#-1,W$:IF W$<>XX$ AND SD<>1 T
     HEN PRINT"SEARCHING FOR ";XX$;".":
     GOTO1400:ELSE IF W$<>XX$ GOTO1400
1220 INPUT#-1,D$,DA,Q
1230 GOSUB25
1240 PRINT"INPUTTING ";B$;", ";L$;" & "
     ;S$;" MENU FROM TAPE."
1250 FOR I=1TOQ:INPUT#-1,H$(I),H1$(I),H
     2$(I):NEXT
1260 PRINT"DATA NOW IN COMPUTER MEMORY."
1270 PRINT"PRESS ENTER TO SEE THE MENU";
1280 INPUT XX:RR=2:CLS:GOTO930
1300 PRINT
1310 PRINT"DO YOU WISH TO SEE ANOTHER M
```

```
      ENU (Y/N)";
1320 INPUT I$
1330 IF I$<>"N" THEN1540
1340 GOTO1660
1400 REM CONTINUE TAPE MOVEMENT FOR DAY
     DESIRED
1410 INPUT#-1,D$,DA,Q
1420 FOR I=1TOQ:INPUT#-1,H$(I),H1$(I),H
     2$(I):NEXT
1430 SD=1:GOTO1210
1500 REM IF MENU HASN'T BEEN MADE
1510 REM YOUR WASTING TIME !!
1540 PRINT
1550 PRINT"PLACE CASSETTE PLAYER IN"
1555 PRINT"PLAY MODE AND ENTER THE DAY
     YOU"
1560 PRINT"WISH TO SEE (MONDAY, TUESDAY
     , ETC.)";
1570 INPUT XX$:PRINT:GOTO1200
1600 CLS:PRINT
1610 PRINT"7 DAY MENU COMPLETED.........."
1620 PRINT
1630 PRINT"DO YOU WISH TO COMPLETE ANOT
     HER 7 DAYS (Y/N)";
1640 INPUT I$
1650 IF I$="Y" THEN FOR I=1TO3:A(I)=0:C
     LS:PRINT:GOTO480
1660 PRINT
1670 PRINT"END OF PROGRAM....."
1680 END
1700 REM SET VARIABLE Q FOR PRINT OUT
1710 IF A(1)>=A(2) AND A(1)>=A(3) THEN
     Q=A(1):GOTO1750
1720 IF A(2)>=A(1) AND A(2)>=A(3) THEN
     Q=A(2):GOTO1750
1730 IF A(3)>=A(1) AND A(3)>=A(2) THEN
     Q=A(3)
1750 RETURN
```

294

RECIPE STORAGE

Ever thumb through a recipe book just to locate one recipe, only to find you've passed it 5 times? This program will end that problem, completely. Each recipe will be stored on cassette tape to be recalled on a moment's notice.

SAMPLE RUN

MENU (RECIPE STORAGE)

VIEW A RECIPE (Y/N)? <u>N</u>

THIS PROGRAM WILL LET YOU
ENTER AND STORE ALL THE RECIPES
YOU DESIRE, AFTERWARDS, YOU CAN
'DUMP' THESE RECIPES ON TAPE FOR
FUTURE REFERENCE.

WHEN ENTERING THE INSTRUCTIONS FOR
A RECIPE, KEEP THEM AS SHORT AS
POSSIBLE, EXAMPLE: ADD 2 TABLESPOONS
OF SHORTENING—STIR WELL. YOU COULD
SHORTEN THIS TO:
ADD 2 TAB. SHORT. —STIR WELL.
YOU MUST KEEP THE AMOUNT OF
INSTRUCTIONS FOR A RECIPE TO NOT
MORE THAN 240 CHARACTERS. (INSTRUCTIONS
ONLY—NOT TITLE OR INGREDIENTS).

PRESS ENTER? <ENTER>

FOLLOW THESE INSTRUCTIONS FOR A RECIPE:
A) DON'T USE ANY COMMAS, USE THE
- OR/
B) ALL ENTRYS WILL BE WITH STRINGS,
SO YOU CAN INPUT ALPHANUMERICS.
C) DON'T CLUTTER THE INGREDIENTS-
PRESS ENTER WHEN FINISHED WITH ONE
LINE OF AN INGREDIENT (IT WILL THEN
BE STORED IN MEMORY).
THE ENTIRE RECIPE WILL BE PRINTED
FOR YOU TO VIEW BEFORE IT IS
'DUMPED' ON TAPE.

PRESS ENTER TO BEGIN? < ENTER >

ENTER TITLE OF RECIPE? WRAPPED HOT DOGS
ENTER AMOUNT OF INGREDIENTS, THAT
IS, AMOUNT OF LINES TO THE
RECIPE (NOT INCLUDING THE INSTRUCTIONS)? <u>4</u>
NOW ENTER THESE 4 INGREDIENTS.

8 SLICES OF BREAD
4 T. BUTTER
8 SLICES AMERICAN CHEESE
8 HOT DOGS

THE INGREDIENTS ARE NOW IN MEMORY.

AFTER YOU ENTER EACH LINE OF THE
INSTRUCTIONS THE COMPUTER WILL PRINT
CHARACTER AMOUNT REMAINING
SO YOU WON'T EXCEED 240 CHARACTERS.
ENTER XX WHEN FINISHED WITH INSTRUCTIONS.

PRESS ENTER WHEN READY TO INPUT INSTRUCTIONS?
<ENTER>

? SPREAD SOFTENED BUTTER ON ONE SIDE

CHARACTER SPACE REMAINING = 206
? OF EACH SLICE OF BREAD, PLACE A SLICE

CHARACTER SPACE REMAINING = 169
? OF CHEESE ON EACH. FOLD OPPOSITE CORNERS

CHARACTER SPACE REMAINING = 129
? OF BREAD - ATTACH WOODEN PICKS. BAKE IN

CHARACTER SPACE REMAINING = 90
? 375 D. OVEN 10 MIN.

CHARACTER SPACE REMAINING = 71
?XX

WHEN FINISHED VIEWING RECIPE,
PRESS ANY KEY.

RECIPE: WRAPPED HOT DOGS

INGREDIENTS:
   8 SLICES OF BREAD   4 T. BUTTER
   8 SLICES AMERICAN CHEESE   8 HOT DOGS

INSTRUCTIONS:
SPREAD SOFTENED BUTTER ON ONE SIDE

OF EACH SLICE OF BREAD. PLACE A SLICE
OF CHEESE ON EACH. FOLD OPPOSITE CORNERS
OF BREAD-ATTACH WOODEN PICKS. BAKE IN
375 D. OVEN 10 MIN.

? <SPACE BAR>

YOU CAN NOW SAVE THE ENTIRE
RECIPE ON TAPE.
PLACE CASSETTE PLAYER IN RECORD
MODE, THEN PRESS ENTER? <ENTER>

OUTPUTTING TO TAPE . . . . .
OUTPUTTING INSTRUCTIONS TO TAPE . . . . .

TRANSFER OF DATA COMPLETED . . . . .
PRESS ANY KEY

WOULD YOU LIKE TO MAKE ANOTHER RECIPE
OR SEE ANOTHER RECIPE (Y/N)? Y

1) MAKE ANOTHER RECIPE
2) SEE ANOTHER RECIPE? 1

PRESS ENTER TO BEGIN? <ENTER>

ENTER TITLE OF RECIPE? SCRAMBLED EGGS
ENTER AMOUNT OF INGREDIENTS, THAT
IS, AMOUNT OF LINES TO THE
RECIPE (NOT INCLUDING THE INSTRUCTIONS)? 3
NOW ENTER THESE 3 INGREDIENTS.

? 4 EGGS
? 4 T. MILK/DASH SALT & PEPPER
? 2 T. MARGARINE

THE INGREDIENTS ARE NOW IN MEMORY.

AFTER YOU ENTER EACH LINE OF THE
INSTRUCTIONS THE COMPUTER WILL PRINT
CHARACTER AMOUNT REMAINING
SO YOU WON'T EXCEED 240 CHARACTERS.

ENTER XX WHEN FINISHED WITH INSTRUCTIONS.

PRESS ENTER WHEN READY TO INPUT INSTRUCTIONS?
<ENTER>

BREAK EGGS IN A SMALL BOWL

CHARACTER SPACE REMAINING = 214
ADD SALT/PEPPER - MILK

CHARACTER SPACE REMAINING = 192
BEAT WELL WITH FORK. PLACE MARGARINE

CHARACTER SPACE REMAINING = 156
IN SKILLET. COOK ABOUT 1 MIN. OVER

CHARACTER SPACE REMAINING = 122
MEDIUM-LOW HEAT. SEASON & SERVE HOT.

CHARACTER SPACE REMAINING = 86
XX

WHEN FINISHED VIEWING RECIPE,
PRESS ANY KEY. <SPACE BAR>

RECIPE: SCRAMBLED EGGS

INGREDIENTS:
    4 EGGS   4 T. MILK/DASH SALT & PEPPER
    2 T. MARGARINE

INSTRUCTIONS:
BREAK EGGS IN A SMALL BOWL
ADD SALT/PEPPER - MILK
BEAT WELL WITH FORK. PLACE MARGARINE
IN SKILLET. COOK ABOUT 1 MIN. OVER
MEDIUM-LOW HEAT. SEASON & SERVE HOT.

YOU CAN NOW SAVE THE ENTIRE
RECIPE ON TAPE.
PLACE CASSETTE PLAYER IN RECORD
MODE, THEN PRESS ENTER?

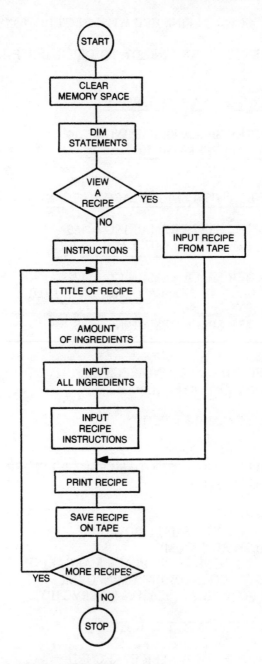

Flowchart for RECIPE STORAGE

Program Listing

```
10 REM PROGRAM TITLE: MENU (RECIPE STORA
   GE)
20 CLS:CLEAR1500:DIM I$(50),A$(25)
30 PRINT@15,"** MENU (RECIPE STORAGE) **"
40 PRINT@87,"PART III"
50 PRINT:IF R=1 THEN60
55 PRINT"VIEW A RECIPE (Y/N)";:INPUT Q$:
   IF Q$="Y" THEN870
58 R=1:CLS:GOTO30
60 PRINT"THIS PROGRAM WILL LET YOU ENTER
    AND STORE ALL THE"
70 PRINT"RECIPES YOU DESIRE. AFTERWARDS,
    YOU CAN 'DUMP' THESE"
80 PRINT"RECIPES ON TAPE FOR FUTURE REFE
   RENCE."
90 PRINT
100 PRINT"WHEN ENTERING THE INSTRUCTIONS
     FOR A RECIPE, KEEP"
110 PRINT"THEM AS SHORT AS POSSIBLE, EXAM
    PLE:"
120 PRINT"ADD 2 TABLESPOONS OF SHORTENING -
     STIR WELL."
130 PRINT"YOU COULD SHORTEN THIS TO:"
140 PRINT"ADD 2 TAB. SHORT. - STIR WELL."
150 PRINT"YOU MUST KEEP THE AMOUNT OF INS
    TRUCTIONS FOR"
160 PRINT"A RECIPE TO NOT MORE THAN 240 C
    HARACTERS."
165 PRINT"(INSTRUCTIONS ONLY -- NOT TITLE
     OR INGREDIENTS)."
166 REM SEE REM STATEMENTS LINES 1200-1250
170 PRINT
180 PRINT"PRESS ENTER";:INPUT X:CLS:PRINT
190 PRINT"FOLLOW THESE INSTRUCTION FOR A
    RECIPE:"
200 PRINT"A) DON'T USE ANY COMMAS, USE TH
    E ";CHR$(45);" OR ";CHR$(47)"
210 PRINT"B) ALL ENTRYS WILL BE WITH STRI
    NGS, YOU CAN MIX"
215 PRINT"NUMERICS WITH THE ALPHABET."
```

301

```
220 PRINT"C) DON'T CLUTTER THE INGREDIENT
    S - PRESS ENTER WHEN FINISHED"
230 PRINT"WITH ONE LINE OF AN INGREDIENT
    (IT WILL THEN BE STORED"
240 PRINT"IN MEMORY)."
280 PRINT"THE ENTIRE RECIPE WILL BE PRINT
    ED FOR YOU TO VIEW"
290 PRINT"BEFORE IT IS 'DUMPED' ON TAPE."
295 PRINT
300 PRINT"PRESS ENTER TO BEGIN";:INPUT X:
    CLS
310 PRINT:PRINT"ENTER TITLE OF RECIPE";:I
    NPUT T$:PRINT
320 PRINT"ENTER AMOUNT OF INGREDIENTS, TH
    AT IS, AMOUNT OF LINES"
330 PRINT"TO THE RECIPE (NOT INCLUDING TH
    E INSTRUCTIONS)";
340 INPUT I
350 PRINT"NOW ENTER THESE";I;"INGREDIENTS.
360 FOR J=1TOI
370 INPUT I$(J)
380 NEXT
390 E=I+1:PRINT
400 PRINT"THE INGREDIENTS ARE NOW IN MEMO
    RY."
410 PRINT
420 PRINT"AFTER YOU ENTER EACH LINE OF TH
    E INSTRUCTIONS"
430 PRINT"THE COMPUTER WILL PRINT CHARACT
    ER AMOUNT REMAINING"
440 PRINT"SO YOU WON'T EXCEED 240 CHARACT
    ERS. ENTER XX WHEN"
450 PRINT"FINISHED WITH INSTRUCTIONS."
460 PRINT
470 PRINT"PRESS ENTER WHEN READY TO INPUT
    INSTRUCTIONS";
480 INPUT X:CLS:PRINT
490 L=0:M=240:I=1:AA=128
500 PRINT@AA,;:INPUT A$(I)
510 IF A$(I)="XX" THEN JJ=I-1:GOTO550
520 L=L+LEN(A$(I))
530 PRINT@1,"CHARACTER SPACE REMAINING ="
    ;M-L
```

```
540 AA=AA+64:I=I+1:GOTO500
550 PRINT"WHEN FINISHED VIEWING RECIPE
    , PRESS ANY KEY."
555 FOR TT=1TO2500:NEXT
560 REM PRINT ENTIRE RECIPE FOR INSPEC
    TION
570 CLS
580 PRINT"RECIPE:     ";T$
590 PRINT
600 PRINT"INGREDIENTS:"
610 I=1:II=2:T=1
615 IF T=INT((E)/2)+1 THEN650
620 PRINTTAB(2);I$(I) TAB(30);I$(II)
630 I=I+2:II=II+2:T=T+1
640 GOTO615
650 PRINT
660 PRINT"INSTRUCTIONS:"
670 FOR K=1TOJJ
680 PRINT A$(K)
700 NEXT:IF RR=1 THEN1010
710 W$=INKEY$:IF W$=""THEN710
720 CLS:PRINT
730 PRINT"YOU CAN NOW SAVE THE ENTIRE
    RECIPE ON TAPE."
740 PRINT"PLACE CASSETTE PLAYER IN REC
    ORD MODE, THEN"
750 PRINT"PRESS ENTER";
760 INPUT W
770 PRINT"OUTPUTTING TO TAPE....."
780 PRINT#-1,T$,I
790 FOR J=1TOI:PRINT#-1,I$(J):NEXT
800 PRINT#-1,E,JJ
810 PRINT"OUTPUTTING INSTRUCTIONS TO T
    APE....."
820 FOR K=1TOJJ:PRINT#-1,A$(K):NEXT
830 PRINT"TRANSFER OF DATA COMPLETED..
    ...."
840 PRINT"PRESS ANY KEY"
850 W$=INKEY$:IF W$=""THEN850
860 GOTO1020
870 REM INPUT RECIPE DATA FROM TAPE
880 CLS:PRINT
890 PRINT"P1ACE CASSETTE PLAYER IN PLA
    Y MODE, THEN PRESS ENTER";
```

```
900  INPUT W$
910  PRINT"INPUTTING FROM TAPE....."
920  INPUT#-1,T$,I
930  FOR J=1TOI:INPUT#-1,I$(J):NEXT
940  INPUT#-1,E,JJ
950  PRINT"INPUTTING INSTRUCTIONS FROM TAP
     E....."
960  FOR K=1TOJJ:INPUT#-1,A$(K):NEXT
970  PRINT"DATA NOW IN MEMORY....."
980  REM PRINT ENTIRE RECIPE
990  W$=INKEY$:IF W$=""THEN990
1000 RR=1:GOTO550
1010 W$=INKEY$:IF W$=""THEN1010
1020 CLS:PRINT
1030 PRINT"WOULD YOU LIKE TO MAKE ANOTHER
     RECIPE"
1040 PRINT"OR SEE ANOTHER RECIPE (Y/N)";
1050 INPUT W$
1060 IF W$<>"Y" THEN1120
1070 PRINT
1080 PRINT"1) MAKE ANOTHER RECIPE"
1090 PRINT"2) SEE ANOTHER RECIPE"
1100 INPUT Q
1110 ON Q GOTO 295,870
1120 PRINT
1130 PRINT"END OF PROGRAM....."
1140 END
1200 REM TRY TO KEEP TITLE, INGREDIENTS AN
     D INSTRUCTIONS
1210 REM TO A RECIPE TO NOT MORE THAN 13 L
     INES AS A
1220 REM CARRIAGE RETURN WILL RESULT AND Y
     OU WILL NOT
1230 REM SEE PART OF THE RECIPE (THE TITLE
     ) OR YOU CAN
1240 REM DELETE THE PRINT STATEMENTS AT LI
     NES 590 & 650
1250 REM BUT YOU WILL LOSE THE 'NEATNESS'
     OF THE PRINTOUT
```

MIXING BEVERAGES

How to mix a simple chocolate shake or a Tom Collins can be filed with this program. All data can be stored on cassette tape for future reference. This program along with the previous three will make your kitchen a much more efficient and productive area, and you'll enjoy it much more, with the help of your computer!

SAMPLE RUN
MIXING BEVERAGES

LIST INSTRUCTIONS (Y/N)? <u>Y</u>

WITH HUNDREDS OF NEW MIXED BEVERAGE
RECIPES COMING OUT EVERY YEAR, YOU'VE
PROBABLY FOUND IT HARDER TO KEEP UP
WITH THEM. THIS PROGRAM, MUCH LIKE
'RECIPE STORAGE' WILL LET YOU ENTER
MIXING INGREDIENTS AND INSTRUCTIONS
FOR ALL YOUR DIFFERENT BEVERAGES. EACH
BEVERAGE CAN BE STORED ON CASSETTE
TAPE, THEN WHEN YOU NEED THE LIST
JUST LOAD THE DATA INTO MEMORY.

PRESS ENTER? <ENTER>

AFTER THE DATA HAS BEEN LOADED INTO
MEMORY, THE COMPUTER WILL PRINT A LIST
OF ALL BEVERAGES CONTAINED IN YOUR
FILE (EACH ONE NUMBERED), MAKE YOUR
SELECTION, AND YOU HAVE ALL BEVERAGE
INSTRUCTIONS. MUCH BETTER THAN THUMBING
THROUGH A RECIPE BOOK, TRYING TO REMEMBER
WHERE THAT ONE BEVERAGE INSTRUCTION
WAS LOCATED.

PRESS ENTER FOR COMMAND LIST? <ENTER>

1) START A BEVERAGE FILE
2) ADD TO BEVERAGE FILE
3) LOAD STORED DATA
4) SAVE CURRENT DATA
5) BEVERAGE SELECT (PRINTOUT)
6) END PROGRAM

MAKE SELECTION? <u>1</u>

TO STOP ENTRYS INTO BEVERAGE FILE
JUST PRESS 'ENTER' FOR A NAME
OF BEVERAGE.

NAME OF BEVERAGE? <u>MILK SHAKE</u>
AMOUNT OF INGREDIENTS? <u>3</u>
INGREDIENT # 1?
<u>1 CUP MILK</u>
INGREDIENT # 2?
<u>1/4 C. CHOCO. SYRUP (OR OTHER FLAVOR)</u>
INGREDIENT # 3?
<u>1 P. VANILLA ICE CREAM</u>
MIXING INSTRUCTIONS?
<u>MIX INGREDIENTS - JUST TO BLEND</u>

NAME OF BEVERAGE? <u>TEA SPICED</u>
AMOUNT OF INGREDIENTS? <u>4</u>
INGREDIENT # 1?
<u>6 CUPS WATER</u>
INGREDIENT # 2?
<u>1 TEA. WHOLE CLOVES</u>
INGREDIENT # 3?
<u>1 IN. STK. CIN.</u>
INGREDIENT # 4?
<u>2 1/2 TAB. BLK. TEA</u>
MIXING INSTRUCTIONS
<u>COMBINE FIRST 3 - BOIL. ADD TEA. STEEP
5 MIN. STRAIN. SERVE HOT.</u>

PRESS ENTER FOR COMMAND LIST? <ENTER>

1) START A BEVERAGE FILE
2) ADD TO BEVERAGE FILE
3) LOAD STORED DATA
4) SAVE CURRENT DATA
5) BEVERAGE SELECT (PRINTOUT)
6) END PROGRAM

MAKE SELECTION? <u>4</u>

PLACE UNIT IN RECORD MODE.
PRESS ENTER? <ENTER>
SAVING BEVERAGE DATA.

BEVERAGE DATA NOW ON TAPE.
PRESS ENTER FOR COMMAND LIST? <ENTER>

307

1) START A BEVERAGE FILE
2) ADD TO BEVERAGE FILE
3) LOAD STORED DATA
4) SAVE CURRENT DATA
5) BEVERAGE SELECT (PRINTOUT)
6) END PROGRAM

MAKE SELECTION? <u>5</u>

SELECT BEVERAGE BY NUMBER ONLY.
1) MILK SHAKE
2) TEA SPICED

INPUT CHOICE? <u>1</u>

BEVERAGE: MILK SHAKE

INGREDIENTS: 1 CUP MILK
    1/4 C. CHOCO. SYRUP (OR OTHER FLAVOR)
    1 P. VANILLA ICE CREAM

MIXING INSTRUCTIONS:
MIX INGREDIENTS - JUST TO BLEND
PRESS ENTER FOR COMMAND LIST? <ENTER>

1) START A BEVERAGE FILE
2) ADD TO BEVERAGE FILE
3) LOAD STORED DATA
4) SAVE CURRENT DATA
5) BEVERAGE SELECT (PRINTOUT)
6) END PROGRAM

MAKE SELECTION? <u>6</u>

END OF BEVERAGE FILE . . . . .

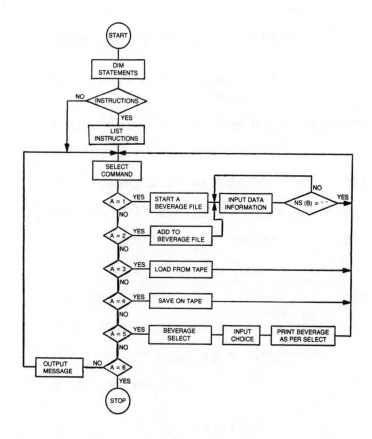

Flowchart for MIXING BEVERAGES

Program Listing

```
10 REM PROGRAM TITLE: MIXING BEVERAGES
20 CLEAR 1000
30 DIM N$(50),I$(25,50),T(50),M$(50)
70 CLS
80 PRINT TAB(15);"** MIXING BEVERAGES
   **"
90 PRINT
120 INPUT"LIST INSTRUCTIONS (Y/N)";A$
130 IF A$="N" THEN 390
140 PRINT
150 PRINT"WITH HUNDREDS OF NEW MIXED B
    EVERAGE"
160 PRINT"RECIPES COMING OUT EVERY YEA
    R, YOU'VE"
170 PRINT"PROBABLY FOUND IT HARDER TO
    KEEP UP"
180 PRINT"WITH THEM. THIS PROGRAM, MUC
    H LIKE"
190 PRINT"'RECIPE STORAGE' WILL LET YO
    U ENTER"
200 PRINT"MIXING INGREDIENTS AND INSTR
    UCTIONS"
210 PRINT"FOR ALL YOUR DIFFERENT BEVER
    AGES. EACH"
220 PRINT"BEVERAGE CAN BE STORED ON CA
    SSETTE"
230 PRINT"TAPE, THEN WHEN YOU NEED THE
    LIST"
240 PRINT"JUST LOAD THE DATA INTO MEMO
    RY."
250 PRINT
260 INPUT"PRESS ENTER";A$
270 CLS:PRINT
280 PRINT"AFTER THE DATA HAS BEEN LOAD
    ED INTO"
290 PRINT"MEMORY, THE COMPUTER WILL PR
    INT A LIST"
300 PRINT"OF ALL BEVERAGES CONTAINED I
    N YOUR"
310 PRINT"FILE (EACH ONE NUMBERED), MA
    KE YOUR"
```

310

```
320 PRINT"SELECTION, AND YOU HAVE ALL
    BEVERAGE"
330 PRINT"INSTRUCTIONS, MUCH BETTER TH
    AN THUMBING"
340 PRINT"THROUGH A RECIPE BOOK, TRYIN
    G TO REMEMBER"
350 PRINT"WHERE THAT ONE BEVERAGE INST
    RUCTION"
360 PRINT"WAS LOCATED."
370 PRINT
380 INPUT"PRESS ENTER FOR COMMAND LIST
    ";A$
390 CLS:PRINT
400 PRINT"1) START A BEVERAGE FILE"
410 PRINT"2) ADD TO BEVERAGE FILE"
420 PRINT"3) LOAD STORED DATA"
430 PRINT"4) SAVE CURRENT DATA"
440 PRINT"5) BEVERAGE SELECT (PRINTOUT)"
450 PRINT"6) END PROGRAM"
460 PRINT
470 INPUT"MAKE SELECTION";A
480 ON A GOTO 500,700,800,900,1000,1400
490 PRINT"ENTER AGAIN - MAKE SELECTION
    1-6.":PRINT:GOTO400
500 REM WITH PROGRAM AS IT IS YOU
510 REM CAN INPUT UP TO 50 DIFFERENT
520 REM MIXING INSTRUCTIONS FOR
530 REM YOUR BEVERAGES. THIS AMOUNT CAN
540 REM BE CHANGED TO YOUR NEEDS BY
550 REM CHANGING THE DIM STATEMENTS
560 REM LOCATED AT LINE --- 30
570 IF I<>0 THEN CLEAR
575 B=1
580 PRINT"TO STOP ENTRYS INTO BEVERAGE
     FILE"
590 PRINT"JUST PRESS 'ENTER' FOR A NAME"
600 PRINT"OF BEVERAGE."
610 PRINT
620 INPUT"NAME OF BEVERAGE";N$(B)
630 IF N$(B)="" THEN 670
635 INPUT"AMOUNT OF INGREDIENTS";A
638 T=A:A=1
```

```
640 PRINT"INGREDIENT #";A;
642 INPUT I$(A,B)
645 IF A<>T THEN A=A+1:GOTO640
650 T(B)=T
655 INPUT"MIXING INSTRUCTIONS";M$(B)
660 R=1:GOTO720
670 B=B-1
675 I=B:B=1:R=0
680 GOTO390
700 REM ADD TO LIST
705 IF I=0 THEN 775
710 B=I
720 IF B>=50 THEN 1300
730 B=B+1
735 IF R=1 THEN 610
740 PRINT
750 PRINT"COMPUTER READY TO RECIEVE"
760 PRINT"MORE FILE DATA."
770 PRINT:GOTO580
775 PRINT"YOU HAVE TO HAVE A FILE STAR
    TED"
780 PRINT"BEFORE IT CAN BE ADDED TO !!"
785 PRINT
790 GOTO380
800 REM LOAD DATA TO MEMORY
805 CLS
810 PRINT
815 PRINT"PLACE CASSETTE UNIT IN PLAY"
820 INPUT"MODE...PRESS ENTER";A$
825 INPUT#-1,I
830 PRINT"LOADING DATA INTO MEMORY."
835 B=1
840 INPUT#-1,N$(B),T(B)
845 A=1
850 INPUT#-1,I$(A,B)
855 IF A<>T(B) THEN A=A+1:GOTO850
860 INPUT#-1,M$(B)
865 IF B<>I THEN B=B+1:GOTO840
870 PRINT
875 GOTO1000
880 INPUT"PRESS ENTER FOR COMMANDS";A$
885 RETURN
```

```
900 REM SAVE DATA IN MEMORY
905 IF I=0 THEN 1010
910 CLS:PRINT
915 PRINT"PLACE UNIT IN RECORD MODE."
920 INPUT"PRESS ENTER";A$
925 PRINT#-1,I
930 PRINT"SAVING BEVERAGE DATA."
935 B=1
940 PRINT#-1,N$(B),T(B)
945 A=1
950 PRINT#-1,I$(A,B)
955 IF A<>T(B) THEN A=A+1:GOTO950
960 PRINT#-1,M$(B)
965 IF B<>I THEN B=B+1:GOTO940
970 PRINT
975 PRINT"BEVERAGE DATA NOW ON TAPE."
980 GOSUB880:GOTO390
1000 REM PRINT BEVERAGE DATA
1005 REM OF BEVERAGE SELECTED
1010 IF I=0 PRINT"NO BEVERAGES IN CURRE
     NT FILE...":PRINT:GOTO380
1020 CLS
1030 PRINT
1040 PRINT"SELECT BEVERAGE BY NUMBER ONLY."
1050 PRINT
1060 FOR B=1TOI:PRINT B;")   ";
1070 PRINT N$(B)
1080 NEXT
1090 PRINT
1100 INPUT"INPUT CHOICE";X
1105 IF X<=(I-I) OR X>=(I+1) PRINT"THAT
     CHOICE ISN'T LISTED. TRY AGAIN.":
     GOTO1030
1110 CLS
1120 A=1:PRINT:D=64:L=D*4
1130 PRINT"BEVERAGE: "TAB(15);N$(X)
1135 PRINT
1140 PRINT"INGREDIENTS:";
1145 PRINT TAB(15);
1150 PRINT I$(A,X)
1160 IF A<>T(X) THEN A=A+1:L=L+D:GOTO11
     45
```

```
1165 PRINT@L+D,;
1170 PRINT"MIXING INSTRUCTIONS:"
1180 L=L+D*2:J=1:W=1:M=(D-14):Q=LEN(M$(
     X)):N=L
1190 PRINT@L,MID$(M$(X),J,1)
1200 IF W>=M AND MID$(M$(X),J,1)=" " TH
     EN 1230
1210 IF J<>Q THEN L=L+1:W=W+1:J=J+1:GOT
     O1190
1220 PRINT:GOSUB880:GOTO390
1230 W=1:L=N:L=L+(D-1):N=N+D
1240 GOTO1190
1300 PRINT
1310 PRINT"YOU HAVE REACHED THE LIMIT"
1320 PRINT"FOR INPUTTING DATA....."
1330 PRINT"TO ADD MORE TO LIST FIRST CH
     ANGE"
1340 PRINT"THE <DIM> STATEMENTS AT LINE"
1350 PRINT"30....."
1360 PRINT
1370 GOSUB880:GOTO675
1400 PRINT
1410 PRINT"END OF BEVERAGE FILE....."
1420 END
```

CALORIE COUNTER

On a diet? Or just want to keep your intake of calories at an even amount everyday? The computer will sort your total calories for the day into three parts, largest at breakfast, medium at lunch and smallest amount of calories at dinner. The computer will then randomly select a menu from the data file containing your choice of foods. You can keep that menu or reject it. If you decide to reject it the computer will select over the foods again. Even if you are not counting calories you'll find this program helpful in selecting food items for your meals!

SAMPLE RUN
<:::CALORIE COUNTER:::>

INSTRUCTIONS? Y
SEEMS LIKE EVERYONE THESE DAYS
ARE COUNTING THE CALORIES OF EVERY
BITE OF FOOD THAT ENTERS THEIR MOUTH.
AND IF YOUR ONE OF THOSE PEOPLE
THIS PROGRAM IS DESIGNED JUST FOR YOU.
FIRST OF ALL YOU SHOULD CONSULT
YOUR FAMILY PHYSICIAN FOR THE AMOUNT
OF CALORIES YOU CAN INTAKE IN ONE
DAY.
SECOND, YOU'LL ENTER THAT AMOUNT
INTO THE COMPUTER, ALSO SELECTING
BREAKFAST, LUNCH OR DINNER.

PRESS ENTER? <ENTER>

AT THAT POINT THE COMPUTER WILL
TAKE OVER (NO IT WON'T COOK THE MEAL!!)
IT WILL SELECT FOODS FOR YOUR MEAL
AND IT WON'T EXCEED THE AMOUNT OF
CALORIES YOU ARE ALLOWED.
YOU CAN EITHER KEEP THE SELECTIONS
OR REJECT THEM, IF YOU DECIDE TO DO
THE LATTER, THE COMPUTER WILL CHOOSE
ANOTHER MENU FOR YOU.

PRESS ENTER? <ENTER>

HOW MANY CALORIES ARE YOU
ALLOWED PER DAY? 850

YOUR HIGHEST CALORIE INTAKE WILL
BE AT BREAKFAST, MIDDLE AT LUNCH
AND SMALLEST CALORIE INTAKE WILL
BE AT DINNER TIME.
AS FOLLOWS:
BREAKFAST: 334
LUNCH: 283
DINNER: 233

TOTAL = 850 CALORIES.

PRESS ENTER FOR MEAL SELECTION?

SELECT MEAL:
1) BREAKFAST
2) LUNCH
3) DINNER

ENTER CHOICE? <u>1</u>

BREAKFAST MENU:
1 SMALL ORANGE 40
1/2 CUP CREAM OF WHEAT 70
4 OUNCE GLASS/TOMATO JUICE 25
1 SLICE WHITE OR RYE BREAD 70
1 TEASPOON BUTTER 45
1 TEASPOON SUGAR 17
BLACK COFFEE OR TEA (NO ADDITIVES) 0

TOTAL CALORIES   = 267
TOTAL CALORIES ALLOWED FOR THIS MEAL = 334

SATISFIED WITH BREAKFAST MENU (Y/N)? <u>Y</u>

WOULD YOU LIKE TO SELECT
ANOTHER MENU (Y/N)? <u>Y</u>

SELECT MEAL:
1) BREAKFAST
2) LUNCH
3) DINNER

ENTER CHOICE? <u>2</u>

LUNCH MENU:
1/2 CUP CANNED SALMON 150
1/4 CUP HEAD LETTUCE 15
3 STALKS FRESH CELERY 24
2 SMALL GREEN PEPPERS 40
1/2 CUP CANTALOUPE 40
BLACK COFFEE OR TEA (NO ADDITIVES) 0

TOTAL CALORIES = 269
TOTAL CALORIES ALLOWED FOR LUNCH = 283

SATISFIED WITH LUNCH MENU (Y/N)? <u>N</u>

MAKING OTHER SELECTIONS . . . . .

LUNCH MENU:
1 EGG 75
1/4 CUP HEAD LETTUCE 15
10 SLICES CUCUMBERS (1/8 IN. THICK) 10
1 SMALL TOMATO 20
1/2 CUP CARROTS CUBED 35
1 SLICE WHITE/RYE BREAD 70
1 TEASPOON BUTTER 45
BLACK COFFEE OR TEA (NO ADDITIVES) 0

TOTAL CALORIES = 270
TOTAL CALORIES ALLOWED FOR LUNCH = 283

SATISFIED WITH LUNCH MENU (Y/N)? <u>Y</u>

WOULD YOU LIKE TO SELECT
ANOTHER MENU (Y/N)? <u>Y</u>

SELECT MEAL:
1) BREAKFAST
2) LUNCH
3) DINNER

ENTER CHOICE? <u>3</u>

MENU FOR DINNER:
1 SLICE BREAST CHICKEN 75
1/2 CUP TOMATO SOUP 50
1 SMALL POTATO BAKED/BOILED 70
1 BISCUIT (HOMEMADE) 20
BLACK COFFEE OR TEA (NO ADDITIVES) 0

TOTAL CALORIES FOR DINNER = 215
TOTAL CALORIES ALLOWED = 233

SATISFIED WITH MENU SELECTED (Y/N)? N

MAKING OTHER SELECTIONS . . . . .

MENU FOR DINNER:
1 SLICE LEAN ROAST BEEF 75
1/2 CUP BOUILLON BROTH 10
1 SMALL POTATO BAKED/BOILED 70
1 TEASPOON BUTTER 45
1 BISCUIT (HOMEMADE) 20
BLACK COFFEE OR TEA (NO ADDITIVES) 0

TOTAL CALORIES FOR DINNER = 220
TOTAL CALORIES ALLOWED = 233

SATISFIED WITH MENU SELECTED (Y/N)? Y

WOULD YOU LIKE TO SELECT
ANOTHER MENU (Y/N)? N

END OF CALORIE COUNTER PROGRAM . . .

<:::CALORIE COUNTER:::>

INSTRUCTIONS? N

PRESS ENTER? <ENTER>

HOW MANY CALORIES ARE YOU
ALLOWED PER DAY? 950

YOUR HIGHEST CALORIE INTAKE WILL
BE AT BREAKFAST, MIDDLE AT LUNCH
AND SMALLEST CALORIE INTAKE WILL
BE AT DINNER TIME.
AS FOLLOWS:
BREAKFAST: 377
LUNCH: 316
DINNER: 256

TOTAL = 949 CALORIES.

PRESS ENTER FOR MEAL SELECTION? <ENTER>

SELECT MEAL:
1) BREAKFAST
2) LUNCH
3) DINNER

ENTER CHOICE? 2

LUNCH MENU:
1 EGG 75
1 CUP COOKED SPINACH 25
2/3 CUP BRUSSELS SPROUTS (COOKED) 40
2 SMALL GREEN PEPPERS 40
1/2 CUP TURNIPS 35
1 SLICE WHITE/RYE BREAD 70
1 BISCUIT (HOMEMADE) 20
BLACK COFFEE OR TEA (NO ADDITIVES) 0

TOTAL CALORIES = 305
TOTAL CALORIES ALLOWED FOR LUNCH = 316

SATISFIED WITH LUNCH MENU (Y/N)? N

MAKING OTHER SELECTIONS . . . . .

LUNCH MENU:
1/2 CUP CANNED SALMON 150
3/4 CUP COOKED CABBAGE 20
10 SLICES CUCUMBERS (1/8 IN. THICK) 10
8 SMALL ASPARAGUS TIPS 24
1/2 CUP TURNIPS 35
1 SLICE WHITE/RYE BREAD 70
BLACK COFFEE OR TEA (NO ADDITIVES) 0

TOTAL CALORIES = 309
TOTAL CALORIES ALLOWED FOR LUNCH = 316

SATISFIED WITH LUNCH MENU (Y/N)? Y

WOULD YOU LIKE TO SELECT
ANOTHER MENU (Y/N)? Y

SELECT MEAL:

1) BREAKFAST
2) LUNCH
3) DINNER

ENTER CHOICE? 3

MENU FOR DINNER:
1 PORTION LEAN RND STEAK 100
1/2 CUP VEGETABLE SOUP 50
1 SMALL POTATO BAKED/BOILED 70
1 BISCUIT (HOMEMADE) 20
BLACK COFFEE OR TEA (NO ADDITIVES) 0

TOTAL CALORIES FOR DINNER = 240
TOTAL CALORIES ALLOWED = 256

SATISFIED WITH MENU SELECTED (Y/N)? Y

WOULD YOU LIKE TO SELECT
ANOTHER MENU (Y/N)? N

END OF CALORIE COUNTER PROGRAM . . .
Even if you are not on a diet this program will prove to be very useful. It can make meal selections for each meal of the day. The data elements can be very quickly changed to food items you prefer. You can select and re-select any meal menu as many times as you want.

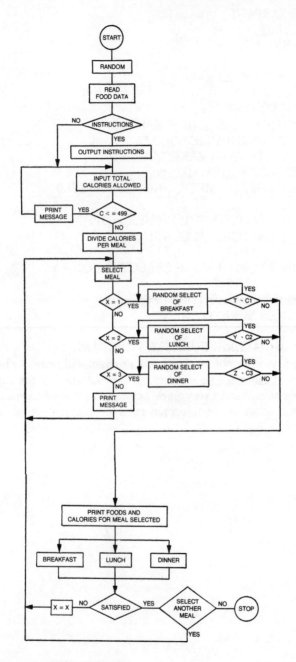

Flowchart for CALORIE COUNTER

Program Listing

```
10 REM PROGRAM TITLE: CALORIE COUNTER
20 CLS:RANDOM
30 DIM B$(16),BB$(15),M(20)
40 DIM L$(20),LL$(21)
50 DIM D$(16),DD$(19)
60 FOR I=1TO15:READ B$(I):NEXT
70 FOR I=1TO20:READ L$(I):NEXT
80 FOR I=1TO16:READ D$(I):NEXT
100 PRINT TAB(15);"<::: CALORIE COUNTE
    R :::>"
110 PRINT
115 INPUT"INSTRUCTIONS (Y/N)";X$:IF X$
    ="N" THEN 420
120 PRINT"SEEMS LIKE EVERYONE THESE DA
    YS"
130 PRINT"ARE COUNTING THE CALORIES OF
    EVERY"
140 PRINT"BITE OF FOOD THAT ENTERS THE
    IR MOUTH."
150 PRINT"AND IF YOUR ONE OF THOSE PEO
    PLE"
160 PRINT"THIS PROGRAM IS DESIGNED JUS
    T FOR YOU."
170 PRINT"FIRST OF ALL YOU SHOULD CONS
    ULT"
180 PRINT"YOUR FAMILY PHYSICIAN FOR TH
    E AMOUNT"
190 PRINT"OF CALORIES YOU CAN INTAKE I
    N ONE"
200 PRINT"DAY."
210 PRINT"SECOND, YOU'LL ENTER THAT AM
    OUNT"
220 PRINT"INTO THE COMPUTER, ALSO SELE
    CTING"
230 PRINT"BREAKFAST, LUNCH OR DINNER."
240 PRINT
250 INPUT"PRESS ENTER";X
260 CLS
270 PRINT
280 PRINT"AT THAT POINT THE COMPUTER W
    ILL"
290 PRINT"TAKE OVER (NO IT WON'T COOK
    THE MEAL!!)"
```

```
300 PRINT"IT WILL SELECT FOODS FOR YOU
    R MEAL"
310 PRINT"AND IT WON'T EXCEED THE AMOU
    NT OF"
320 PRINT"CALORIES YOU ARE ALLOWED."
330 PRINT"YOU CAN EITHER KEEP THE SELE
    CTIONS"
340 PRINT"OR REJECT THEM, IF YOU DECID
    E TO DO"
350 PRINT"THE LATTER, THE COMPUTER WIL
    L CHOOSE"
360 PRINT"ANOTHER MENU FOR YOU."
370 REM SEE REM STATEMENTS FOR FURTHER
380 REM INFORMATION ON MEAL SELECTIONS
390 REM LINES 5000-5080
400 PRINT
410 INPUT"PRESS ENTER";X
420 CLS
430 PRINT
440 PRINT"HOW MANY CALORIES ARE YOU"
450 PRINT"ALLOWED PER DAY";
460 INPUT C
465 IF C<=499 PRINT"TRY AGAIN, MUST BE
     AT LEAST 500 CALORIES.":GOTO430
470 GOSUB2000
475 PRINT
480 PRINT"YOUR HIGHEST CALORIE INTAKE
    WILL"
490 PRINT"BE AT BREAKFAST, MIDDLE AT L
    UNCH"
500 PRINT"AND SMALLEST CALORIE INTAKE
    WILL"
510 PRINT"BE AT DINNER TIME."
520 PRINT"AS FOLLOWS:"
530 PRINT"BREAKFAST: ";C1
540 PRINT"LUNCH:     ";C2
550 PRINT"DINNER:    ";C3
560 PRINT
570 PRINT"TOTAL =";C4;"CALORIES."
580 PRINT
590 INPUT"PRESS ENTER FOR MEAL SELECTI
    ON";X
600 CLS
610 PRINT
620 PRINT"SELECT MEAL:"
630 PRINT"1) BREAKFAST"
```

324

```
640  PRINT"2) LUNCH"
650  PRINT"3) DINNER"
660  PRINT
670  PRINT"ENTER CHOICE";
680  INPUT X
690  ON X GOTO 700,1000,1500
695  PRINT"SELECT AGAIN, ENTER A NUMBER
     LISTED.":GOTO660
700  REM BREAKFAST
710  FOR I=1TO15:M(I)=I:NEXT:T=0:Z=3:F=
     1
720  A=RND(Z)
730  IF M(A)=0 THEN 720
735  BB$(F)=B$(A):GOSUB740:GOTO745
740  T=T+VAL(RIGHT$(BB$(F),3)):RETURN
745  IF F=4 THEN 800
760  ON F GOTO 770,780,790
770  Z=7:FOR V=1TO3:M(V)=0:NEXT:GOTO795
780  Z=10:FOR V=4TO7:M(V)=0:NEXT:GOTO79
     5
790  Z=12:FOR V=8TO10:M(V)=0:NEXT
795  F=F+1:GOTO720
800  IF ABS(T-C1)>=45 THEN F=F+1:GOTO94
     0
810  IF ABS(T-C1)>=17 THEN F=F+1:GOTO96
     0
820  IF T>C1 GOSUB1800:GOTO700
830  F=F+1:BB$(F)=B$(15)
835  CLS:PRINT
840  PRINT"BREAKFAST MENU:":FOR I=1TOF:
     PRINTBB$(I):NEXT:PRINT
850  PRINT"TOTAL CALORIES =";T
855  PRINT"TOTAL CALORIES ALLOWED FOR T
     HIS MEAL =";C1:PRINT
860  PRINT"SATISFIED WITH BREAKFAST MEN
     U (Y/N)";
870  INPUT A$
880  IF A$="Y" THEN 2200
885  FOR I=1TOF:BB$(I)="":NEXT:GOSUB900
890  GOTO700
900  CLS
910  PRINT
920  PRINT"MAKING OTHER SELECTIONS....."
930  RETURN
940  BB$(F)=B$(13):GOSUB740
950  GOTO810
```

```
960 BB$(F)=B$(14):GOSUB740
970 GOTO820
1000 REM LUNCH
1010 FOR I=1TO20:M(I)=I:NEXT:X=4:L=1:Y=
     0
1020 A=RND(X)
1030 IF M(A)=0 THEN 1020
1040 LL$(L)=L$(A):GOSUB1050
1045 GOTO1090
1050 Y=Y+VAL(RIGHT$(LL$(L),3))
1060 RETURN
1090 IF L>=5 THEN 1210
1100 ON L GOTO 1110,1120,1130,1140
1110 FOR I=1TO4:M(I)=0:NEXT:X=7:GOTO120
     0
1120 FOR I=5TO7:M(I)=0:NEXT:X=11:GOTO12
     00
1130 FOR I=8TO11:M(I)=0:NEXT:X=16:GOTO1
     200
1140 FOR I=12TO16:M(I)=0:NEXT:X=19
1200 L=L+1:GOTO1020
1210 IF ABS(Y-C2)>=70 THEN L=L+1:GOTO13
     20
1215 IF ABS(Y-C2)>=45 THEN L=L+1:GOTO13
     70
1216 IF ABS(Y-C2)>=20 THEN L=L+1:GOTO14
     10
1218 L=L+1
1220 LL$(L)=B$(15)
1222 IF Y>C2 GOSUB1800:GOTO1000
1225 CLS:PRINT
1226 PRINT"LUNCH MENU:"
1230 FOR I=1TOL:PRINTLL$(I):NEXT
1235 PRINT
1240 PRINT"TOTAL CALORIES =";Y
1250 PRINT"TOTAL CALORIES ALLOWED FOR L
     UNCH =";C2
1260 PRINT
1270 PRINT"SATISFIED WITH LUNCH MENU (Y
     /N)";
1280 INPUT A$
1290 IF A$="Y" THEN 2200
1292 GOSUB900
1295 FOR I=1TOL:LL$(I)="":NEXT:GOTO1000
1320 LL$(L)=L$(20)
1330 GOSUB1050
```

```
1350 GOTO1215
1370 LL$(L)=B$(13)
1380 GOSUB1050
1400 GOTO1216
1410 LL$(L)=B$(11)
1420 GOSUB1050
1430 GOTO1218
1500 REM DINNER
1510 FOR I=1TO16:M(I)=I:NEXT:J=10:D=1:Z
     =0
1520 A=RND(J)
1530 IF M(A)=0 THEN 1520
1540 DD$(D)=D$(A)
1550 GOSUB1560:GOTO1580
1560 Z=Z+VAL(RIGHT$(DD$(D),3))
1570 RETURN
1580 IF D=3 THEN 1660
1600 ON D GOTO 1610,1620
1610 FOR I=1TO10:M(I)=0:NEXT:J=14:GOTO1
     650
1620 FOR I=11TO14:M(I)=0:NEXT:J=16:GOTO
     1650
1650 D=D+1:GOTO1520
1660 IF ABS(Z-C3)>=45 THEN D=D+1:GOTO17
     50
1670 IF ABS(Z-C3)>=20 THEN D=D+1:GOTO17
     70
1680 D=D+1
1690 DD$(D)=B$(15)
1691 IF Z>C3 THEN XX=XX+1:GOSUB1800:IF
     XX<=6 GOTO1500 ELSE 2300
1694 CLS:PRINT
1695 PRINT"MENU FOR DINNER:"
1698 FOR I=1TOD:PRINTDD$(I):NEXT
1699 PRINT
1700 PRINT"TOTAL CALORIES FOR DINNER ="
     ;Z
1710 PRINT"TOTAL CALORIES ALLOWED =";C3
1720 PRINT
1730 INPUT"SATISFIED WITH MENU SELECTED
     (Y/N)";A$
1740 IF A$="Y" THEN 2200
1742 FOR I=1TOD:DD$(I)="":NEXT:GOSUB900
1745 GOTO1500
1750 DD$(D)=B$(13)
1760 GOSUB1560:GOTO1670
```

327

```
1770 DD$(D)=B$(11)
1780 GOSUB1560:GOTO1680
1800 CLS
1810 PRINT
1820 PRINT"CALORIE COUNT TO HIGH..."
1830 PRINT"SELECTING ANOTHER MENU..."
1840 FOR Q=1TO900:NEXT
1850 RETURN
2000 REM CALORIES PER MEAL
2010 R=RND(100)
2020 C1=INT((C/3)+R)
2030 C2=INT(C1/3)
2040 C3=ABS(C1-C2)
2050 IF C3<=100 THEN 2000
2060 C2=C2+INT(C1/2)
2070 C4=C1+C2+C3
2080 C5=INT(ABS(C-C4)/3)
2090 C1=C1+C5
2100 C2=C2+C5
2110 C3=C3+C5
2120 C4=C1+C2+C3
2130 IF C4>C THEN 2150
2140 RETURN
2150 C1=0:C2=0:C3=0:C4=0:C5=0
2160 GOTO2000
2200 PRINT
2210 PRINT"WOULD YOU LIKE TO SELECT"
2220 PRINT"ANOTHER MENU (Y/N)";
2230 INPUT A$
2240 IF A$="Y" THEN 600
2250 PRINT
2260 PRINT"END OF CALORIE COUNTER PROGR
     AM..."
2270 END
2300 PRINT
2310 PRINT"THE AMOUNT OF CALORIES YOU H
     AVE"
2320 PRINT"ENTERED CANNOT MAKE-UP A MEN
     U"
2330 PRINT"FOR THE DINNER MEAL. WOULD Y
     OU"
2340 PRINT"LIKE TO TRY AGAIN, ENTERING
     GREATER"
2350 PRINT"THAN";C;"CALORIES FOR AN ENT
     IRE DAY (Y/N)";
2360 INPUT A$
```

```
2365 XX=0
2370 IF A$="Y" THEN 420
2380 PRINT
2390 PRINT"PRESS ENTER";
2400 INPUT A$
2410 GOTO600
5000 REM DATA ELEMENTS FOR MENU ITEMS
5010 REM CAN BE QUICKLY CHANGED TO
5020 REM YOUR OWN NEEDS BY CHANGING
5030 REM TITLE OF ITEM FOLLOWED BY
5040 REM AMOUNT OF CALORIES. THE LIST
5050 REM CONTAINED HEREIN IS A RANDOM
5060 REM SELECTION OF MANY DIFFERENT
5070 REM CALORIE LISTS
5080 REM DATA FOR BREAKFAST
5090 DATA 1 SMALL ORANGE 40,1/2 SMALL G
     RAPEFRUIT 40
5100 DATA 3 COOKED PRUNES (LARGE) 75
5130 DATA 1/2 CUP CREAM OF WHEAT 70
5140 DATA 1/2 CUP OATMEAL 70
5150 DATA 1/2 CUP CORNFLAKES 50
5155 DATA 1 EGG 75
5160 DATA 4 OUNCE GLASS / TOMATO JUICE
     25
5170 DATA 6 OUNCE GLASS MILK 125
5180 DATA 6 OUNCE GLASS SKIMMED MILK 65
5210 DATA 1 BISCUIT (HOMEMADE) 20
5215 DATA 1 SLICE WHITE OR RYE BREAD 70
5216 DATA 1 TEASPOON BUTTER 45
5220 DATA 1 TEASPOON SUGAR 17
5230 DATA BLACK COFFEE OR TEA (NO ADDIT
     IVES) 0
5240 REM DATA FOR LUNCH
5250 DATA 1/2 CUP CANNED TUNA  150
5260 DATA 1/2 CUP CANNED SALMON 150
5270 DATA 1 EGG  75
5280 DATA 1/4 CUP COTTAGE CHEESE  75
5300 DATA 3/4 CUP COOKED CABBAGE  20
5310 DATA 1/4 CUP HEAD LETTUCE  15
5320 DATA 1 CUP COOKED SPINACH  25
5330 DATA 3 STALKS FRESH CELERY  24
5340 DATA 10 SLICES CUCUMBERS (1/8 IN.
     THICK)  10
5350 DATA 2/3 CUP BRUSSELS SPROUTS (COO
     KED)  40
5360 DATA 1 CUP EGGPLANT  25
```

```
5370 DATA 8 SMALL ASPARAGUS TIPS   24
5380 DATA 1 CUP STRING BEANS   25
5390 DATA 2 SMALL GREEN PEPPERS   40
5400 DATA 1 SMALL TOMATO   20
5410 DATA 1 SMALL APPLE   40
5420 DATA 1/2 CUP CARROTS CUBED   35
5430 DATA 1/2 CUP TURNIPS   35
5440 DATA 1/2 CUP CANTALOUPE   40
5450 DATA 1 SLICE WHITE/RYE BREAD   70
5460 REM DATA FOR DINNER
5470 DATA 1 SLICE LEAN ROAST LAMB   75
5480 DATA 1 SLICE LEAN ROAST BEEF   75
5490 DATA 1 CAKE HAMBURGER STEAK   100
5500 DATA 1 PORTION LEAN RND STEAK   100
5510 DATA 1 SLICE ROAST VEAL   100
5520 DATA 1/2 SMALL CHICKEN BROILER 200
5530 DATA 1 SLICE BREAST CHICKEN   75
5540 DATA 1 SMALL PIECE HADDOCK   75
5550 DATA 6 MEDIUM OYSTERS   120
5560 DATA 1 PIECE BROOK TROUT   75
5570 DATA 1/2 CUP CHICKEN NOODLE SOUP
     100
5580 DATA 1/2 CUP VEGETABLE SOUP   50
5590 DATA 1/2 CUP TOMATO SOUP   50
5600 DATA 1/2 CUP BOUILLON BROTH   10
5610 DATA 1 SMALL POTATO BAKED/BOILED
     70
5620 DATA 1/2 CUP MASHED POTATOES (WHITE
     )  100
```

COUPON STORING FILE

Millions of people each year are using more and more coupons. This program will organize all of your coupons, and leave the storage up to you. To see if you have a coupon, for say, coffee, simply enter the letter 'C'. Any or all coupons that begin with the letter 'C' will be listed. You should find this program quite useful!

SAMPLE RUN

RECAL DATA FROM TAPE? <u>N</u>

PRINT INSTRUCTIONS? <u>Y</u>

COUPON STORING FILE

TIRED OF SEARCHING THROUGH YOUR COUPONS
FOR A DISCOUNT ON AN ITEM YOU NEED
THEN TO DISCOVER YOU HAVEN'T A COUPON
FOR THAT ONE ITEM?
THIS PROGRAM WILL HELP YOU PUT AN
END TO THAT PROBLEM (OF COURSE HOW
YOU ORGANIZE THE ACTUAL COUPONS IS
LEFT UP TO YOU, BUT THIS PROGRAM WILL
NEATLY STORE ALL THE COUPON INFORMATION).

PRESS ENTER? <ENTER>

YOU CAN LIST UP TO 25 COUPONS (TITLE,
AMOUNT, EXPIRATION DATE, IF ANY). THE
COMPUTER WILL PLACE ALL OF THESE IN
ALPHABETICAL ORDER, THE COMPLETED LIST
WILL BE PRINTED OUT, THEN YOU CAN
STORE IT ON TAPE FOR FUTURE REFERENCE.
WHEN YOU RECALL THE COUPON LIST AND
YOU'RE LOOKING FOR A PARTICULAR ITEM,
SUCH AS <COFFEE> ALL YOU NEED INPUT
IS THE LETTER <C>, IF YOU HAVE ANY
COUPONS LISTED UNDER <C> THE COMPUTER
WILL PRINT ALL OF THEM.

PRESS ENTER TO BEGIN FILE? <ENTER>

TO CANCEL BUILDING OF FILE
ENTER <XX> FOR <NAME OF COUPON>.

TITLE OF COUPON? <u>TISSUE-BATHROOM</u>
AMOUNT OF COUPON? <u>.2</u>
EXPIRATION DATE
(IF NONE—ENTER NONE)? <u>NONE</u>

332

TITLE OF COUPON? <u>TOWELS (GENERIC)</u>
AMOUNT OF COUPON? <u>.15</u>
EXPIRATION DATE
(IF NONE—ENTER NONE)? <u>01/01/81</u>
TITLE OF COUPON? <u>CHOCO. MORSELS</u>
AMOUNT OF COUPON? <u>.1</u>
EXPIRATION DATE
(IF NONE—ENTER NONE)? <u>NONE</u>

COUPON	AMOUNT	EXPIRATION DATE
CHOCO. MORSELS	.10	NONE
TISSUE-BATHROOM	.20	NONE
TOWELS (GENERIC)	.15	01/01/81

PRESS A KEY <SPACE BAR>

SAVE DATA ON TAPE? <u>YES</u>

PLACE A FRESH CASSETTE IN
PLAYER, THEN PRESS ENTER?
SAVING DATA . . . . .

TRANSFER COMPLETED . . . . .

(1) ENTIRE COUPON FILE
(2) SELECT LETTER AREA

SELECT (1 OR 2)? <u>2</u>

ENTER LETTER FOR SECTION? <u>T</u>

COUPON AMOUNT EXPIRATION DATE

TISSUE-BATHROOM .20   NONE

TOWELS (GENERIC) .15 01/01/81

THAT IS THE LISTING, UNDER
THE LETTER T, WOULD YOU
LIKE TO SEE MORE (Y/N)? <u>N</u>

WOULD YOU LIKE TO ADD TO
THE PRESENT LIST OF COUPONS?

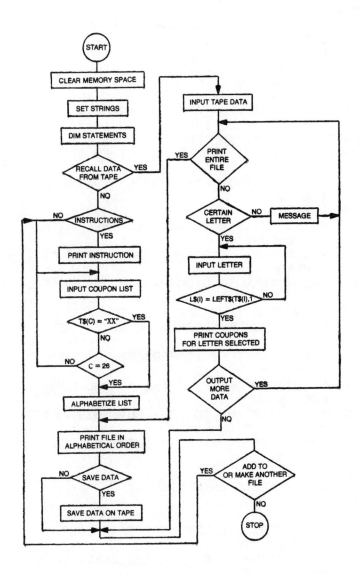

Flowchart for COUPON STORING FILE

```
Program Listing
10 REM PROGRAM TITLE: COUPON STORING
   FILE
20 CLEAR1000
30 CLS:PRINT
40 A$="$$###.##"
50 DIM T$(26),A(26),W$(26)
60 INPUT"RECALL DATA FROM TAPE";I$
70 IF I$="YES" OR I$="Y" THEN 1400
80 INPUT"PRINT INSTRUCTIONS";I$
90 IF I$<>"YES" AND I$<>"Y" THEN 390
95 CLS
100 PRINTTAB(15);"*** COUPON STORING F
    ILE ***"
130 PRINT
140 PRINT"TIRED OF SEARCHING THROUGH Y
    OU COUPONS"
150 PRINT"FOR A DISCOUNT ON AN ITEM YO
    U NEED"
160 PRINT"THEN TO DISCOVER YOU HAVEN'T
     A COUPON"
170 PRINT"FOR THAT ONE ITEM ?"
180 PRINT"THIS PROGRAM WILL HELP YOU P
    UT AN"
190 PRINT"END TO THAT PROBLEM (OF COUR
    SE HOW"
200 PRINT"YOU ORGANIZE THE ACTUAL COUP
    ONS IS"
210 PRINT"LEFT UP TO YOU, BUT THIS PRO
    GRAM WILL"
220 PRINT"NEATLY STORE ALL THE COUPON
    INFORMATION)."
230 PRINT
240 INPUT"PRESS ENTER";X
250 CLS
260 PRINT
270 PRINT"YOU CAN LIST UP TO 25 COUPON
    S (TITLE,"
280 PRINT"AMOUNT, EXPIRATION DATE, IF
    ANY). THE"
290 PRINT"COMPUTER WILL PLACE ALL OF T
    HESE IN"
300 PRINT"ALPHABETICAL ORDER, THE COMP
    LETED LIST"
```

```
310 PRINT"WILL BE PRINTED OUT, THEN YO
    U CAN"
320 PRINT"STORE IT ON TAPE FOR FUTURE
    REFERENCE."
330 PRINT"WHEN YOU RECALL THE COUPON L
    IST AND"
340 PRINT"YOUR LOOKING FOR A PARTICULAR
     ITEM,"
350 PRINT"SUCH AS <COFFEE> ALL YOU NEE
    D INPUT"
360 PRINT"IS THE LETTER <C>, IF YOU HA
    VE ANY"
370 PRINT"COUPONS LISTED UNDER <C> THE
     COMPUTER"
380 PRINT"WILL PRINT ALL OF THEM."
390 PRINT
400 INPUT"PRESS ENTER TO BEGIN FILE";X
410 CLS
420 PRINT
430 PRINT"TO CANCEL BUILDING OF FILE"
440 PRINT"ENTER <XX> FOR <NAME OF COUP
    ON>."
450 C=1
460 PRINT
470 INPUT"TITLE OF COUPON";T$(C)
480 IF T$(C)="XX" THEN 580
490 INPUT"AMOUNT OF COUPON";A(C)
500 PRINT"EXPIRATION DATE"
510 INPUT"(IF NONE -- ENTER NONE)";W$(
    C)
520 PRINT
525 IF C>=26 THEN 550
530 C=C+1
540 GOTO470
550 PRINT
560 PRINT"YOU HAVE ENTERED THE AMOUNT
    OF"
570 PRINT"COUPONS THAT WAS PERMITTED..
    ..."
580 REM ALPHABETIZE / INTERCHANGE LIST
590 C=C-1
600 K=C
605 IF K=1 THEN 725
610 C=1:X=0
620 IF T$(C)<=T$(C+1) THEN 700
630 Q$=T$(C+1):T$(C+1)=T$(C)
```

337

```
640 T$(C)=Q$
650 A=A(C+1):A(C+1)=A(C)
660 A(C)=A
670 M$=W$(C+1):W$(C+1)=W$(C)
680 W$(C)=M$
690 X=10
700 C=C+1
710 IF C<>K THEN 620
720 IF X=10 THEN 610
725 CLS:PRINT
730 REM PRINT ENTIRE FILE
740 REM IN ALPHABETICAL ORDER
750 PRINT"C O U P O N";
760 PRINT TAB(18);"A M O U N T";
770 PRINT TAB(35);"E X P I R A T I O N
    D A T E";
780 FOR X=0TO127:SET(X,0):SET(X,6):NEXT
790 FOR Y=1TO5:SET(30,Y):SET(65,Y):NEXT
800 IF G=2 THEN 830
820 I=1
830 PRINT
835 IF G=2 AND LEFT$(T$(I),1)<>L$ THEN
    900
840 PRINT T$(I);
850 PRINTTAB(18);USING A$;A(I);
860 PRINTTAB(45);W$(I)
870 IF I<>K THEN 890
875 IF G=2 THEN 1700
880 GOTO1000
890 IF I=11 OR I=22 THEN GOSUB 1500:PR
    INT@192,;
900 I=I+1
905 IF G=2 AND LEFT$(T$(I+1),1)<>L$ TH
    EN 1700
910 GOTO840
1000 REM DATA TO TAPE ?
1010 GG=1:GOSUB1500
1020 CLS:PRINT
1030 IF G=1 THEN 1800
1040 PRINT"SAVE DATA ON TAPE";
1050 INPUT I$
1060 IF I$="YES" OR I$="Y" THEN 1080
1070 GOTO1800:REM END
1080 PRINT
1090 PRINT"PLACE A FRESH CASSETTE IN"
1100 PRINT"PLAYER, THEN PRESS ENTER";
```

338

```
1110 INPUT I$
1120 PRINT#-1,K
1130 PRINT"SAVING DATA....."
1140 FOR I=1TOK
1150 PRINT#-1,T$(I),A(I),W$(I)
1160 NEXT
1170 PRINT
1180 PRINT"TRANSFER COMPLETED....."
1190 GOTO1800
1200 CLS
1205 GOTO1400
1210 PRINT
1220 PRINT"(1) ENTIRE COUPON FILE"
1230 PRINT"(2) SELECT LETTER AREA"
1240 PRINT
1250 PRINT"SELECT (1 OR 2)";
1260 INPUT Z
1270 ON Z GOTO 1275,1300
1275 G=1
1280 GOTO725
1300 REM SELECT LETTER
1310 INPUT"ENTER LETTER FOR SECTION";L$
1315 I=1
1320 IF L$<>LEFT$(T$(I),1) THEN 1330
1325 GOTO1380:REM TO PRINTOUT
1330 IF I<>K THEN 1340
1335 GOTO1345:REM LETTER NOT IN FILE
1340 I=I+1:GOTO1320
1345 PRINT
1350 PRINT"THE LETTER YOU ENTERED ";L$
1355 PRINT"CANNOT BE LOCATED IN YOUR FI
     LE."
1360 PRINT
1365 INPUT"TRY AGAIN (Y/N)";I$
1370 IF I$="Y" THEN 1300
1375 GOTO1800:REM END
1380 G=2
1385 GOTO725:REM PRINTOUT
1400 REM DATA FROM TAPE
1405 PRINT
1410 PRINT"PLACE CASSETTE IN PLAYER, SE
     T"
1415 PRINT"IN PLAY MODE, THEN PRESS ENT
     ER";
1420 INPUT I$
1425 INPUT#-1,K
```

```
1430 PRINT
1435 PRINT"INPUTTING COUPON FILE....."
1440 FOR I=1TOK
1445 INPUT#-1,T$(I),A(I),W$(I)
1450 NEXT
1455 PRINT
1460 PRINT"TRANSFER COMPLETE...DATA IN
     MEMORY."
1465 PRINT
1470 G=1
1475 GOTO1210
1500 REM ERASE VIDEO FOR NEATNESS
1510 FOR X=0TO127:SET(X,44):NEXT
1520 PRINT@980,"PRESS A KEY";
1530 X$=INKEY$:IF X$="" THEN 1530
1535 IF G=1 OR GG=1 THEN RETURN
1540 X=15552:Y=15615
1550 FOR L=XTOY:POKE L,132:POKE L,192
1560 NEXT
1570 IF X<>16192 THEN 1590
1580 GOTO1650
1590 X=Y+1:Y=Y+64
1600 GOTO1550
1650 FOR X=40TO62:SET(X,45):RESET(X,45)
1660 NEXT
1670 RETURN
1700 PRINT
1705 FOR X=1TO2500:NEXT
1710 PRINT"THAT IS THE LISTING, UNDER"
1720 PRINT"THE LETTER ";L$;". WOULD YOU"
1730 INPUT"LIKE TO SEE MORE (Y/N)";I$
1740 IF I$<>"Y" THEN 1800
1750 L$=""
1760 GOTO1210
1765 PRINT"WOULD YOU LIKE TO ADD TO"
1770 PRINT"THE PRESENT LIST OF COUPONS";
1775 INPUT I$
1780 IF I$="N" THEN 1800
1785 CLS
1790 PRINT
1795 C=C+1:GOTO460
1800 REM END
1810 PRINT
1820 PRINT"END OF COUPON FILE PROGRAM.
     ..."
1830 END
```

SHOPPING LIST

This program can be used in different ways, but, it all boils down to helping you make a more organized shopping list. You can (by request) have the computer add the price of each food item (including local tax for your area) to give you the total of your shopping bill before you go shopping.

SAMPLE RUN

****SHOPPING LIST****

SEE INSTRUCTIONS? <u>NO</u>

ENTER SHOPPING ITEM # 1 ?
<u>MILK (1 GAL.)</u>
ENTER AMOUNT OF THIS ITEM? <u>2.5</u>
ENTER SHOPPING ITEM # 2 ?
<u>BREAD (2 LOAVES)</u>
ENTER AMOUNT OF THIS ITEM? <u>1.2</u>
ENTER SHOPPING ITEM # 3 ?
<u>LAUNDRY DETER.</u>
ENTER AMOUNT OF THIS ITEM? <u>3.39</u>
ENTER SHOPPING ITEM # 4 ?
<u>DISH SOAP</u>
ENTER AMOUNT OF THIS ITEM? <u>1.29</u>
ENTER SHOPPING ITEM # 5 ?
<u>GROUND BEEF (3 LBS.)</u>
ENTER AMOUNT OF THIS ITEM? <u>4.5</u>
ENTER SHOPPING ITEM # 6 ?
<u>CHICKEN (2/WHOLE)</u>
ENTER AMOUNT OF THIS ITEM? <u>5.75</u>
ENTER SHOPPING ITEM # 7?
<u>CHEESE (SLICED)</u>
ENTER AMOUNT OF THIS ITEM? <u>3.3</u>
ENTER SHOPPING ITEM # 8 ?
<u>CHIPS</u>
ENTER AMOUNT OF THIS ITEM? <u>1.3</u>
ENTER SHOPPING ITEM # 9 ?
XX

SHOPPING ITEM	AMOUNT	TAX ON ITEM
MILK (1 GAL.)	$2.50	$0.10
BREAD (2 LOAVES)	$1.20	$0.05
LAUNDRY DETER.	$3.39	$0.14
DISH SOAP	$1.29	$0.05
GROUND BEEF (3 LBS.)	$4.50	$0.18
CHICKEN (2/WHOLE)	$5.75	$0.23
CHEESE (SLICED)	$3.30	$0.13
CHIPS	$1.30	$0.05

```
SUB-TOTAL FOR ITEMS:    $23.23
TAX ON ITEMS:       $0.93
TOTAL FOR ITEMS:    $24.16

1) SEE LIST
2) SEE COMMANDS
3) MAKE HARD COPY OF LIST
2

1) STORE LIST ON TAPE
2) LOAD LIST FROM TAPE
3) MAKE A SHOPPING LIST
4) ADD TO PRESENT LIST
5) END PROGRAM

SELECT FROM ABOVE? 5

END OF SHOPPING LIST . . . . .
```

Input with or without amounts, the choice is yours. You can start your list at the beginning of the week and add to it during the week, finishing it the day you do the actual shopping. A very handy way to make and store your shopping list.

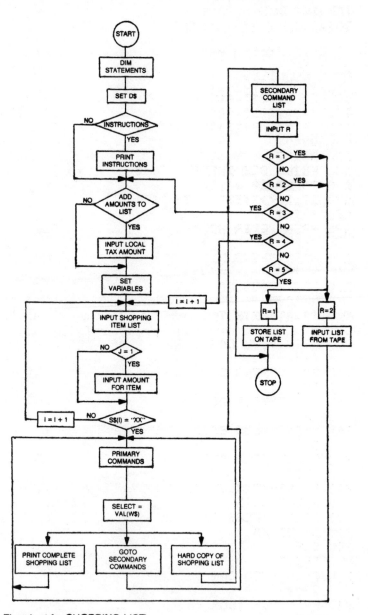

Flowchart for SHOPPING LIST

Program Listing

```
10 REM PROGRAM TITLE: SHOPPING LIST
20 CLS
30 CLEAR 1000
40 DIM S$(31),A(31)
50 D$="$$####.##"
100 PRINTTAB(15);"**** SHOPPING LIST *
    ***"
110 PRINT
150 PRINT"SEE INSTRUCTIONS";
160 INPUT I$
170 IF I$<>"YES" THEN 1130
180 PRINT
190 PRINT"EVER WONDER WHY YOU WENT SHO
    P-"
200 PRINT"PING WITHOUT A LIST, THEN SP
    ENT"
210 PRINT"$50.00 MORE THAN YOU HAD PLA
    NNED?"
220 PRINT"WITH THE HELP OF THIS PROGRA
    M"
230 PRINT"YOU CAN LIST ALL OF YOUR SHO
    P-"
240 PRINT"PING ITEMS DAYS BEFORE YOU D
    O"
250 PRINT"YOUR ACTUAL SHOPPING, YOU CA
    N"
260 PRINT"ALSO ENTER THE AMOUNTS OF EA
    CH"
270 PRINT"ITEM AND RECEIVE A TOTAL AMO
    UNT"
280 PRINT"(INCLUDING / EXCLUDING TAX),"
290 PRINT
300 PRINT"PRESS ENTER";
310 INPUT X$
320 CLS
330 PRINT
340 PRINT"YOU CAN ALSO RECEIVE A HARD
    COPY"
350 PRINT"OF YOUR SHOPPING LIST BY FOL
    LOWING"
```

```
360 PRINT"THE <COMMAND LIST>."
370 PRINT"OF COURSE, TO DO THIS YOU MU
    ST HAVE"
380 PRINT"ACCESS TO A LINE PRINTER."
390 PRINT"TOTAL AMOUNT OF ITEMS YOU CA
    N ENTER"
400 PRINT"IS 30 (MORE BY CHANGING THE
    DIM"
410 PRINT"STATEMENTS LINE 40). AFTER Y
    OU HAVE"
420 PRINT"FINISHED, ENTER <XX> FOR AN
    ITEM"
430 PRINT"THE COMPUTER WILL PRINT YOUR
    TOTAL"
440 PRINT"SHOPPING LIST, THEN A COMMAN
    D LIST."
450 PRINT
460 PRINT"PRESS ENTER";
470 INPUT X$
480 CLS
490 PRINT
500 PRINT"YOU CAN 'DUMP' THE SHOPPING
   LIST ON"
510 PRINT"CASSETTE TAPE AND ADD MORE T
    O IT AT"
520 PRINT"A LATER DATE OR RECALL THE L
    IST WHEN"
530 PRINT"YOU ARE READY TO DO YOUR SHO
    PPING."
540 PRINT
550 PRINT"PRESS ENTER TO BEGIN";
560 INPUT X$
570 CLS
580 PRINT
600 PRINT"DO YOU WISH TO ADD AMOUNTS T
    O THE"
610 PRINT"SHOPPING ITEMS YOU ENTER";
620 INPUT I$
630 IF I$="YES" THEN 650
635 IF J=1 J=0
640 GOTO710
650 PRINT"WHAT IS THE TAX AMOUNT FOR Y
    OUR"
```

```
660 PRINT"AREA (ENTER WITH THE % SIGN)
    ";
670 INPUT T%
675 T=T%/100:J=1
680 PRINT"WHEN YOU ENTER THE AMOUNT FO
    R AN"
690 PRINT"ITEM ENTER <WITHOUT> THE LEA
    DING"
700 PRINT"$ <DOLLAR> SIGN."
705 FOR X=1TO2500:NEXT
710 CLS:I=1
720 TX=0:Q=1
730 PRINT@64,"ENTER SHOPPING ITEM #";I;
740 INPUT S$(I)
745 IF S$(I)="XX" THEN 820
750 IF J<>1 THEN 800:REM NO AMOUNT/NO
    TAX
760 PRINT@128,"ENTER AMOUNT OF THIS IT
    EM";
770 INPUT A(I)
780 TX(I)=T*A(I)+A(I)
800 I=I+1
810 PRINT@84,"                        ";
815 PRINT@153,"            ";
816 GOTO730
820 I=I-1:Q=I
830 CLS
840 PRINT:IF J<>1 THEN 1500
850 PRINTTAB(0);"SHOPPING ITEM" TAB(32
    );"AMOUNT";
860 PRINTTAB(50);"TAX ON ITEM"
870 PRINT
880 I=1
890 PRINTTAB(0);S$(I) TAB(29);USING D$
    ;A(I);
895 PRINTTAB(50);USING D$;T*A(I)
900 IF I<>Q THEN 920
910 GOTO930
920 I=I+1
925 GOTO890
930 REM PRINT-OUT WITH TOTAL AMOUNTS
940 FOR I=1TOQ:SB=A(I)+SB:NEXT
```

```
950  FOR I=1TOQ:TX=T*A(I)+TX:NEXT
955  TT=SB+TX
960  PRINT
965  IF Q>=10 THEN FOR X=1TO1500:NEXT
970  PRINTTAB(20);"SUB-TOTAL FOR ITEMS:
     ";
980  PRINTTAB(45);USING D$;SB
990  PRINTTAB(20);"TAX ON ITEMS: ";
1000 PRINTTAB(45);USING D$;TX
1010 PRINTTAB(20);"TOTAL FOR ITEMS: ";
1020 PRINTTAB(45);USING D$;TT
1030 FOR X=1TO4500:NEXT
1040 FOR X=0TO127:SET(X,44):NEXT
1050 PRINT@960,"1) SEE LIST";
1060 PRINT@975,"2) SEE COMMANDS";
1070 PRINT@996,"3) MAKE HARD COPY OF LI
     ST";
1080 W$=INKEY$
1090 IF W$="" THEN 1080
1100 ON VAL(W$) GOTO 1110,1130,1650
1110 SB=0:TX=0
1120 GOTO830
1130 CLS
1140 PRINT
1150 PRINT"1) STORE LIST ON TAPE"
1160 PRINT"2) LOAD LIST FROM TAPE"
1170 PRINT"3) MAKE A SHOPPING LIST"
1175 PRINT"4) ADD TO PRESENT LIST"
1180 PRINT"5) END. PROGRAM"
1190 PRINT
1200 PRINT"SELECT FROM ABOVE";
1210 INPUT R
1220 ON R GOTO 1230,1370,1490,1595,1900
1230 REM LIST TO TAPE
1240 PRINT"PLACE PLAYER IN RECORD MODE"
1250 PRINT"AND PRESS ENTER";
1260 INPUT X$
1270 PRINT
1280 PRINT"STORING DATA LIST ON TAPE..."
1300 PRINT#-1,T,Q,J
1310 FOR I=1TOQ
1320 PRINT#-1,S$(I),A(I)
```

```
1330 NEXT
1340 PRINT"DATA ON TAPE....."
1350 FOR X=1TO1500:NEXT
1360 GOTO1130
1370 PRINT"READY CASSETTE PLAYER (PLACE
     IN"
1380 PRINT"PLAY MODE) AND PRESS ENTER";
1390 INPUT X$
1400 PRINT
1410 PRINT"LOADING DATA FROM TAPE....."
1420 INPUT#-1,T,Q,J
1430 FOR I=1TOQ
1440 INPUT#-1,S$(I),A(I)
1450 NEXT
1460 PRINT"DATA IN MEMORY....."
1470 FOR X=1TO1500:NEXT
1480 GOTO1040
1490 SB=0:TX=0
1495 GOTO570
1500 REM SHOPPING LIST PRINT-OUT
1510 REM WITHOUT AMOUNTS
1520 I=1:K=2
1530 PRINTTAB(10);"SHOPPING LIST OF ITE
     MS"
1540 PRINT
1545 IF S$(I)="XX" THEN 1600
1550 PRINTTAB(0);S$(I) TAB(30);S$(K)
1560 IF K+1<=Q THEN 1580
1570 GOTO1600
1580 I=I+2:K=K+2
1590 GOTO1545
1595 I=Q+1:CLS:GOTO730
1600 GOTO1040
1650 REM LINE PRINT HARD COPY
1660 REM OF SHOPPING LIST
1670 CLS
1680 PRINT
1690 PRINT"READY LINE PRINTER, THEN"
1700 PRINT"PRESS ENTER";
1710 INPUT X$
1720 I=1:K=2
1730 LPRINT TAB(0);"SHOPPING LIST"
```

```
1740 LPRINT CHR$(138)
1750 LPRINT TAB(0);S$(I);
1760 LPRINT TAB(15);S$(K)
1770 IF K+1<=Q THEN 1790
1780 GOTO1130
1790 I=I+2:K=K+2
1800 GOTO1750
1900 REM END OF PROGRAM
1910 CLS
1920 PRINT
1930 PRINT"END OF SHOPPING LIST....."
1940 END
```

Some BASIC Commands Used

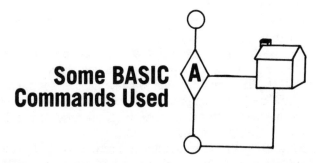

CLEAR—Used without an argument (e.g., CLEAR - press ENTER) this command will reset all numeric values to zero and all strings to null. When used with an argument (e.g. CLEAR 1000) it makes a specified number of bytes available for string storage.

CLS—Clears the video display.

PRINT—Prints an item or a list of items on the video display. These items include, string constants (messages enclosed within quotes), string variables, numeric constants (numbers), variables, or expressions involving part or all of the preceding items.

PRINT —Specifies exactly where printing is to begin on the video display.

PRINT TAB—Moves the cursor to a specified TAB position on the video.

PRINT USING—With this statement you can specify a format for printing string and numeric values.

INPUT—Causes computer to stop execution until you enter the specified number of values via the keyboard. This includes strings or numeric variables.

DATA—Lets you store data inside your program to be accessed by a READ statements. The DATA list will be read from first to last.

READ—Instructs the computer to read a value (or values) from the DATA list.

PRINT#-1—Prints the values of the variables specified onto cassette tape. The #-1, specifies that the DATA will be transferred to cassette number 1. Player must be in the RECORD position.

INPUT #-1—Inputs a specified number of values that have been stored on cassette tape. The INPUT list must be identical to the PRINT list that created the tape or an out-of-data error (OD?) will occur.

351

DIM—Lets you set the depth of an array or list of arrays. If no DIM is used, a depth of 11 (subscrips 0-11) is allowed for each dimension of each array used.

END—Terminates execution of program. END can be used anywhere in a BASIC program.

STOP—Interrupts execution of a BASIC program. During this break you can examine or change variable values.

GOTO—Transfers program to a line number specified.

GOSUB—Transfers program execution to a specified subroutine line number. Stores calling line so that program can go back there when a RETURN is encountered.

RETURN—Ends a subroutine and returns control to the line immediately following the most recently executed GOSUB.

ON GOTO—Specifies program to branch to a certain line depending on the value of the current variable.

ON GOSUB—Works like ON GOTO but branches to a certain SUBROUTINE specified by the line number in the line-number list.

FOR . . . NEXT—Opens a repetitive loop so that a sequence of program may be executed over and over.

REM—Instructs the computer to ignore the rest of the program line.

IF—Instructs the computer to test the following relational or logical expression.

THEN—Initiates the action clause of an IF-THEN type statement.

ELSE—Used after IF to specify an alternative action in case the IF test fails.

ASC—Returns the ASCII code (decimal form) for the first character of the specified string.

CHR$—Performs the inverse of the ASC function. Returns a one-character string whose character has the specified ASCII code.

INKEY$—Returns a one-character string determined by an instantaneous keyboard strobe.

LEFT$—Returns the first n characters of a string.

LEN—Returns the character length of a string, in numeric form.

MID$—Returns a substring of the argument string with length n and starting at p. The string name, length and starting position must be enclosed in parentheses. Example:
MID$ (A$,2,5) refers to a five character string beginning with the 2nd character of A$.

RIGHT$—Returns the last n characters of a string.

VAL—Returns the number represented by the characters in a string argument.

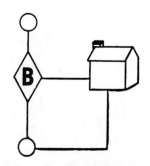

Relational Operations

< Less than
> Greater than
= Equal to
<> Not Equal to
<= Less than or Equal to
>= Greater than or Equal to

These operators are useful both for logical arithmetic and for IF...THEN statements
Example: IF I<=K THEN I=K*2

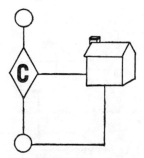

ASCII Character Codes 32-126

32	53 5	74 J	95 _	116 t
33 !	54 6	75 K	96 `	117 u
34 "	55 7	76 L	97 a	118 v
35 #	56 8	77 M	98 b	119 w
36 $	57 9	78 N	99 c	120 x
37 %	58 :	79 O	100 d	121 y
38 &	59 ;	80 P	101 e	122 z
39 '	60 <	81 Q	102 f	123 {
40 (	61 =	82 R	103 g	124 |
41)	62 >	83 S	104 h	125 }
42 •	63 ?	84 T	105 i	126 ~
43 +	64 @	85 U	106 j	
44 ,	65 A	86 V	107 k	
45 –	66 B	87 W	108 l	
46 .	67 C	88 X	109 m	
47 /	68 D	89 Y	110 n	
48 0	69 E	90 Z	111 o	
49 1	70 F	91 [	112 p	
50 2	71 G	92 \	113 q	
51 3	72 H	93]	114 r	
52 4	73 I	94 ∧	115 s	

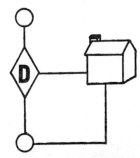

Flowchart Symbols

TERMINAL. Marks the beginning or the end of a flowchart.

PROCESSING. Indicates the performance of a given task.

DECISION. Indicates a juncture at which a choice must be made.

CONNECTOR. Used to indicate common points in the flow when connecting points cannot be drawn.

INPUT/OUTPUT. This is the general symbol for INPUT/OUTPUT. The processing symbol is sometimes used for this symbol.

DIRECTION OF FLOW. Always show the direction of program flow.

355

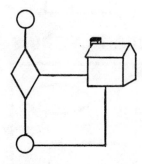

Index